Social Interaction and the Development of Children's Understanding

edited by

Lucien T. Winegar

Department of Psychology
Randolph-Macon College

ABLEX PUBLISHING CORPORATION
NORWOOD, NEW JERSEY

Library of Congress Cataloging-in-Publication Data

Social interaction and the development of children's understanding /
    Lucien Winegar, editor.
        p.   cm.
    Bibliography: p.
    Includes index.
    ISBN 0-89391-533-5
        1. Social interaction in children.   2. Child development.
3. Child psychology.   I. Winegar, Lucien.
HQ784.S56S63   1989
155.4—dc20   89-31305
                                                                        CIP

Ablex Publishing Corporation
355 Chestnut Street
Norwood, New Jersey 07648

55.4
soc

Table of Contents

iii

Contributors

Teresa Blicharski, Laboratory of Human Ethology, 919 Cherrier St., Montreal, Quebec, Canada H2L 1J1

Celia A. Brownell, Department of Psychology, 460 Langley Hall, University of Pittsburgh, Pittsburgh, PA 15260

Mary Gauvain, Department of Psychology, Scripps College, 1030 Columbia Ave., Claremont, CA 91711

Melanie Killen, Department of Psychology, Wesleyan University, Middletown, CT 06457

John R. Mergendoller, Far West Laboratory for Educational Research and Development, 1855 Folsom St., San Francisco, CA 94103

Ellen Moss, Department of Psychology, University of Quebec at Montreal, Montreal, Quebec, Canada, H3C 3P8

Martin J. Packer, School of Education, 4421 Tolman Hall, University of California at Berkeley, Berkeley, CA 94720

K. Ann Renninger, Program in Education, Swarthmore College, Swarthmore, PA 19081

F. F. Strayer, Laboratory of Human Ethology, 919 Cherrier St., Montreal, Quebec, Canada H2L 1J1

Jaan Valsiner, Department of Psychology, Davie Hall 013A, University of North Carolina at Chapel Hill, Chapel Hill, NC 27514

Lucien T. Winegar, Department of Psychology, Randolph-Macon College, Ashland, VA 23005

Introduction

Lucien T. Winegar

Theoretical and empirical work in developmental psychology has begun to focus on the role played by more competent others in the development of children's knowledge. Guided by Piaget's (1962) discussion of "contradiction," Vygotsky's (1978) description of "zone of proximal development," and Hunt's (1961) proposal of "optimal mismatch," researchers have investigated the influence of adults and more competent peers on the development of a variety of children's abilities (e.g., Bearison, 1986; Hinde, Perrot-Clermont, & Stevenson-Hinde, 1985; Rogoff & Lave, 1984; Rogoff & Wertsch, 1984; Wertsch, 1985). Specific abilities of interest have included conservation ability, logical reasoning, language development, and categorization performance. Most studies have reported clear evidence for the influence of expert others on children's developing abilities.

The contributions to the present volume follow from this previous body of work, but the current studies differ from many previous investigations in two important ways. First, the studies here do not address the influence of others on changes in children's cognition, but rather focus on the role others play in children's use of metacognitive strategies. understanding of social events, moral and affective development, use of planning skills, knowledge of social conventions, and development of play interests. Second, and more importantly, these discussions proceed from the assumption that children's understanding of their world, as reflected by their performance in it, need not be considered only as following from structural changes in their knowledge, but rather also can be fruitfully construed in terms of social transactions which characterize members of social groups. It is thus the intent of contributions to this volume to discuss children's performance in social settings not solely as caused by knowledge structures in the children's heads, but additionally as supported by social processes within cultural environments.

The goal of this book is to bring together research and theoretical work that addresses the relations between social interaction and the development of children's understanding. Representing a wide range of theoretical perspectives from ethological to hermeneutic, contributors to this volume present and discuss research on the roles adults and/or peers play in preschool-aged and elementary school children's development in a variety of areas.

Chapter 1 (Valsiner) presents a theoretical account of the role of multiple caretakers on children's development. The heterogeneity inherent in the actions of multiple caregivers is interpreted as serving as both challenge and resource for development of the child's understanding of the world. Since the activity of children constructs their future development within the constraint structures set by others, development is characterized by "bounded indeterminacy."

Chapters 2 through 4 discuss the role of social interactions between adults and children in children's development. Chapter 2 (Strayer, Moss, & Blicharski) reports and discusses the implications of a study examining how the social experience of home-reared and day-care children differentially influences problem-solving tactics expressed during semistructured play in the home setting. Results differ from previously reported findings which minimize the cognitive impact of early day-care experience. To the extent that day-care stimulates the acquisition of skills in expression of problem-solving tactics as necessary means for effectively communicating with others, day-care children seem to benefit cognitively from this more complex social experience. On the other hand, the questioning tactics of the home-reared children may reflect the influence of the basic complementary roles in the mother-child dyad, where the mother serves both as source of emotional security and problem-solving information. Such findings underscore the importance of observing and analyzing the development of intellectual abilities in social contexts which more adequately reflect natural cognitive adaptation.

Chapter 3 (Winegar) presents and discusses research on the development of children's understanding of social events and procedural conventions. Theoretical observations suggested by two studies of preschool children in social events are presented: first, an event investigated more experimentally—preschool children purchasing an item at an experimentally established store setting; and second, an event observed in a natural setting—preschool children at snacktime in their school. These studies are used to illustrate processes of socialization that occur in daily settings and are interpreted as suggesting complementary capabilities in children and processes in social interaction that support child's developing understanding of social events.

Chapter 4 (Packer & Mergendollar) describes an innovative elementary school curriculum and its influence on children's affective and moral development. Employing a hermeneutic approach, the authors suggest that children should be viewed as skilled practitioners, who construct practical skills and concerns in collaboration with peers and adults. Thus, moral development is viewed not as a matter of increased autonomy through articulation of ethical principles, but as an increased interdependence and sensitivity to social concerns that develops through participation in social activities.

Chapters 5 through 7 discuss the role of social interaction between children and peers in children's development. Chapter 5 (Gauvain) discusses the influence of social organization in the classroom on the development of children's planning skills. Analysis of patterns of social involvement across planning sessions suggests that an important consideration for children in organizing their activities is the activities of other children in the class. Apparently, children have preferences as to what they want to do, as well as with whom they want to spend time, and they seek situations that favor both of these goals. This suggests that even when a situation is not explicitly instructional, social organization and coordination with others may influence children's problem-solving skills, or at least their knowledge about different problem domains.

Chapter 6 (Killen) discusses the nature and development of children's social knowledge in diverse contexts. The focus is on how young children structure their social interactions in peer exchanges and the role that contextual features play in such interactions. The ways in which children structure their interactions in examined through analyses of how children relate to each other in peer group sessions and how they resolve conflicts as a means towards regulating their interactions. The major context variables examined include the presence or absence of adults and the type of activities in which children are engaged. It is proposed that understanding of how young children organize their social interactions and the influences that context variables have on this process will provide information about the behavioral foundation of social development.

Chapter 7 (Renninger) presents and discusses studies of children's sustained dyadic interactions around play objects during naturally-occurring free play at nursery school. Findings are interpreted as suggesting that children's social interactions are schooled both by children's previous interactions with others and by their interest in play objects. Thus, the process of perceiving and responding to possible actions involving others and objects is conceptualized as guiding changes in children's social interaction that, in turn, influence their subsequent social interactions as well as their understanding of possible actions.

Chapter 8 (Brownell) provides concluding critical discussion of the preceding seven chapters. Individual chapters are reviewed and their emerging themes are considered. She concludes that conceptual systems and social systems do not operate independently, and she discusses the implications of her conclusion.

Throughout the volume, the role of others is discussed in terms of provision of support, direction, or challenge for children's developing understanding. Changes in children's understanding, in turn, simultaneously inform interactional adjustments by both children and others. It is the recognition and consideration of this complementary relationship between developing understanding and organization of social interactions that provides the unifying theme for this volume.

ACKNOWLEDGEMENTS

While only a single editor's name appears on this book, the preparation of this volume was supported by numerous organizations and individuals who deserve acknowledgement. The initial concept of this volume was formed during the preparation of a symposium entitled *Social Interaction and the Development of Understanding* presented at the 16th Annual Meeting of the Jean Piaget Society in May, 1986. I would like to extend my appreciation to the Jean Piaget Society for its continuing provision of a forum at which emerging theory in developmental psychology can be presented and discussed.

The editoral preparation of this volume was funded by a grant from the Walter Williams Craigie Foundation. Two individuals, Thomas W. Porter and Jerome H. Garris, were particularly instrumental in assisting me in attaining this grant. I thank them and Ladell Payne for this assistance and for providing me with general institutional support without which the preparation of this volume would have been much hindered.

Most of the chapter contributors to this book are colleagues of mine of long standing; my association with many of them extends back to our graduate school days. I thank all the authors for taking the often considerable time and effort to contribute to my first edited volume. I hope the experience has been as valuable for them as it has been for me.

Two of the authors in particular were especially instrumental in the conception and completion of this volume. Jaan Valsiner unselfishly shared his considerable knowledge of the publishing world with me. He guided me through preparation of a prospectus and contact with publishers, and listened to my complaints about delays with a sympathetic ear. Without his initial support and direction, it is doubtful that this book would ever have gotten out of my head and into print. My discussions with Jaan on matters theoretical and practical continue to contribute to my own development and his example of a generous practitioner and colleague provides a model toward which, on my best days, I continue to strive. K. Ann Renninger has been an invaluable collaborator on almost every project I have undertaken since graduate school. While her contribution is not always formally acknowledged, her influence is always felt. She served as collaborator on the original formulation of this volume and the symposium which preceeded it. She advised me at all stages of this project from conception to completion, displaying an amazing ability to both listen and suggest, and, more importantly, a knowledge of when to do which. She is, at least in spirit, the true second editor of this book.

More generally, the hands and minds of two of my teachers are clearly evident in this volume and my contribution to it. My education and development in psychology was guided first by John C. Greenwood and later by Robert H. Wozniak. They provided an empowering context for my professional development, and the professional and personal knowledge which I have developed through my association with them will continue to be expressed in my actions for a long time to come. It is to both of them that I dedicate this volume.

Finally, I would like to acknowledge the contribution of Renée J. Cardone. Her patience, encouragement, and support contribute to my work both here and elsewhere, and to my own continuing development within a context of complementary interaction.

REFERENCES

Bearison, D. (1986). Transactional cognition in context: New models of social understanding. In D. Bearison & H. Zimiles (Eds.), *Thinking and emotions: Developmental perspectives* (pp. 129–146). Hillsdale, NJ: Erlbaum.

Hinde, R.A., Perrot-Clermont, A-N., & Stevenson-Hinde, J. (Eds.). (1985). *Social relationships and cognitive development*. Oxford: Clarendon Press.

Hunt, J.McV. (1961). *Intelligence and experience*. New York: Ronald Press.

Piaget, J. (1962). *The language and thought of the child*. New York: Meridian.

Rogoff, B., & Lave, J. (Eds.). (1984). *Everyday cognition: Its development in social context*. Cambridge: Harvard University Press.

Rogoff, B., & Wertsch, J.V. (Eds.). (1984). *Children's learning in the "zone of proximal development."* San Francisco: Jossey-Bass.

Vygotsky, L.S. (1978). *Mind in society: The development of higher psychological processes*. Cambridge: Harvard University Press.

Wertsch, J.V. (Ed.). (1985). *Culture, communication, and cognition: Vygotskian perspectives*. Cambridge: Cambridge University Press.

CHAPTER 1

Collective Coordination
of Progressive Empowerment*

Jaan Valsiner

Developmental psychology is aimed at explaining the work of fundamental processes that underlie psychological development. However, in its explanations it has made use of relatively few folk models that have been available within occidental cultures. Since these folk models have been based on dualistic thinking about the world, theoretical models of development have in the past faithfully followed the tradition of either intrinsic (genetic), or extrinsic (environmental) determinism in explaining development. An alternative to such bifurcation in theoretical thought, which constitutes the basis of the present synthetic exercise, is the recognition of *bounded indeterminacy* of development. The present perspective is founded on the axiom that all developmental processes take place within environments that are organized (qualitatively structured). The structure of the environment at any given moment limits the set of possible further courses of development. It guides the developmental process by eliminating excess uncertainty at every moment of time, thus allowing the organism to develop further within a limited range of possible events that can take place at the next moment. Viewed from this perspective, constraining (which has a negative connotation in the common sense of occidental cultures) becomes a theoretical concept that reflects the process that leads towards progressive future development of organisms. Hence the concept of constraining as used in the present theoretical system is seen as a term with positive common-sense flavor. All development is possible thanks to the existence of constraint structures that reduce the uncertainty of the set of possible events, and guide the developing organism further towards actively proceeding along one or another trajectory that is available to the organism at the given time. In other terms, constraints are partitions in the set of possible events that can occur, so that some of these events become more possible than

* Terry Winegar's constructive comments on an earlier version of this chapter are gratefully appreciated.

7

the others, and some are made practically impossible in the given time (and environment). Constraints occur in structural configurations (hence the use of the term "constraint structure"), the form of which changes in the course of development. Constraint structures of a given developmental state empower the developing organism to proceed toward transformation into a future state. The particular future state need not be predictable from the given constraint structure in any particular way, since the developing organism's activity within the constrained environment constructs that actual future developmental state thorough a possibly unique trajectory of development. In this respect, development is indeterministic, but within the limits specified by the constraint structure at the given time. This is the basic meaning of the concept of *bounded indeterminacy* of development.

In the case of human development, the environment of the developing person is culturally organized. Other people arrange (and rearrange) the constraint structures that the developing person encounters in life. Children's development is socially guided through constraint structures that empower children to explore novel ways of acting and thinking, as they actively relate to their (constrained) environments. The developing child can relate to the constraint structures in different ways. First, he or she can accept the limiting role these constraints play in the child's relationship with the environment. Second, he or she can act upon the given constraint structure with the aim of modifying it, transforming it into another form. Dependent on circumstances, such efforts may, or need not, succeed. Either way, the child's activity towards changing the constraint structures is of relevance for the child's development. The child develops through accepting most of the constraining some of the time, challenging other aspects of constraining from time to time, and occasionally succeeding with these challenges. Constraint structures both guide and challenge children's acting and reasoning in the course of development.

Looking at child development through the prism of constraint structures, and emphasizing their empowerment function, opens new theoretical alleys that are worth exploring. However, it also leads to a number of complex issues. The task of this chapter is to outline one of those—how does progressive empowerment through differential constraining take place under conditions of multiple caregivers of the developing child?

THE PROBLEM: INDIVIDUAL VERSUS COLLECTIVE CAREGIVING

A child is likely to encounter a multitude of "social others" who perform caregiving functions, and who set up constraint structures to guide the child's relationships with the environment. The particular structures constructed by different caregivers are likely to differ from one another. The child is constantly confronted with that difference, as a hypothetical case presented in Table 1.1 demonstrates.

Table 1.1.   A Hypothetical Example of the Multiplicity of Constraining Conditions of a Hypothetical Child. (X, Y, Z, and W are Different Activities; + and − Denote Acceptable and Unacceptable Nature of Those as Decided Upon by the Given Caregiver)

Child's Activity:	X	Y	Z	W
Caregiver:				
Mother	+	+	+	−
Father	+	−	−	−
Grandmother	−	+	+	+
Grandfather	+	+	+	+

For instance, the mother may allow the child to do X, Y, and Z, but not W. The father may be more "restrictive" and allow the child to act in way X, but not in ways Y, Z, and W. However, during a visit to the grandparents, the child realizes that his grandmother is willing to let him act in way W, aside from Y and Z. Furthermore, the grandfather is even more "liberal," letting the grandchild do everything.

The situation described in Table 1.1 is quite realistic, and poses serious problems for the investigator of child development. First, it eliminates the myth of a homogeneous "child socialization system" that is supposed to lead the child's development to the culturally expected outcomes in a uniform way. Second, how does the child integrate these different sets of constraints into a "working model" of acting in the given setting? It is inevitable that the child gradually integrates the information about the constraining structure into his knowledge system, and may begin to use it in efforts to change his or her environment. This is a general Vygotskian postulate, the specifics of which remain unknown to us. How is that information assimilated into the child's developing knowledge structure? How is the heterogeneity of the constraint structure represented in the child's knowledge? How does the child accommodate his knowledge structure to the demands of the constraint structure? What are the ways in which that knowledge can be used by the child at different levels of cognitive development? These are all questions worth addressing in the brand of research efforts that bears the label of 'social cognition' research.

Finally, an essential question remains—how do the caregivers coordinate their constraint structures? Issues of such coordination can be seen at every step in everyday reality: parents complain about the grandparents who supposedly "spoil the child" in ways that the parents don't like; or they look for teachers in preschools and schools who seemingly share their educational philosophies and child-management strategies. Even when general agreement is reached between different caregivers as to how to "handle the child," the particular ways of treating the child are likely to remain inconsistent across caregivers. Different caregivers may share the general "philosophy" of taking care of the given child, but may look after the child in different environmental settings (e.g., teachers at school, parents at home). They have no directly shared information basis for unifying their particular ways of handling the child—the parent does not see how the teacher acts in the classroom, and the teacher has no observations of the parent's handling of the child at home. Of course, they may rely heavily on indirect sharing of such information—in teacher-parent communication, or making inferences about what happens at home (or school) from the child's conduct at school (or home).

However, *some* subgroup of all the caregivers may have more access to each other's ways of child-minding. Thus, the father and the mother of the child can observe each other's child-rearing efforts, and coordinate those, more often than the mother and grandmother can (unless the latter shares the parents' household). Thus, the group of multiple caregivers constitutes a variably structured collective, in which some members have more opportunities than others to access the child-minding activity of other members. Some substructures of that collective may be very closely intertwined, whereas others have only loose ties. A hypothetical example of the group of caregivers is provided in Figure 1.1.

Obviously, the uneven connectedness of different members of the group is partially due to the residence patterns of the members of the group, and to the extent of experience that each member shares with some other member in taking care of the child. Since "parallel caregiving" is likely to be rather limited in scope, it follows that every member of the group has in principle limited amount

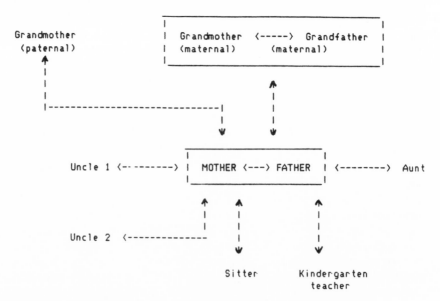

Figure 1.1.   The structure of a hypothetical group of child caregivers.

of information available about the child-care strategies of every other member. The only possible case for which this would not be true is a group member who observes every other member's activities with the child during the whole time the latter member is with the child. Of course, there is a person, who, however, does not belong to the group of caregivers, but who has such full information available—*the child himself*! Whereas every caregiver in the group has to operate on the basis of limited knowledge about what his or her peers have done, the child has full experience of it. That experience may be observable by other caregivers, as they watch the child's conduct and listen to the child's stories about the events that have taken place when the other caregivers were in charge of the child. However, the child's conduct and stories need to reflect "the truth, and nothing but the truth." First, the child reflects upon the world from his own perspective, which is necessarily different from that of any of the members of the caregiving collective. The way the child understands different events may differ greatly from his parents' way. What, for a young child, may seem a "fun play" with a daycare provider who is generous afterwards in providing the child with candies may, for the parents, be immediately recognized as a case of "sexual abuse of the child." Second, the child need not be motivated to provide some of the caregivers with accurate information about what happens when the child is with the other caregiver(s). It may be seen by the child to be to his advantage to withold some information, or to misinform some caregivers about the events that take place in conjunction with others. Thus, a child protesting to parents against being sent to bed at a reasonable hour, after returning from a stay in grandparents' house, may use the argument that "my grandma always let me stay up until X." The child may well know that this information is untrue, but expect that parents will not immediately proceed to verify it at that moment, when the child's goal is to extend the bedtime for a bit longer. In more dramatic cases, increased knowledge by children of the adults' understanding of what qualifies as 'child abuse' (and of its legal consequences) may easily become a powerful weapon in the hands of some children who set themselves the goal of harming a caregiver whom they dislike for some reason. The children's "monopoly" for knowledge about the events that take place in the caregiving network can be used in different ways, depending on the particular goals the children set themselves (or are guided to set).

How, then, can the group of caregivers coordinate their activities? And how can we think of the ways in which the child perceives the activities of different caregivers, and attempts to alter those?

PARTIALLY COORDINATED CONSTRAINT STRUCTURES

An answer to the question posed above may be in the *partially coordinated* nature of the activities of different caregivers. What does that concept mean? Why "partial" instead of "full" coordination?

Let us assume that in the common-sense-based understanding of the world, members of the caregiving collective strive towards achieving *full* coordination of their activities. They worry that other members of the collective "have different standards," or "behave differently" in a similar situation, and so on. They may try to persuade, instruct, or force the other members of the collective to handle the child similarly to the way they do it. For instance, parents may try to persuade the teacher at school to use disciplinary techniques that correspond to the ones they prefer to use at home. Of course, such uniformity of child-handling activities is impossible to achieve, since each member of the caregiving collective is a unique person, each event that occurs when the child is handled by the given caregiver is unique, and the caregivers vary their conduct from one moment to another. Therefore, only a limited extent of coordination of activities (and their respective constraint structures) of the caregivers is realistically possible. In actuality, the caregiving collective strives towards *sufficient* degree of coordination of their activities, which is always *partial* in its nature. The heterogeneity of constraint structures that are set up by the caregiving collective follows from the unequal access to the organization of child-environment relations on behalf of different caregivers.

Let us illustrate the partial coordination of constraint structures by a hypothetical example, using the caregiving collective described in Figure 1.1. First, the possibilities for coordination of caregiving activities are organized by different amounts of time that the child spends under care of some combination of caregivers from the collective. In Table 1.2, a hypothetical distribution of the percentages of time of caregiving by different persons is provided.

Table 1.2 is meant to illustrate a possible case of how all the time that the (hypothetical) child spends with an adult caregiver, or a group of caregivers, is distributed between different subunits of the caregiving network. Of course, the

Table 1.2.   Time (in %) of Caregiving by Different Subgroups of Caregivers (a Hypothetical Case).

Subgroup of Caregivers	% of Time
Mother	20
Father	2
Mother + Father	8
Grandmother(p) + Father	5
Grandmother(m) + Grandfather(m)	15
Uncle 1	1
Uncle 1 + Mother	5
Uncle 2	1
Aunt	1
Sitter	20
Teacher	22
Total	100%

formal extent of time sharing in a caregiving collective only creates a possibility for different caregivers coordinating their actions, and does not reflect the actual extent of coordination of caregiving activities.

In the example given in Table 1.2, the child spends 30 percent of the time with parents only, and 42 percent of the time with caregivers who are not related to him by kinship ties (sitter, teacher). What is more important in the present context, however, is the extent of parallel caregiving by two or more persons. Table 1.2 informs us about four such groups (Mother + Father; Grandmother (parental) + Father, Grandmother (maternal) + Grandfather (maternal), and Uncle 1 + Mother), all of which are dyadic in their composition. It is only within these dyadic caregiver-groups that immediate coordination of particular constraint structures between caregivers can be accomplished. Thus, the maternal grandfather and grandmother have the opportunity of observing each other's activities with the child to their full extent (neither of them is reported to be involved with the child separately, hence their overlap is 100 percent). At the same time, the Mother and Uncle 1 have only partial overlap in their handling of the child—Uncle 1 does it alone at times, and the Mother does it alone, or together with the Father. The Mother/Uncle 1 overlap is 17.2 percent (calculated by dividing the overlapping time of the two, by the sum of all times each individually or in other groups spends with the child). Likewise, the Mother/Father overlap is 20 percent.

As was pointed out earlier, all the cases of partial overlap in cargivers' time allocation to the child create *possibilities* for coordination of caregiving actions. It leads to partial coordination of these actions. Of course, the extent of mere exposure to one another's ways of caregiving is not sufficient in and by itself, for coordination purposes. The *actual* coordination of caregivers' child-directed actions depends on the goals and roles of the persons involved. For instance, despite the 100 percent time sharing in caregiving, the maternal Grandmother and Grandfather of the child may agree to disagree on how to constrain the child's actions, whereas the Mother and Father (despite relatively low time sharing) may coordinate their actions in full. Whatever form any particular dyadic coordination may take, it is obvious that the uneven time sharing within the caregiving group *in toto* defines the *partial* nature of the coordination within the group. Caregivers have only limited observational access to one another's actions in particular settings, and even if they possess it, they may disagree about their ways of interpreting the child's actions.

Of course, communication between caregivers serves as a channel to improve the coordination of the caregiving group. However, if observationally available experiences can be shared directly, then communication *about* individual caregivers' experiences with the child can be shared only indirectly, in *post factum* communication about what has happened, and in preemptive communication of how to deal with a possible situation. When observing the other, a caregiver has full and immediate (''on-line'') information input. In contrast, when talking to the other about the other's experiences with the child, the information exchange is no longer context-specific, and includes generalization partially due to the reliance on language use. Thus, both the limited actual time sharing in caregiving, and the mediated nature of communication between different members of the collective with no overlap in time sharing, makes the coordination of constraint structures within the caregiving collective partial in its nature.

CHILD'S ACTIVITY UNDER THE CONDITIONS OF PARTIALLY COORDINATED CAREGIVING

As was demonstrated above, the child is the only person who has full observational access to the heterogeneity of the actions of the caregiving group. Furthermore, the child is not just a passive target of these actions, but an active coconstructor of the constraint structures that different subgroups of the caregiving group set up to regulate child-environment relations. In the beginning of this chapter, the principle of bounded indeterminacy of development was briefly outlined. How does that principle function in the child's relationships with differentially constrained environments, where that constraining is the natural result of partial coordination of caregiving activities? How are constraint structures transformed as a result of the child's active relationship with the partially coordinated constraint structures of the caregiving collective?

A formal hypothetical description of a case of transformation of the constraint structures of the caregiving group is presented in Table 1.3.

Table 1.3 contains two kinds of information. First, it elaborates the idea of how situation (behavior setting) specificity of constraint structures can lead to heterogeneity of caregiving by the group. The child encounters different (only occasionally overlapping) situations while being given care by different caregivers. In our example, situation E at Time 1 is encountered only when either Uncle 1 or Uncle 2 takes care of the child. The constraint structures of the two uncles for the child's actions in situation E are diametrically opposite! Situation F occurs at Time 1 only in the extra-kinship part of the caregiving group (with the Sitter and with the Teacher). Other situations (e.g., A, B) occur when the child is with many different caregivers, although the particular constraint structures of the caregivers obviously differ (see, as an example, the difference at Time 1 between maternal grandmother's and grandfather's structuring of child's actions in the same situations).

The second kind of information depicted in Table 1.3 pertains to transformation of constraint structures from Time 1 to Time 2. In our example, a new situation (F) emerges at Time 2 in the home conditions (with Father and Mother). That situation had previously been present only in the child's relations with the Teacher and the Sitter (at Time 1 as well as Time 2). Furthermore, parents' ways of constraining the child's actions in situation F at Time 2 proceed somewhat

Table 1.3. Selective, Situation-Bound Transformation
of the Constraint Structures that the Group of Caregivers
Sets Up for a Child (a Hypothetical Example)

Caregiver	Time 1 Situation: Constraints	Time 2 Situation: Constraints
Mother	A: $X+$ $Y+$ $Z-$ $W-$	A: same
	B: $X+$ $Y+$ $Z+$ $W-$	B: same
	C: $X-$ $Y+$ $Z+$ $W+$	C: same
		F: $X+$ $Y-$ $Z+$ $W-$
Father	A: $X+$ $Y+$ $Z-$ $W-$	A: same
	B: $X+$ $Y-$ $Z+$ $W-$	B: same
		F: $X-$ $Y-$ $Z+$ $W+$
Grandmother(p)	A: $X-$ $Y-$ $Z-$ $W+$	A: same
	B: $X+$ $Y+$ $Z-$ $W-$	B: $X+$ $Y+$ $Z+$ $W-$
	D: $X+$ $Y-$ $Z-$ $W-$	D: same
Grandmother(m)	A: $X+$ $Y+$ $Z+$ $W+$	A: $X+$ $Y-$ $Z+$ $W+$
	B: $X+$ $Y+$ $Z+$ $W+$	B: $X+$ $Y+$ $Z-$ $W+$
	C: $X+$ $Y+$ $Z-$ $W-$	C: same
	D: $X+$ $Y+$ $Z+$ $W+$	D: same
Grandfather(m)	A: $X-$ $Y-$ $Z+$ $W-$	A: $X+$ $Y-$ $Z+$ $W-$
	B: $X-$ $Y-$ $Z-$ $W+$	B: $X+$ $Y+$ $Z+$ $W+$
	C: $X+$ $Y+$ $Z-$ $W-$	C: same
	D: $X+$ $Y+$ $Z+$ $W+$	D: same
Uncle 1	E: $X+$ $Y+$ $Z-$ $W+$	E: same
Uncle 2	E: $X-$ $Y-$ $Z+$ $W-$	E: same
Aunt	A: $X+$ $Y+$ $Z+$ $W-$	A: $X+$ $Y+$ $Z-$ $W-$
Sitter:	A: $X+$ $Y+$ $Z-$ $W-$	A: same
	B: $X+$ $Y+$ $Z+$ $W-$	B: same
	F: $X-$ $Y-$ $Z+$ $W+$	F: same
Teacher:	C: $X+$ $Y-$ $Z-$ $W-$	C: same
	F: $X+$ $Y-$ $Z-$ $W-$	F: same
	G: $X-$ $Y+$ $Z-$ $W-$	G: same
	H: $X-$ $Y-$ $Z+$ $W-$	H: same

Note: A . . . H denote different situations, X, Y, Z, W—different actions of the child, and $+$, $-$ mark acceptability and unacceptability of the given action in the particular situation by the given caregiver.

similarly to the Sitter's and Teacher's constraining efforts at Time 1: the Father, at Time 2, happens to use the same constraint structure as the Sitter at Time 1, and the Mother has developed her own strategy that partially overlaps with those of the Sitter and the Teacher.

From the transformation in Table 1.3 it is also possible to reveal an increase in the coordination of child-care strategies between the maternal grandparents. If, at Time 1, the Grandmother (m) and Grandfather (m) differed greatly in case of situations A and B, then by Time 2 that difference has diminished. Their only discordance is in case of actions W (in A) and Z (in b) at Time 2, which one of them allows to happen and the other does not. Finally, it can be observed that the

Aunt has become more restrictive of child's actions over time in situation A—but in the direction that matches the parents' handling of that situation.

CHILDREN'S COGNITION WITHIN ITS (CAREGIVEN) ENVIRONMENT

The presence of the heterogeneity in constraint structures, as evidenced in Table 1.3, presents the developing coognitive system of the child with a formidable task—to analyze the information from different sources on what is possible to do in different situations, how these situations can be transformed, and who of the caregivers could be better targets for active efforts towards such transformation than others, and to synthesize all that information into a holistic model that can be used to guide their conduct. The development of such models—in the form of structured knowledge about one's own "life space" that is organized by constraint structures—takes place through internalization of external social experience, along the lines put forward by Pierre Janet and Lev Vygotsky in the past. Here, the cognitive structures ("knowledge structures") are viewed as internalized transformations of external experiences of the developing child, and they become the means for organizing the child's further conduct—which leads to further development, in conjunction with the external constraint structures. As transformations based on the experience in relations with the environment, the internalized knowledge structures also follow the principle of bounded indeterminacy: some aspects of the knowledge structure are strictly fixed (and serve as cognitive constraints), whereas others remain in indeterminate state and are only temporarily clarified as the person tries to reason about a problem that needs to be solved internally, in the mind. Knowledge structures, in our use of the term, are not algorithms or scripts in the sense that contemporary cognitive psychology has often depicted them. The basic theoretical limitation of contemporary cognitive science is the assumption inherited from the history of computer engineering that the principle by which human consciousness works must resemble that of a deterministic hardwiring scheme of a computer.

We do not know how children, at different ages, in reality solve the analytic/synthetic problem of integrating the information about different context-bound constraint structures of the group of caregivers. We can try to analyze some possible ways in which a child might handle this task—not for a moment pretending that there is any reality behind our mental exercise.

For the sake of simplicity of presentation, let us simplify our hypothetical example (in Table 1.3) by not considering cross-situational heterogeneity, and by concentrating only on one situation (A). Information about that situation is presented in Table 1.4.

As can be seen from Table 1.4, the changes in the constraint structures from Time 1 to Time 2 involve the Aunt becoming more restrictive (disallowing Z),

Table 1.4. Selective Transformation of the Constraint Structures of the Group of Caregivers in Situation A (a Hypothetical Example)

Caregiver	Time 1 Constraint Structure	Time 2 Constraint Structure
Mother	(1.1) X+ Y+ Z− W−	(1.2) X+ Y+ Z− W−
Father	(2.1) X+ Y+ Z− W−	(2.2) X+ Y+ Z− W−
Grandmother(p)	(3.1) X− Y− Z− W+	(3.2) X− Y− Z− W+
Grandmother(m)	(4.1) X+ Y+ Z+ W+	(4.2) X+ Y− Z+ W+
Grandfather(m)	(5.1) X− Y− Z+ W−	(5.2) X+ Y− Z+ W−
Aunt	(6.1) X+ Y+ Z+ W−	(6.2) X+ Y+ Z− W−
Sitter:	(7.1) X+ Y+ Z− W−	(7.2) X+ Y+ Z− W−

Note: X, Y, Z, W denote different actions of the child, and +, − mark acceptability and unacceptability of the given action by the specific caregiver.

and the maternal grandparents moving to agree upon allowing X. How could we think of the child's active role in transformation of constraint structures, like those depicted in Table 1.4?

There are different ways that the child can handle the constraint structures at any time. First, the child may adjust his actions to the differences in constraint structures, making the most of these differences. That could be called *Maximal Contextual Exploitation* (MCE) rule. For example, a child may eat as much ice cream as possible while being cared for by the grandmother (knowing that she allows her to do so), but never asks for a second serving of a dessert at home (knowing that the parents are strictly limiting his consumption of sweets).

Under the MCE rule, the child only adjusts his actions to the existing constraint structures, without attempting to modify those. Although this rule is used by children quite often, it need not be presented as the major way in which constraining by caregivers guides child development. Child's actions under the MCE rule do not cross the boundaries of the constraint structures. However, much of child development includes such "boundary crossing" efforts. Let us look at different possible strategies that can be used by the child in active efforts to change his or her world.

CHILDREN'S DECISION MAKING AS A DEMOCRATIC PROCESS?

First, let us consider the least realistic version of those ways, which we call *undifferentiated majority rule* (UMR). It is based on the assumption that children's reasoning and acting is based on their acceptance of democracy (that is, dominance of the majority over the minority). If the child at Time 1 (in Table 1.4) acts in accordance with the UMR, we would expect him to act in situation A in accordance with whatever the quantitative majority of the caregivers approve. Thus, action X is approved in A by 5 of the caregivers, action Y by 5 caregivers, action Z by 3 caregivers, and action W by 2 of the caregivers. Following this distribution, the child may be interested in X and Y, and less so in Z or W. If the child follows this rule, his performing of X leads to discrepancy with the paternal Grandmother's and maternal Grandmother's constraint structures, which the child may try to modify in the direction of the "majority opinion" concerning X. In the case of maternal Grandmother at Time 2, that may be seen as having been successful. Likewise, the child may accept the majority's opinion concerning disallowance of some actions. Thus, action W may be attempted rarely, since it is not allowed by the majority of caregivers.

It is obvious that UMR is context-independent—what is (or is not) to be done by the child is determined by the majority of allowance (or disallowance) of the caregivers in the group. Furthermore, the collective nature of the caregiving group is not taken into account in case of UMR: each member of the group "votes" for or against a given action of the child in situation A, and the child merely "counts the votes" in some unspecified cognitive manner. If UMR were an adequate representation of reality, then children's conduct would look relatively problemless and conformity-oriented. That, of course, is rather different from reality. Children often oppose the restrictions imposed by the majority of caregivers, and try to find ways of removing those restrictions. How can this "clandestine revolutionary activity" be planned on behalf of the child?

THE "WEAK LINK" RULE (WLR)

The child may be interested (at Time 1) in some action (for example, W) that is disallowed by the majority of the caregivers' group in situation A. Despite W being ruled out by the majority, the child is highly motivated to perform it (often, limitation is highly motivating to keep the person to persevere in efforts to get it), and has experienced limited possibilities of performing it (in our example, only with paternal Grandmother, and—possibly—with the maternal Grandmother in case the Grandfather does not intervene). In this respect, the child knows where the "weak link" (in respect to W in A) is in the constraint structure of the caregiving collective. The child may (a) enjoy doing W in A when under the care of the two allowing grandmothers, and (b) try to negotiate with other caregivers the change of their constraint structures, so that W would become included in the set of actions that are allowed. In our example, however, such negotiation process has been to no avail—at Time 2 the persons who allow W in A are still the same. Anyway, at times the child may succeed. The WLR works like a basic tactic of locating the few "social others" who are open to the child's interest, and use them to get others to agree. Most likely, the use of the WLR starts from the peripheral region of the social group of caregivers, and moves gradually towards the core of the group. It resembles the "foot in the door" technique described in social psychology as a means towards recruitment of members of cults, or in attitude change. Only in our case, the "agent" is the presumed "novice" (the child—whom adults may consider "naive" or unknowledgeable in general), who uses his privileged position of possessing the full information about constraint structures of áll members of the caregiving group in order to try to modify these structures. This may include child's use of information about a certain member of the caregiving group against another in the most opportune times of negotiation.

EPISODIC NATURE OF THE EFFORTS TO TRANSFORM CONSTRAINT STRUCTURES

Both the UMR and WLR assume *constancy* of the application of these rules. Children are represented either as good followers of democratic principles all the time, or as clever strategists who are constantly looking for "weak links" in the caregiving system. Such representation is undoubtedly overlooking the playful inconsistency that is so characteristic of children's handling of the adult world.

More realistically, children's efforts to transform the constraint structures of the caregiving collective may be episodic in nature. The child, on one occasion in situation A, may set up a goal that necessitates action W (which is rarely allowed), and then move to use the WLR. On other occasions in situation A where his goals do not require W, the same child may elect to behave in the ways that are expected by the majority (UMR), and not try to perform W at all. Not only is the caregiving system (its superimposition of the constraint structures) inconsistent, but so is the child's effort to change it! However, the child's inconsistency stems from his developing motivational system, and interests, whereas that of the caregiving collective is primarily due to differential experiences and child-rearing goals of its members.

CONCLUSIONS: EMPOWERMENT THROUGH HETEROGENEITY OF THE COLLECTIVE CONSTRAINING SYSTEMS

This chapter has guided the reader through a series of hypothetical examples to demonstrate that heterogeneity of the constraint systems that caregivers collectively set up for the developing child is an inevitable and unavoidable phenomenon. We can actually argue that this heterogeneity assists in the process of development *by providing constant challenges* to the child by way of the partial coordination of caregivers' actions.

We can distinguish three kinds of heterogeneity that are present in the guidance of child development by a caregivers' group. All these three were represented in the example in Table 1.3. First, there exists *interpersonal* heterogeneity within the group, in respect to comparable caregiving situations. The child experiences it, and may learn to use it for his own purposes (e.g., try to perform a certain action in the given situation while given care by a person who allows it;

or learn to set up one caregiver against another, (e.g. "Mommy always lets me do that, Grandma!"). Second, the caregiving activities involve *intrapersonal (cross-situational)* heterogeneity—the same person uses different sets of constraints in different situations. The child experiences this kind of heterogeneity while moving from one situation to another under the guidance of the same caregiver. The child may try to insist upon preservation of a constraint structure from a previous situation in a new setting, only to find out that all constraint structures, although transformable in principle, are context-bound. Third, our example involved a demonstration of *intertemporal* heterogeneity: different caregivers transformed their constraint structures for some (but not other) situations into new form over time, because the child renegotiated the structure, or because of their own convenience.

How can these three kinds of heterogeneities be a resource in the process of development. They guarantee *variable* experiences for the child, even in otherwise similar situations. It gradually extends the child's horizons by making his relationships with the environment dynamic and potentially modifiable. On the cognitive side of the child, the nonhomogeneous nature of the caregivers' constraint structures challenges the child to coordinate knowledge about these structures, and to use the knowledge in efforts to change them.

We are left with a paradoxical result of our analysis, namely, that *partial coordination of the constraint structures within a collective of caregivers may perform the empowerment role for the child's development*, beyond the particular functions of these constraints. The heterogeneity inherent in caregivers' actions serves as a challenge, and as a resource, for the child's understanding of the world. It also creates possibilities for compensatory social assistance, when some parts of the caregiving collective are functioning in a nonoptimal manner. A young child, caught in the middle of parents' hostilities at home, is unlikely to make an appointment with a therapist. However, spending time with his favorite uncle, aunt, grandparents, sitter, or teacher may compensate for the potentially deleterious effects of observing parental discord at home. All through human history, it is the functional social network of the child (including both kin-group members and selected nonrelatives) that serves as the social mechanism for helping the child through good and bad times during growing up. The flexibility of that network is its asset, which may be put to different uses in the course of child development. Developmental psychology is still far from understanding the ways in which caregiving collectives guide the child towards becoming an adult, under very different environmental circumstances. Perhaps the main reason our knowledge of that matter has remained limited is our overly enthusiastic reliance on empirical research along the line of methodological traditions that are inappropriate for the study of complex dynamic phenomena. In order to distance our thinking from inductive empiricism, the analyses outlined in this chapter are purposefully deductive in their nature. We hope that this deductive analysis may increase our understanding of the complexity of child development under complex constraint structures introduced by the "social others" of the child.

CHAPTER 2

Biosocial Bases of Representational Activity During Early Childhood

F. F. Strayer
Ellen Moss
and Teresa Blicharski

BIOLOGICAL BASES OF HUMAN INTELLIGENCE

Biological theories about the origins of human intelligence postulate that selective pressures leading to the rapid emergence of complex cognitive processes emanated from phylogenetic adjustments to an increasingly complex social world. Mutual adaptation within stable social groups favored transformations in representational abilities where thinking about relationships with others and variability of events within collective contexts contributed increasingly to individual fitness (Humphrey, 1976). Experimental research with nonhuman primates has shown that both the quality and quantity of early social experience has strong determining influences on problem-solving activity. Animals deprived of early social contact have greater difficulty in learning simple stimulus-response associations (Jarrard, 1971; Sackett, 1970). From a biological perspective, children's cognitive development can be viewed as a species-specific process involving individual adaptation to particular constraints imposed by interpersonal relations. These relations require continual coadjustments between social partners in order to regulate interpersonal communication and to assume optimal levels of cooperative interaction.

Instead of emphasizing the fundamental role of inherent intellectual abilities, a biosocial model of cognitive growth places primary emphasis upon variations in social contexts that orient individual growth and produce phenotypic variability in children's representational activity. Differences in early social experience canalize individual growth and lead to differences in children's representational activity. According to cognitive ethologists working with young children, the social basis of human intelligence is most apparent during infancy, when we find direct correspondence between the diversity of the child's early social experiences and the complexity of emerging problem-solving skills (Charlesworth, 1976; Hinde, 1979; Schaffer, 1984; Strayer, 1980, 1984). The early development of information-processing skills is shaped during repeated exchanges with familiar social partners who structure the child's attention, memory, and interpretation of immediate experience. Early concept formation depends upon the interpersonal coordination of mutual perceptions, actions, and feelings. The meaning and interest of such psychological experience is constructed from information drawn from the past history of a particular social relationship and from the recognition of mutual intentions that govern future shared action.

The primacy of social experience as a pacesetter for cognitive growth has provocative implications for traditional approaches to early intellectual development. This view of the origins of cognitive activity differs in important ways from psychometric approaches to intelligence that place primary emphasis upon individual differences in performance (Cattell, 1947; Terman, 1925), as well as from recent information-processing models that examine activities such as recall and organization as basic components of problem solving ability (Meacham, 1984; Miller, Galanter & Pribram, 1960). However, a biosocial analysis of early cognitive development focusing upon processes underlying the acquisition and transfer of information between active agents accords well with the theories of Lev Vygotsky (1962) who emphasized that intellectual functioning develops through a process of internalization where representational capacities are both activated and structured through social exchange with familiar others.

A biosocial perspective suggests that most of the fundamental cognitive activities (such as classification, seriation, and conservation) as well as basic mental operations (such as perspective taking, decentration, and abstract reflection) are both socially focused and socially constructed abilities that are progressively extended to the world of objects. Current psychological assessment of such representational activities is usually based upon the children's manipulation of objects, rather than upon their strategic adjustments in daily encounters with natural social partners. Such object-centered, rather than person-centered assessments of representational capacities may in fact underestimate developmental changes in cognitive activity. Contemporary preoccupations with the abstract representations of objective information seems to have shifted research attention away from basic processes that facilitate the acquisition of representational activity, and towards the study of how individuals differ in what appear to be *native* intellectual capacities.

SOCIAL CONSTRAINTS AND COGNITIVE DEVELOPMENT

Accepting that social adaptation is the prime mover of cognitive development also has direct implications for how we interpret the effects of early stimulation on later cognitive development. From a social perspective, enriched stimulation involves both qualitative and quantitative changes in the regulation of the child's attention. Reported evidence for the beneficial effect of early environmental enrichment on cognitive development may reflect the indirect influence of such changes on the quality of early social experience. In the natural setting, physical objects usually serve as instruments for facilitating social participation (Musatti, 1986). Both adults and children use objects to focus interpersonal communication, and to actively modulate the nature of ongoing social exchange. The strategic shifting of attention between a social partner and a physical object permits maximizing both play and exploration while conserving the ongoing coordination of a social episode. Thus, the greater variety of information in complex environments leads to concomitant changes in the quantity and diversity of early social experiences and in cognitive performance.

The child's simultaneous awareness of mutual interest in particular objects and of the objects themselves entails a basic aspect of almost all dyadic communication after the first five months of life (Trevarthen, 1974). At this early age, the mental representation of both objects and people involves abstracting *figurative representations* of perceived information. Primitive mental organization entails a coordinated representation of perceptions and movement that are not yet differentiated as mature abstract concepts (Boesch, 1984). However, to communicate effectively the child must be able to abstract a diversity of pertinent features from the perceived world, to manipulate these different patterns of figurative information, and to exchange resulting representations with the social partner. The capacity to coordinate such diverse cognitive demands involves basic representational skills that are practiced on a regular basis with almost all social partners in the child's early entourage.

In comparison to dyadic communication, adaptation within a stable peer group generates even more impressive cognitive demands for the child. As a group member, the child must repeatedly calculate and anticipate the behavior of multiple social partners weighing the advantages and disadvantages of possible actions and the potential responses that such actions might elicit. The social skills that are essential for regular participation in a peer play group seem in many ways to surpass the representational capacities of a Grand Master playing multiple, but independent, games of chess with many familiar adversaries. Mastery of chess depends on careful monitoring of one's own behavior as well as attention to the adversary's current and anticipated actions. Subtle discrepancies from expected response patterns serve as cues for updating prevailing representations of the ongoing social episode and adjusting previously planned strategies. Similarly, the child's competent participation with familiar peers requires cognitive distancing from the present set of events in order to revise representations of the nature of ongoing interaction, as well as to anticipate and plan future activity. Cognitive distancing contributes to the growth of decentration skills by separating the child psychologically from the immediate present (Sigel, 1982). Verba, Stambak, and Sinclair (1982) have examined the progressive distancing which occurs during social exchanges among a small group of toddlers. In order to maintain shared activity, these children often repeated the action of their peer using a slightly different object, combined two successive actions by the partner into a single complex response, and/or corrected their partner's unsuccessful problem-solving activity by substituting more appropriate actions. Mutual imitation, social comparison, and joint verification of actions provide the continuity of social involvement that becomes the basis for emerging interpersonal relationships among young peers. From a cognitive perspective, the progressive coordination at a group level corresponds with increasing metacognitive awareness on an individual level (Nadel-Brulfert & Baudonnière, 1982; Musatti, 1986).

EARLY SOCIAL RELATIONS AND COGNITIVE GROWTH

The majority of research that has attempted to demonstrate direct links between children's early cognitive functioning and early social experience has focused almost exclusively upon the possible relations between quality of primary attachment and the emergence of individual differences in cognitive styles. The figurative representation of events has been studied in terms of affective qualities which in early infancy appear to be tied to the regulation of basic biological needs (Boesch, 1984; Hofer, 1987). By three months, infants are capable of encoding at a sensorimotor level the reliability of homeostatic regulation associated with nine caregivers' actions towards them (Main, Kaplan, & Cassidy, 1985; Pipp & Harmon, 1987). In parallel with the acquisition of informational signs and symbols, growth in representational ability is associated with progressive internalization of the affective quality of the primary attachment relationship. Preliminary evidence suggests that the infant's modal style of transacting with the object world may be closely related to dyadic relational styles with primary caregivers. Recent studies exploring the influence of attachment on infant cognition have reported that security of attachment at 12 months is associated with more active exploration and greater spatial and conceptual abilities at two years (Hazen & Durrett, 1982), greater skill in negotiating the physical environment at 18 months (Cassidy, 1986) greater task persistence at 12 and 24 months (Frodi, Bridges, & Grolnick, 1985) and higher levels of exploratory play (Harmon, Suwalsky & Klein, 1979).

Correspondingly, insecure primary attachment relationships have been linked to poorer mastery motivation in play with objects at age two (Harmon et al., 1979). Although insecure-avoidant toddlers manifest a high level of object-oriented behavior, they do so in a less planful goal-oriented fashion (Frodi et al., 1985). Their relatively higher investment in objects reflects a lack of equilibration between dependency and exploration since these infants do not direct attention away from the object and towards the mother even when security is threatened (Bretherton, 1985). Such inflexible, monotonic object play may provide a predictable alternative to an incoherent, disorganized relationship with the primary caregiver. Insecure-resistant toddlers show the least object engagement (Main, 1973) and the most attempts to orient the mother toward them while at the same time resisting positive responses (Frodi et al., 1985). As Bretherton (1985) has suggested, such infants seem unable to direct attention to the environment, and perserverate in focusing attention anxiously toward the parent. These reported effects of attachment on patterns of cognitive processing are consistent with the idea that behavioral and attentional mechanisms activated through repeated social transactions structure representational activity in qualitatively different ways.

In spite of these preliminary findings on the potential effects of early social experience on the quality of early representational activity, an exclusive focus upon primary attachment relationships cannot adequately portray the biological bases of cognitive development. A biosocial analysis of early cognitive development also requires revising some of our most basic views about early affective development. Traditionally, theoretical models of social development have placed central importance on the primary role of mother-child bonding (Ainsworth, 1972; Bowlby, 1969; Bretherton, 1985; Matas, Arend, & Sroufe, 1978; Waters & Deane, 1985). Under the influence of psychoanalytic theory (Freud, 1940), psychologists have usually construed the quality and relative exclusivity of the primary attachment relationship as the cornerstone for all subsequent growth and development. The quality of primary social bonds has been assumed to determine basic patterns of social interaction and affective development, and indirectly to influence exploration, social play, and emotional reactivity. These latter experiences, in turn, are assumed to shape the child's emerging cognitive abilities. However, from a phylogenetic perspective, extended neotony in the human species suggests that survival needs of the infant probably exceed the normal capacities of any single caregiver. Parental investment theory predicts that the central role of maternal responsivity in models of socioaffective development should be attenuated by a more general consideration of the diversity of other available social resources (Strayer, 1984; Trivers, 1972). This biosocial model of early social development predicts that the multiplicity of agents in the infant's social entourage should be as important to early social and cognitive development as the quality of primary nurturing by the biological mother.

A critical question in current research on the social construction of cognitive activity entails the testing of the generalizability of attachment effects with regard to a diversity of social partners and a variety of social settings (Bretherton, 1985). Hofer (1987) hypothesizes that elaboration of the attachment system is associated not only with changes in the structure of representational activities but also with the reorganization of homeostatis regulatory mechanisms underlying all stable relationships. Components of social skills learned in the course of interactions with primary attachment figures are restructured in the context of social relations with other regular partners. The resulting interpersonal generalization of rudimentary regulatory skills permits the infant to benefit from multiple sources of external information. Such restructuring enables the child to develop greater autonomy on both a socioaffective and cognitive plane.

The contribution of other social partners to the establishment of children's auto-regulatory abilities might be especially important for infants who have a less then optimal relation with their biological mother. Pipp & Harmon (1987) emphasize that an insecure attachment relationship with the mother does not necessarily predispose a child to the same problematic bonding with other adults. Evidence of change in attachment classification with changing family circumstances and differences in the quality of infant attachment to caregivers such as mother and father (Lamb, 1978; Lamb, Thompson, Gardner, Charnov, & Estes, 1984) support such a view. The cognitive implications of developmental plasticity lead to predictions of at least a partial recuperation of nonadaptive styles of object engagement and environmental exploration as a result of more diversified socioaffective contacts. Evidence of improved cognitive performance among deprived preschoolers exposed to quality day-care programs in comparison to home-reared control groups also supports predictions from a biosocial model (Belsky & Steinberg, 1978).

THE DESCRIPTIVE ANALYSIS OF REPRESENTATIONAL SKILLS

Empirical investigation of the reciprocal influences between patterns of early experience and the development of representational skills requires identification and measurement of interactive social and cognitive processes in naturalistic settings. It is generally recognized that global outcome measures of cognitive and social development do not permit the evaluation of particular functional skills related to adaptation in real-life settings (Belsky & Steinberg, 1978; Wachs & Gruen, 1982). Recent theories of intelligence have emphasized the central role of problem-solving abilities in accounting for the growth of both social and intellectual competence (Newell & Simon, 1972; Sternberg & Powell, 1983). The importance of developing more comprehensive techniques for studying early problem-solving behavior during this period is born out by recent evidence demonstrating that the only measures of intellectual performance showing strong continuity between infancy and the remainder of the life span are those linked to problem creation, development, and solution skills (Fagen & McGrath, 1981; Lewis & Brooks-Gunn, 1981; Sternberg & Powell, 1983). The lack of more extensive information about problem-solving tactics among very young children in everyday settings represents a major gap in modern research on cognitive development (Charlesworth, 1976; Harris, 1983).

Specific components of problem solving which have been studied systematically include rule structuring (Siegler, 1978), goal-targeting, and subgoal sequencing (Case, 1978; Klahr, 1985), grouping objects and actions according to perceptual and functional characteristics (Trabasso, Isen, Dolecki, Mc Lanahan,

Riley, and Tucker, 1978) and metacognitive or executive components which direct and monitor the problem-solving process (Brown & Deloache, 1978; Flavell, 1981). Although the heuristic utility of analyzing each component of intellectual functioning is apparent, few researchers have been able to reintegrate the diversity of separate findings to provide a representative description of how children coordinate cognitive tactics in the generation of effective solutions to problems. A more adequate developmental model of psychological functioning should include factors that explain individual differences in the coordinated use of such representational tactics, as well as account for age-related trends in the use of both specific cognitive tactics and more general problem-solving strategies. For example, Main et al. (1985) have noted the overconcentration on objects and activities characterizing the verbal interactions of parents with their six-year-olds classified as insecure-avoidant in infancy. As noted previously, these children showed an inappropriately high degree of attention to inanimate objects in early childhood (Cassidy, 1986).

Another category of problem-solving behavior refers to task orientation which in joint activity includes careful monitoring and directing of the partner's activity and attention to the relationship between the ongoing activity and common goals. Attempts to jointly coordinate problem solving activity are disrupted by overconcentration on personal attributes of the partner or aspects of the relationship which do not facilitate co-construction of problem solving strategies. For example, disapproval which is not contingent on the attainment of task subgoals or unnecessary conduct management is disruptive for joint problem solving. As discussed above, such patterns are associated with the dyadic interaction of insecure-resistant toddlers and their mothers (Frodi et al., 1985). These dyads showed a dysfunctional preoccupation with relationships and feelings during joint play which was incompatable with mutual collaboration in the solution of problems.

Although working models of intellectual development postulate interdependence of component processes of problem solving (e.g. Sternberg & Powell, 1983), empirical studies that articulate the exact nature of such dependencies are extremely rare. Studies of metacomponents of problem-solving ability that have been undertaken (e.g. Brown, 1982; Moss, 1985; Wertsch et al., 1980) have varied so widely in their conceptual and methodological approaches that any single synthesis is difficult. While certain researchers have looked only at nonverbal behavior in lab contexts, others have emphasized verbal exchanges during social interaction. Of particular importance to the elaboration of cognitive and affective representational structures are metacognitive strategies which enable distancing from particular actions in order to restructure plans in the service of goal attainment. Strategies such as predicting consequences, checking results, monitoring activity, and reality testing are critical to the child's ability to be self-regulating in a variety of problem-solving situations (Brown, 1978; 1988; Mischel, 1981).

Although these metacognitive skills are often assumed to be deficient in the very young child (Brown, 1978), our research suggests that precursors of later more independent abilities are evident in the patterns of peer interaction discussed above and in certain patterns of adult-child joint problem solving. The latter are characterized by adult modeling of specific metacognitive strategies and sensitivity to emerging child social and cognitive autonomy (Moss, 1985). As Wertsch, McNamee, McLane and Budwig (1980), and Brown, Palinscar, and Armbruster (1984), have shown, the young child is largely dependent on adult regulation and coordination of complex problem-solving activity. As the child matures and becomes more capable of generating and monitoring plans, the sensitive caregiver should assume a more indirect role allowing maximal opportunities for the child to test and practice emerging skills. This pattern of progressive empowerment has been associated with the interaction styles of parents with high-IQ preschoolers (Moss, 1985), and with children of the same age demonstrating consistent ability to delay gratification (Moss, Strayer, Cournoyer & Trudel, 1988); it is also related to the flexible, fluid conversational style of parents and their securely-attached school-aged children (Main et al., 1985).

RESEARCH QUESTIONS

A synthesis of these views about the nature of human sociability and intelligence raises intriguing questions about the interaction between patterns of attachment, out-of-home care, and the development of problem-solving skills. The hypothesis that strategies learned in the course of social transactions are generalized to problems encountered during play with objects provides a set of novel predictions about the early development of representational skills. From this perspective, we expect that both social intelligence and social competence depend on the complexity and diversity of early social relations as well as on the socioaffective equilibrium of the child's primary attachment bond.

In accordance with traditional attachment theory, we predicted that a secure primary relationship with mother would be associated with greater diversity and complexity of representational tactics during problem solving. Moreover, the development of problem-solving skills has also been associated with opportunities to participate in joint activity with both adults and peers. Adaptation to the peer group should require distancing from particular actions in order to analyze and plan appropriate social strategies, and thus offer more direct occasions for the development of metacognitive ability. For securely attached infants who begin day care in the fourth quarter of the first year, a time of consolidation of the attachment system, we expected that the growth of goal-oriented object-interaction patterns should be accelerated by social demands in the day care situation.

For insecurely attached infants, exposure to more responsive adults in the day care situation and object-oriented interactive demands from peers might introduce more adaptive occasions for both social and cognitive development, and thus indirectly compensate for deficits in interaction patterns developed at home. Given day care children's greater social experience with a diversity of social partners, we predicted that they would have a greater tendency to employ representational tactics that include distancing, or metacognitive forms of information exchange when compared to insecurely-attached infants reared at home.

To explore some of these predictions in greater depth, we examined how the quality of primary bonding and the diversity of early social relations outside of the family setting contribute to the child's use of specific representational tactics in common, everyday problem-solving situations. To provide the most ecologically valid assesment of these early cognitive abilities, our research focused upon problem solving during structured dyadic play at home with mother. We chose to study the problem-solving behavior of mothers and infants who differed in both attachment and early care environments in order to examine the coherence and diversity in cognitive and social representational activity during the first three years of life.

RESEARCH METHODS

The quality of the mother-child bond was evaluated using the Attachment Q-Sort Questionaire (Waters & Deane, 1985). The questionaire was completed by 93 middle-class, French-speaking mothers within a few weeks of their child's second birthday. Approximately half of these children had been enrolled in an infant day care program during their first year of life, while the others had no regular day care experience during the course of the research.

The Attachment Q-Sort provided a profile of the child's social functioning based upon the relative weighting of 100 descriptive items that characterized children's social adjustment during the first three years. Indices of socioaffective security, interpersonal dependency, and general sociability were computed by comparing obtained individual profiles with theoretically optimal profiles for each of these developmental constructs (Waters & Deane, 1985). However, in this study, rather than selecting children on the basis of their deviation from mean construct scores, we decided to assess to what extent the Q-Sort procedure provided homogenous categories of children who could be characterized by specific differences in the quality of the early attachment relationship. This ethological approach to classification permitted us to identify natural groupings of toddlers who were similar with respect to a variety of attachment-related behaviors.

Using complete linkage hierarchical clustering techniques with correlation matrices as indices of similarity between individual profiles, we identified three classes of children with similar Q-Sort scores. These initial findings were validated in split-half analyses which showed that the classification scheme was stable across randomly selected subsamples of subjects. In order to evaluate whether the three empirical clusters corresponded to qualitatively different patterns of primary attachment, groups of children were contrasted with respect to security, dependency, and sociability socores. One-way analyses of variance indicated that attachment classes differed in a linear manner on each of the three theoretical constructs measured by the Q-Sort Questionaire [F's (2,91) = 23.72, p's < .001]. Class I children were the most secure, most sociable, and least dependent, while Class III were the least secure, least sociable, and most dependent. Since the three clusters showed the strongest mean difference on the security dimension, they were labeled the Secure, Average, and Insecure groups. In our subsequent analyses of problem-solving activity, a subsample of 34 children (17 from Class I; 17 Class III) was selected to represent the two extreme clusters in this attachment classification analysis. In each group, approximately half of the subjects were from the day care group and half from the home-reared. Table 2.1 outlines the distribution of subjects in the four subsamples.

All subjects had been videotaped with their mother during semistructured play sessions at home when the children were 18 and 30 months old. Three modalities of information exchange (Nonverbal gestures, Statements, and Questions) were coded separately using a taxonomy of specific problem-solving tactics. These descriptive categories were regrouped on an *a priori* basis into four classes of problem-solving behaviors (see Table 2.2) which reflected the mother's and child's relative investment in objects, action sequences, conduct management of the dyadic partner and metacognitive activity.

The description of problem-solving activity required simultaneous coding by two highly trained observers. One observer focused upon the mother while the other followed the child. Observers noted all instances of the above tactics that were used by their respective focal subjects, as well as whether a recorded act was directed to a social partner or towards an object. Interobserver reliability in coding this information was assessed regularly using Cohen's Kappa; all Kappa indices were greater than 0.85.

Data were entered separately into two OS-3 data loggers that were connected to a common digital time signal written on one of the audio tracks of the VHS video recording system. This device permitted accuracy to a tenth of a second. Since the original data records included both the coded forms of individual activ-

Table 2.1. Description of Subjects in Problem-Solving Sample

Group Membership	Secure (Class I)	Insecure (Class III)	Total
Home Reared			
Girls	4	4	8
Boys	4	5	9
Day Care			
Girls	4	4	8
Boys	4	5	9
Total	16	18	34

Table 2.2.   Coding Taxonomy for Dyadic
Exchange of Information

Classes of Activity		Problem Solving Tactics
A. Metacognitive	1.	Planning Action Sequences
	2.	Predicting Consequences
	3.	Verifying results
	4.	Reality Testing
B. Action-Based	5.	Subgoal Specifications
	6.	Solution Attainment
	7.	Rule Elaboration
C. Object-Based	8.	Perceptual Cues
	19.	Functional Cues
	10.	Contextual Cues
	11.	Labeling
D. Conduct	12.	Orientation to Task
Management	13.	Disapproval
	14.	Approval

ity and their exact time of appearance, it was possible to recompose a literal, temporally-based transcript of all dyadic exchange during the entire problem-solving session. Computer software that merged the two data files also identified separate sequences of social problem solving. Whenever more than five seconds elapsed without any activity emitted by either the mother or child, a special code was automatically inserted to denote sequence transitions.

RESEARCH FINDINGS

Repeated measure analyses of variance ($2 \times 2 \times 2$; day care experience, age, and attachment category) were conducted to examine group differences in rates of overall and specific problem-solving activity, relative use of the three response modalities, and the differential use of different problem-solving tactics.

Figure 2.1 shows the mean hourly rates of social sequences as a function of age for both socialization and attachment groups. Day care children were involved in significantly more sequences of dyadic information exchange at both age levels (main effect for socialization group, $F (1,30) = 6.86$, $p < .02$), and initiated significantly more activity during the problem-solving sessions (main effect for socialization group, $F(1,30) = 6.59$, $p < .02$). Although there was a slight decrease at 30 months in the hourly rate of problem-solving sequences for three of the four contrast groups in Figure 2.1, these mean differences were not significant.

Group differences in the rate of problem-solving activity and in the rate of dyadic sequences were clarified by examining the relative contribution of the mother and child to total dyadic activity at each age level. Given the strong dif-

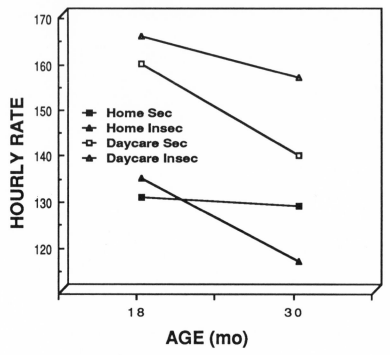

Figure 1. Hourly Rate of Dyadic Sequences for Social Groupings

ferences between the day care and home-reared children in rate of problem-solving activity, subsequent analyses of how problem-solving styles might be influenced by early social experience were conducted using relative frequency measures which control for differences in activity level. Figure 2.2 shows the proportion of problem-solving tactics that were initiated by the mother as a function of age for each of the experimental groups.

There was a significant interaction between age and socialization experience in the relative investment of home and day care mothers during dyadic problem-solving activity [F(1,30,) = 8.06, p.<.01]. At 18 months, day care mothers initiated nearly two-thirds of the recorded activity in each sequence, while home mothers were responsible for only slightly more than half of all dyadic activity. Such group differences in maternal involvement were no longer apparent at 30 months. A possible explanation of these early but temporary group differences is that they reflect efforts by the daycare mothers to initiate communication about their children's extrafamilial experiences. Such maternal probing may be less present at the later age, owing to the more spontaneous and sophisticated verbal skills of the 30-month-old child.

To explore this possibility, our second set of questions focused upon children's relative use of verbal and nonverbal response modalities. The relative use

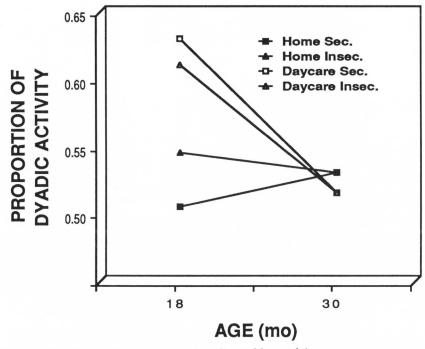

Figure 2.   Maternal Investment in Dyadic Problem Solving

of nonverbal activity declined as a function of age [F(1,30) = 112.40, p<.001] for all children while the relative use of both statements and questions increased [F's (1,30) = 23.54, p's <.001]. However, the rate of change for the latter two measures differed as a function of early social experience [F's (1,30) = 4.66, p's <.05]. Day care children used more statements, while home-reared children used more questions during information exchange with mother.

Day care children's greater facility in the verbal expression of problem-solving tactics may have resulted from their more extensive experience in a complex social group where the expression of problem-solving tactics is a necessary means for effectively communicating with others during play. Problem-solving tactics which may first develop as a response to varying environmental demands in the daycare center become part of the child's cognitive repertoire and are later generalized in the home context. On the other hand, the questioning tactics of the home children may reflect the influence of the basic complementary roles in the mother-child dyad, where the mother serves both as a source of emotional security and information.

Analyses of children's relative use of specific tactics revealed a series of age effects for Labeling [F(1,30) = 12.48, p<.001], Function Cues [F(1,30) = 14.11, p. <.001], Subgoal Identification [F(1,30), df = 19.16, p<.001] and

Metacognitive activity [F(1,30) = 10.89, p. <.01]. These analyses revealed only a single socialization effect for the relative use of metacognitive activity [F (1,30) = 6.53, p <.05]. There were no significant effects relating to the security of primary attachment. Group differences in the relative use of metacognitive tactics as a function of age are illustrated in Figure 2.3. Visual inspection of the performance for each subgroup reveals that both the day care groups and the secure home children contribute more to the reported age trend than do the insecure home children.

These results suggest the existence of broad zones of problem-solving development which can be considered normative during the third year of life. The acquisition of object labels, extended exploration of the relation between objects and particular problem-solving activities as well as increased capacity to to coordinate different elements of the problem space can be considered to be in the zone of proximal development during this period. As hypothesized, day care experience appears to have the greatest impact on the stimulation of distancing processes which permit overall coordination of activity. Insecurity of attachment appears to have a minor depressing effect on the emergence of these basic cognitive abilities which is somewhat attenuated by the day care experience.

Similar analysis of mothers' relative use of specific problem-solving tactics also showed a number of general age effects. At 30 months, mothers used rela-

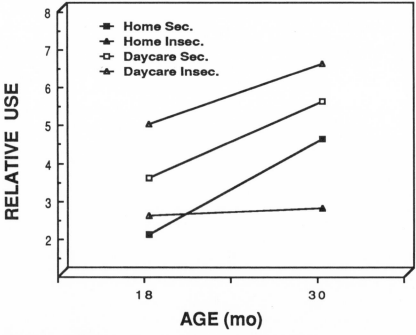

Figure 3.   Children's Relative Use of Metacognitive Tactics

tively more Labeling [F(1,30) = 5.08, p <.05), Perceptual Cues [F(1,30) = 13.03, p <.001] and Metacognitive tactics [F(1,30) = 36.39, p <.001], suggesting a general relation between emerging child object-exploratory and coordination abilities and complementary maternal scaffolding. In addition, day care mothers showed a greater proportion of metacognitive activity at both 18 and 30 months [F(1,30) = 4.95, p <.05]. The more frequent metacognitive questions asked by day care mothers may reflect their efforts to understand activities and expressions that their children may have learned outside of the home. These tactics may encourage the children to better conceptualize experiences not shared with mother and thus stimulate further cognitive growth. Although the graphic illustration of these results in Figure 2.4 suggests a possible interaction between attachment classification and early socialization experience in the rate of maternal metacognitive activity, analysis of this effect revealed only a marginal trend [attachment by experience effect, F(1,30) = 3.18, p <.10].

The anticipated differences in the relative use of metacognitive tactics as a function of early social experience provided direct support for the psychobiological hypothesis that the nature and complexity of early social relations impacts directly upon children's emerging representational abilities. To a large extent, differences in the use of problem-solving tactics appear more related to age and extrafamilial experience than to the quality of the primary attachment bond.

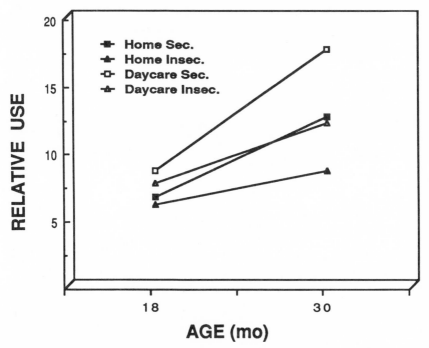

Figure 4. Mothers' Relative Use of Metacognitive Tactics

However, to obtain more precise measures of the influence of quality of attachment on representational ability, we carried out an exchange analysis of dyadic communication. In keeping with coconstruction developmental models, we hypothesized that measures of mother and child mutual responsivity to initiatives by the partner to jointly coordinate information exchange would constitute a more sensitive index of the possible contribution of primary attachment and early experience to the development of metacognitive tactics. Sequential exchanges involving such distancing strategies were examined with reference to modal response patterns within each of the four contrast groups.

Table 2.3-A provides a summary of the mean likelihood of each maternal response class. These first-order probabilities reflect the relative use of each class of information exchange as a response to child initiated tactics. An overview of these maternal profiles shows that for all groups, the largest proportion of behaviors involves references to task objects while the next most frequent are action-oriented. Mothers of insecure children use relatively more references to conduct than to metacognitive activity, whereas mothers of secure children show the opposite tendency. Home mothers are generally more action-oriented than are daycare mothers. Mothers of insecure children are generally lower in metacognitive responses than are mothers of the secure group with the daycare insecure group slightly higher than their home counterparts.

Table 2.3-B shows how these baseline probabilities change when the preceeding action of the child was a metacognitive tactic. Comparison of maternal baselines with contingent response probabilities enables us to look at the responsiveness of the four mother groups to child demonstrations of higher-order

Table 2.3. Dyadic Contingencies for Maternal Reactions

A). Baseline Probabilities for Maternal Responses

Group Membership	Metacognition	Action	Object	Conduct	Total Frequency
Day Care Secure	.18	.23	.44	.15	(1160)
Homecare Secure	.17	.29	.36	.18	(1024)
Day Care Insecure	.13	.23	.42	.21	(1019)
Homecare Insecure	.10	.27	.44	.19	(1098)

B). Probability of Maternal Response to Child Metacognitive Tactics

Group Membership	Metacognition	Action	Object	Conduct	Total Frequency
Day Care Secure	.40	.28	.22	.10	(98)
Homecare Secure	.34	.25	.21	.20	(61)
Day Care Insecure	.26	.24	.32	.16	(105)
Homecare Insecure	.26	.17	.38	.19	(47)

coordinating attempts. In parallel with the findings of others who have associated maternal responsivity with the imitation of antecedent child behaviors (Brome & Uzgiris, 1985; Moran & Symon, 1987; Schaffer, 1984) we observed a general trend for child metacognitive tactics to elicit maternal matching.

Mothers of day care children were more likely than home mothers to match their children's metacognitive initiations. This trend is strongest for the day care secure children, slightly lower for the home secure, and weakest for the two insecure groups. Accordingly, we expected a decrease in maternal baseline levels of object responses following child demonstrations of distancing ability indicating scaffolding of these higher-order skills. Alternatively, responding with an object cue to a higher-order metacognitive behavior indicates that the mother is focusing the child back to the level of a single object after the child is demonstrating competence at coordinating the object with other elements of the problem space. Mothers of secure children show more substantial decreases in object references when compared to the insecure group. The insecure home mothers, who reduce their object references the least, show the most rigidity of style. This group is also least likely to complement child metacognitive initiatives with orientations to actions. Day care insecure mothers more closely resembled the other three subgroups with their respective use of these tactics.

Finally although all mothers have a similar baseline rate of personal conduct references (approval, disapproval and task-orientation), day care mothers show a lower tendency to use these responses consequent to child metacognitive initiations.

Comparable descriptions of children's responses in dyadic exchange are summarized in Table 2.4. Baseline scores in Table 2.4-A show that the vast majority of children's responses involved either object or action tactics. This distribution reflects general age-appropriate representational competence which permits sharing information about object attributes and employing objects to achieve subgoals in ongoing activity. In accordance with earlier analyses, day care children have a higher proportion of metacognitive references. Secure children were observed to make relatively more object references. When compared to the other three subgroups, day care insecure children were more likely to respond with conduct management tactics and less likely to use action tactics.

Examination of the dyadic contingencies in Table 2.4-B indicate that children also moderately increased their probability of metacognitive activity following maternal use of a metacognitive tactic. Such behavior can be considered developmentally appropriate since at 30 months, verbalization of metacognitive strategies such as reality testing or activity monitoring would be most likely to occur directly following adult modeling (Moss, 1985). Homecare secure children show greater recuperation of their lower baseline level of metacognitive activity than do insecure home children suggesting more effeetive adult scaffolding. Whereas secure children show a slightly higher level of on-task activity following maternal distancing cues, the insecure group shows the opposite response. As a result,

Table 2.4.   Dyadic Contingencies for Child Reactions

A). Baseline Probabilities for Child Responses

Group Membership	Metacognition	Action	Object	Conduct	Total Frequency
Day Care Secure	.08	.43	.41	.08	(1157)
Homecare Secure	.05	.45	.41	.08	(1031)
Day Care Insecure	.08	.33	.46	.13	(1024)
Homecare Insecure	.04	.42	.45	.09	(1098)

B). Probability of Child Response to Maternal Metacognitive Tactics

Group Membership	Metacognition	Action	Object	Conduct	Total Frequency
Day Care Secure	.14	.45	.30	.11	(214)
Homecare Secure	.12	.47	.35	.06	(155)
Day Care Insecure	.16	.27	.39	.18	(141)
Homecare Insecure	.08	.37	.31	.24	(110)

insecure children have a lower probability of action responses to maternal metacognitive initiations with day care insecure children lowest of all four subgroups. Day care insecure children show the highest proportion of object references consequent to maternal metacognitive cues and the least decrease as compared to baseline measures.

With regards to person-oriented references, insecure home children show the most dramatic change in their baseline level consequent to maternal metacognitive cues. Whereas home secures decrease slightly on this measure and both day care groups increase moderately, the home insecures increase their probability by two and a half times.

DISCUSSION

These results suggest the existence of broad maturational zones of early representational development which are subject to variation as a result of the influence of both quality of attachment and early day care experience. Between 18 and 30 months, there is substantial increase in cognitive activity associated with the representation and communication of object attributes and relations between objects and problem-solving subgoals. In addition, there is evident emergence of planning and monitoring skills crucial to more independent coordination of problem-solving activity. Mothers appear to be coparticipants in the construction of these abilities during this developmental period since changes in the component tactics of their behavior during play with their toddlers in general parallel growth in child abilities.

Day care experience appears to have an impact primarily on the development of children's verbal and metacognitive skills, and on the structure of information flow in the mother-child dyad. Day care children's proportion of metacognitive activity was higher than that of home children both in overall and mother-elicited behavior. Day care children act more often as information sources and initiate more social sequences with mother. Mothers of day care children ask a greater proportion of questions which further encourage the coordination of event representations. Such mutual facilitation of higher-order cognitive skills seems related to the necessity to reconstitute separate experiences. Relational constraints were also evident in the greater use of questions by home-reared children. Such tactics may reflect these children's punctual adaptation to the asymmetrical demands that characterize the complementary roles in early adult-child social relations (Youniss, 1980). These views are supported by recent studies which have investigated the effects of experience with peer and adult partners on children's discourse competence. Hay (1982) found that young children who had attended preschool used more sophisticated discourse skills than those who had remained at home. French (1985), in a detailed analysis of the language skills used by a 30-month year-old girl, found that she used considerably more sophisticated conversational devices when interacting with her peer than with her more responsive and conversationally-skilled mother. The author suggested that these sophisticated discourse skills develop when they are needed to maintain an interaction and are therefore likely to be facilitated by social contacts with conversationally unskilled peers rather than adults.

Although our first ANOVA analyses did not reveal any significant attachment effects, sequential analyses offered more precise information about how the quality of primary bonding and the diversity of early social relations influence the child's representational activity during episodes of structured play with mother. Although day care children had a higher baseline level of metacognitive activity, mothers of day care insecure children did not respond with complementary higher-order tactics any more readily than did mothers of home insecure children. They were also considerably lower than both secure groups. Given this lower level of maternal scaffolding, it is surprising that day care insecure toddlers still maintain a higher metacognitive response rate than do both home groups. This suggests that experiences in the day care context compensate for less adequate stimulation in the home environment. On the other hand, mothers of secure day care children appear to build on their children's acquired metacognitive competence by imitating and thereby reinforcing its growth.

Security of attachment appears to influence attention mechanisms. Insecure children are more object-oriented than secure children and their mothers are most likely to reorient dyadic interaction towards simple objects even when their children show evidence of higher-order cognitive skills. Day care experience does not substantially alter these dyadic patterns but may affect the relative contribution of each partner since overinvestment in objects is most evident in both home insecure mothers' responses and insecure daycare children's responses. The net result appears to be greater avoidance of a coconstructive context and less optimal collaboration in goal-oriented problem-solving endeavors when compared with secure dyads.

Home mothers are more likely to reorient their children's attention to some aspects of their conduct than are day care mothers. Moreover, insecure children in both groups show higher levels of maternal conduct management. Home insecure children show extreme increases in maternal monitoring when their mothers are the most-task-oriented, suggesting considerable inaccuracy in these children's functional understanding of the coordination of the respective input of different participants in a common endeavour.

This deficit which has been associated with the cognitive style of insecure-resistant children (Frodi et al., 1985; Main et al., 1985) is less evident in the responses of daycare insecure children. It is possible that greater opportunities to engage and observe more cohesive group dynamics has attenuated the development of this relational dysfunction.

Finally, security of attachment appears to have an impact on dyadic representation and execution of task activities related to subgoals. Mothers of insecure home children are least likely to respond with an action tactic to their children's metacognitive initiatives while daycare insecure children show the lowest level of activity referencing. Further studies are necessary to confirm and explain these differences.

CONCLUSION

These findings strongly support predictions from a cognitive ethological model of early representation that gives primacy to the social construction of intellectual activities. Interpersonal relations constrain the transfer of information and shape the child's emerging representational skills. Past studies of social constraints on intellectual functioning have generally emphasized that parent-child communication establishes basic patterns of socioaffective adjustment which only indirectly shape the child's subsequent cognitive development (Matas, et al, 1978; Shatz, 1983). Our result show more direct links between representational activity and early social experience. From a psychobiological perspective, these findings suggest that early social relations provide a species characteristic setting for the development of skills in the expression and representation of problem-solving tactics.

In our study, both the diversity and the quality of this social experience was associated with the more rapid emergence of complex problem-solving tactics. The day care secure group was, in many instances, more advanced in communicative and representational competence. Clearly we found no support for the hypothesis that out-of-home care in the first year of life has a disorganizing effect on a secure attachment relationship. Rather, our results support the view that early day care experience may complement, or even compensate for, an emerging style of interpersonal communication that does not optimize the toddler's emerging intellectual functioning. In this regard, it is important to stress that in many instances, the problem-solving style of insecurely attached toddlers who had more extensive day care experience was equivalent to that of their securely attached peers who had been socialized only in the more restricted home setting. This finding suggests that human infants are able to benefit from multiple parental resources, and under adverse conditions supplementary parental care may facilitate normal cognitive and affective development. Such an interpretation is consistent with predictions from sociobiological parental investment theory. Both the diversity and the quality of interpersonal relations constrain the acquisition of information and thus shape the child's emerging representational abilities. These results demonstrate the utility of a coadaptation model of information exchange as the prime mover for early cognitive development and the emergence of social skill.

REFERENCES

Ainsworth, M.D. (1972). Attachment and dependency: A comparison. In J.L. Gewirtz (Ed.), *Attachment and dependency* (pp. 97–132). Washington, DC: Winston.

Belsky, J., & Steinberg, L. (1978). The effects of day care: A critical review. *Child Development, 49*, 929–949.

Boesch, E.E. (1984). The development of affective schemata. *Human Development, 27*, 119–124.

Bowlby, J. (1969). *Attachment and loss*. New York: Basic Books.

Bretherton, I. (1985). Attachment Theory: Retrospect and Prospect. In I. Bretherton & E. Waters (Eds.), Growing points of attachment theory and research. *Monograph of the Society for Research in Child Development, 50*, 3–39.

Brome, S., & Uzgiris, I. (1985). *Imitation in mother–child conversations*. Paper presented at the meeting of the Society for Research in Child Development, Toronto, Canada.

Brown, A.L., & Deloache, J.S. (1987). Skills, plans and self-regulation. In R. Siegler (Ed.), *Children's thinking: what develops?* (pp. 3–37). Hillsdale, NJ: Erlbaum.

Brown, A., Palinscar, A., & Armbruster, B. (1984). Inducing comprehension-fostering activities in interactive learning situations. In H. Mandl, N. Stein, & T. Trabasso (Eds.), *Learning from texts*. Hillsdale, NJ: Erlbaum.

Brown, A.L. (1982). Inducing strategic learning from texts by means of informed self-control training. In *Topics in Learning Disabilities, 1–17*.

Case, R. (1978). Intellectual development from birth to adulthood: A Neo-piagetian interpretation. In R. Siegler (Ed.), *Children's thinking: What develops?* (pp. 37–73). Hillsdale, NJ: Erlbaum.

Cassidy, J. (1986). The ability to negotiate the environment: An aspect of infant competence as related to quality of attachment. *Child Development, 57*, 331–338.

Cattell, P. (1947). *The measurement of intelligence of infants and young children.* New York: Psychological Corporation.

Charlesworth, W.R. (1976). Human intelligence as adaptation: An ethological approach. In L. Resnick (Ed.), *The nature of intelligence,* (pp. 147–169). Hillsdale NJ: Erlbaum.

Fagen, J.F., & McGrath, S.K. (1981). Infant recognition memory and later intelligence. *Intelligence, 5,* 121–130.

Flavell, J.H. (1981). Cognitive monitoring. In W.P. Dickson (Ed.), *Children's oral communication skills* (pp. 35–61). New York: Academic Press.

French, L. (1985). *Effects of partner and setting on young children's discourse competence.* Paper presented at the meeting of the Society for Research in Child Development, April, Toronto, Canada.

Freud, S. (1940). An outline of psychoanalysis. In J. Strachey (Ed. and trans.), *The standard edition of the complete psychological works of Sigmeund Freud, Vol. 23,* (pp. 137–207). London: Hogarth.

Frodi, A., Bridges, L., & Grolnick, W. (1985). Correlates of mastery-related behaviour: A short-term longitudinal study of infants in their second year. *Child Development, 56,* 1291–1299.

Harmon, R., Suwalsky, J., & Klein, R. (1979). Infant's preferential response for mother versus an unfamiliar adult. *Journal of the American Academy of Child Psychiatry, 18,* 437–449.

Harris, P.L. (1983). Infant cognition. In M. Haith & J. Campos (Eds.), *Mussen handbook of child psychology* (pp. 689–783). New York: Wiley.

Hay. A. (1982). *The role of interactive experience in the development of discourse skills.* Unpublished doctoral dissertation, University of Illinois at Urbana-Champaign.

Hazen, N., & Durrett, M. (1982). Relationship of security of attachment to exploration and cognitive mapping ability in two-year-olds. *Developmental Psychology, 18,* 751–759.

Hinde, R.A. (1979). *Towards understanding relationships.* New York: Academic Press.

Hofer, M. (1987). Early social relationships: A psychobiologist's view. *Child Development, 58* (3), 633–647.

Humphrey, N.K. (1976). The social function of intellect. In P. Bateson & R. Hinde (Eds.), *Growing points in ethology* (pp. 303–317). Cambridge: Cambridge University Press.

Jarrard, L.E. (1971). *Cognitive processes of nonhuman primates.* New York: Academic Press.

Klahr, D. (1985). Solving problems with ambiguous subgoal ordering: Preschooler's performance. *Child Development, 56,* 940–953.

Lamb, M.E. (1978). Qualitative aspects of mother-and father-infant attachments. *Infant Behavior and Development, 1,* 265–275.

Lamb, M., Thompson, R., Gardner, P., Charnov, E., & Estes, D. (1984). Security of infantile attachment as assessed in the strange situation: Its study and biological interpretation. *The Behavioral and Brain Sciences, 7,* 127–171.

Lewis, M., & Brooks-Gunn, J. (1981). Visual attention at three months as a predictor of cognitive functioning at two years of age. *Intelligence 5,* 131–140.

Main, M., Kaplan, N., & Cassidy, J. (1985). Security in infancy, childhood and adulthood: A move to the level of representation. In I. Bretherton & E. Waters (Eds.),

Growing points of attachment theory and research. *Monograph of the Society for Research in Child Development, 50,* 41–65.

Matas, L., Arend, R.A., & Sroufe, L.A. (1978). Continuity of adaptation in the second year: The relationship between quality of attachment and later competence. *Child Development, 49,* 547–556.

Meacham, J.A. (1984). The social basis of intentional action. *Human Development, 27* (3–4), 119–124.

Mischel, W. (1981). Metacognition and the rules of delay. In J. Flavell & L. Ross (Eds.), *Cognitive and social development: Frontiers and possible futures* (pp. 240–271). New York: Cambridge University Press.

Miller, G., Galanter, E., & Pribram, K. (1960). *Plans and the structure of behavior.* New York: Holt, Rhinehart & Winston.

Moran, G., & Symon, D. (1987). *Using sequential analyses to quantify maternal responsiveness in early mother–infant interactions.* Paper presented at the biannial meeting of the Society for research in Child Development, Baltimore, MD.

Moss, E., Strayer, F., Cournoyer, M., & Trudel, M. (1988). Social roots of metacognition and self-regulation, *Canadian Journal of Early Childhood Education,* 3–9.

Moss, E. (1985). Transfer of metacognitive strategies in mother-child dyads. Paper presented at the meeting of the Society for Research in Child Development, Toronto, Canada.

Musatti, T. (1986). Early peer relations: The perspectives of Piaget and Vygotsky. In E. Mueller & C. Cooper (Eds.), *Process and outcome in peer relationships.* New York: Academic Press 25–50.

Nadel-Brulfert, J., & Baudonnière, P.M. (1982). The social function of reciprocal imitation in 2-year-old peers, *International Journal of Behavioral Development, 5,* 1, 95–109.

Newell, A. & Simon, H. (1972). *Human problem-solving.* Englewood Cliffs, NJ: Prentice-Hall.

Pipp, S. & Harmon, R. (1987). Attachment as regulation: A commentary. *Child Development, 58,* 633–647.

Sackett, G.P. (1970) Unlearned responses, differential rearing experiences, and the development of social attachments by Rhesus monkeys. In *Primate Behavior: Developments in field and laboratory research.* In L.A. Rosenbloom (Ed.), Academic Press: New York, 112–138.

Schaffer, H.R. (1984). *The child's entry into a social world.* New York: Academic Press.

Shatz, M. (1983). Communication. In P. Mussen (Ed.), *Handbook of child psychology, 4th ed.* New York: Wiley 495–544.

Siegler, R.S. (1978). The origins of scientific thinking. In R.S. Seigler (Ed.), Children's thinking: what develops? Hillsdale, NJ: Erlbaum 109–147.

Sigel, I. (1982). The relationship between distancing strategies and the child's cognitive behavior. In L. Laosa & I. Sigel (Eds.). *Families as learning environments for young children.* New York: Plenum 47–87.

Sternberg, R.J., & Powell, J.S. (1983). The development of intelligence. In J.H. Flavell and E.M. Markman (Eds.), *Mussen handbook of child psychology, Vol. 3* (pp. 341–419). New York: Wiley.

Strayer, F.F. (1980). Social ecology of the preschool peer group. In A. Collins (Ed.), *Cognition, affect and social relations.* Hillsdale, NJ: Erlbaum 165–193.

Strayer, F.F. (1984). Biological approaches to the study of the family. In R. Parke, R. Emde, H. McAdoo, & G. Sackett (Eds.), *Review of child development research, 7* (pp. 1–19). Chicago: University of Chicago Press.

Terman, L.M. (1925). *Genetic studies of genius. Vol. 1. The mental and physical traits of a thousand gifted children*. Stanford: Stanford University Press.

Trabasso, T., Isen, A., Dolecki, P., McLanahan, A.G., Riley, C.A., & Tucker, T. (1978). How do children solve class-inclusion problems? In R. Siegler (Ed.), *Children's thinking: what develops?* (pp. 151–181). Hillsdale, NJ: Erlbaum.

Trevarthen, C. (1974). Conversations with a two month old. *New Scientist, 62*, 230–265.

Trivers, R. (1972). Parental investment and sexual selection. In B. Campbell (Ed.), *Sexual selection and the descent of man, 1871–1971*. Chicago: Aldine.

Verba, M., Stambak, M., & Sinclair, H. (1982). Physical knowledge and social interaction in children from 18 to 24 months of age. In G. Forman (Ed.), *Action and thought* (pp. 267–296). New York: Academic Press.

Vygotsky, L. (1962). *Thought and language*. Chicago: M.I.T. Press.

Wachs, T.D., & Gruen, G.E. (1982). *Early experience and human development*. New York: Plenum.

Waters, E., & Deane, K.E. (1985). Defining and assessing individual differences in attachment relationship: Q-methodology and the organization of behavior in infancy and early childhood. In I. Bretherton & E. Waters (Eds.), Growing points of attachment theory and research. *Monograph of the Society for Research in Child Development, 50*, 39–41.

Wertsch, J.V., McNamee, G., McLane, J.B., & Budwig, N.A. (1980). The adult-child dyad as a problem-solving system. *Child Development, 51*, 1215–1221.

Youniss, J. (1980). *Parents and peers in social development: A Sullivan-Piaget perspective*. London: The University of Chicago Press.

CHAPTER 3

Organization and Process in the Development of Children's Understanding of Social Events*

Lucien T. Winegar

Perhaps the most functionally adaptive activity engaged in by children is the effective coordination of their actions with the actions of others. Successful social interaction gives children access to material and/or affilio-affective resources that are important for continuing development. However, the social world within which children must coordinate their actions is dynamic and complex. Children interact with a variety of different individuals in a multitude of settings. Even interactions with the same individual or in the same setting can be quite complex as interpretations, expectations, and evaluations of children's performance change as children develop and gain additional experience.

In spite of this complexity, children at very young ages often act within social settings as if they know the rules. They appear to generate expectations, recognize role requirements, assume reciprocity, and behave acceptably in a wide variety of social situations. Furthermore, children usually learn the rules of new social situations very quickly, often beginning to demonstrate newly acquired understanding after only a single exposure to a new event. Having learned the rules of one situation, children typically attempt to apply this understanding to new situations.

One way to begin to understand the apparent ease with which children learn social conventions is to think in terms of complementary processes in social in-

* Data collection for some of the research reported in this chapter was supported by a Faculty Research Grant from Haverford College. Additional support for data analyses was provided by the Maurice L. Mednick Memorial Foundation. I would like to thank the children and teachers who participated in these studies, Polly Stephens, Rachel R. Rothschild, and Chris Bjornsen for their assistance in data collection and analysis, and Renée Cardone, Chris Bjornsen, and K. Ann Renninger for their comments on early drafts of this chapter.

teraction and capabilities in children that support the child's developing understanding of social events. Specifically, it has been claimed that social partners
and social situations provide boundary conditions within which some perceptions, representations, and actions of the child are promoted and others are discouraged (Valsiner, 1984, 1987; Winegar & Renninger, 1985; Winegar, 1988).
Through these constraining processes, others channel children toward socially
appropriate performance in, and understanding of, their cultural environment. At
least as importantly, children also bring to social events a sensitivity to constraints on perception, representation and action provided by social others. They
also rely on such social constraining to highlight relevant aspects of social exchange. It is through these complementary processes that children come to understand their world.

In this chapter, I will make theoretical observations about the organization
of social environments within which children's understanding of social events
develops and about the nature of the social processes through which such understanding emerges. I will illustrate these observations using two studies of
preschool children in social events: first, an event investigated
experimentally—preschool children purchasing an item in a store setting and
second, an event observed in a natural setting—preschool children at snacktime
in their school. Throughout, my goal will be to lead to the conclusion that children's participation in and understanding of their world are intrinsically social
and emerge from an individual/social dialectic process of co-construction.

PROCESS AND ORGANIZATION OF SOCIAL INTERACTION

Most studies of children's understanding of social events have used event knowledge as a vehicle to investigate children's memory. Initially, the domain of event
knowledge was chosen because children seemed to demonstrate capabilities in
this area which were not exhibited in other areas (Nelson & Gruendel, 1981).
Thus, early investigations of children's knowledge of social events were not interested primarily in the content of children's memory as a means to illuminate
children's knowledge of events *per se*, but rather to illuminate processes and
contents of children's memory in an area with which children had experience and
familiarity.

An important discovery of this research program is that children are able to
provide general descriptions of events with which they have experience (Nelson,
1986). Thus, children's descriptions of events is characterized as flowing from
"generalized event representations." However, while often findings from such
studies are taken as indications of children's knowledge of events, such findings
are actually about children's memory for events or, even more accurately, about
children's verbal expression of their memory for events. Unless it is assumed
that verbal reports of memory equals knowledge (or at least that verbal reports of

memory directly reflect knowledge), these studies reveal very little about children's knowledge of events (Beilin, 1983; Winegar, 1988).

The usefulness of describing children's knowledge of routine social exchanges in terms of "generalized event representations" must be reconsidered as, increasingly, investigators have found important differences in children's reporting of "What happens in an event?" depending upon how the question is asked and by whom, as well as the mode of child response (e.g., Fivush, Hudson, & Nelson, 1984; Fivush & Fromhoff, 1988; Gray & Fivush, 1987). Many of the same researchers who originally investigated children's memory for general events have turned to the study of autobiographical memory. The findings of these later investigations of children's verbal reports of memory for events can be interpreted as casting doubt on the very construct of generalized event representations from which they arose. Thus, the questions that originally drove the early event knowledge research are in many ways less clearly answered now that they were 10 years ago.

Further, there is increasing evidence from other lines of research that what children say about what happens in an event and what children do in that event may have little predictable relationship to each other. This lack of predictability from language to action is suggested by numerous studies of possible relations between judgement and action (e.g., Damon, 1977; Kassin & Ellis, 1988).

These points suggest the importance of considering the context-relative nature of children's knowledge of events. It appears that what children "know" about an event depends not only on the amount and type of experience children have in the event in question, but also on who asks the question, how the question is asked, and the mode of child response. For these reasons I have begun to consider children's *understanding* of social events rather than their knowledge. For me, the consideration of understanding rather than knowledge serves as a reminder of two important, related points about children and social events. First, it may not be most fruitful to consider children's verbal descriptions, actions, or other expressions of level of familiarity with social events as flowing from abstract, generalized, reflectively-accessible knowledge. Second, such verbal descriptions, actions, and other expressions do not reside solely in the child's head; rather, they are active negotiations between a child and his or her social environment.

Such a reconceptualization has important implications for the investigation of children's understanding of social events. Most importantly, it requires the constant recognition that understanding and the expression of understanding are constructed and given meaning within social interaction. For this reason the nature of the social interaction of the investigation itself (e.g., interviews conducted by adults with children), and the influence of this social interaction on the expression of children's understanding of social events must be considered. Children are meaning-makers. Just as they try to make sense and construct order out of kindergarten daily routines, trips to museums, and trips to the store, they similarly try to make sense out of investigative interviews. The recognition of this meaning-making helps clarify why children may say something different when their mother asks them about an event than when an experimenter asks them about an event.

Thus, if we want to begin to make sense of children's understanding of social events, instead of children's memory for social events, we might best start with a consideration of the social processes within which this understanding emerges. Children gain understanding of social events through exposure to social situations. Occasionally this exposure is through a narrative medium (e.g., a story), and children are passive observers. More usually, exposure to an event is direct and children are active participants. Nelson (1981) has described this latter process as one of participatory interaction. She suggests that children's understanding of their social world develops through dynamic, interactive activities within contexts that are highly structured. Further, "although adults direct the action and set the goals, they do not necessarily provide direct tuition for the child, rather *they provide conditions under which the child fills in the expected role activity*" (pp. 106, emphasis added).

Far from being a type of learning that is peculiar to the acquisition of event knowledge, participatory interaction would seem to be a common method for the transmission of many classes of cultural understanding. It is process whereby novices (children) learn from interactions with experts (adults and often peers) through repeated experience. Though explicit directions and explanations may occasionally be offered by the expert, it is more usual that only the minimum amount of information necessary for compliance by the novice is provided. With experience children come to perform adequately in situations and eventually become experts in their own right.

The general nature of social interaction between experts and novices (or in this case, teachers and children) has been discussed elsewhere. It was observed that in a variety of formal and informal teaching/learning situations, there appears to be a complementarity between the actions of the expert and the actions of the novice (Renninger & Winegar, 1985a; 1985b). Specifically, with experience, experts increasingly relinquish control over novices' actions and novices take increasing responsibility for their own performance. This complementarity in process between expert and novice is referred to as "differential constraining/ progressive empowerment."

While this approach is similar to recent discussions of "scaffolding" (e.g., Wood, 1980), it differs in its explicit recognition of the co-contribution made to this learning process by both the adult and child.[1] Specifically, "differential constraining" refers to the tendency of more expert others to adjust the level and form of support they provide for the performance of less expert others. This con-

---

[1] See Winegar (1988) for a discussion of additional differences between scaffolding and differential constraining/progressive empowerment.

straining is characterized as "differential" since experts adjust both the degree and type of support they provide as novices exhibit increasing responsibility for acceptable performance in an event. "Progressive empowerment" refers to the increasing ability for socially acceptable performance demonstrated by the actions of the novice. During development, novices internalize environmental support and constraints originally provided by experts, and thus become increasingly "self-constraining." This increased responsibility assumed by the novice itself necessitates further differential adjustment on constraining processes provided by the expert. Thus, differential constraining/progressive empowerment describes complementary aspects of a social process in which experts provide direction and support for novices' performance. It is this direction and support which enable a novice to accomplish the action at hand while simultaneously developing understanding of the general actions and activities which constitute social events.

However, the use of the terms "constraints" or "constraining" within this approach should not be read as implying a restriction placed on the child's actions by an oppressive adult. As indicated by the label "differential constraining/progressive empowerment," the complement to constraining is empowerment. Constraining of the range or type of actions in a setting enables an individual to complete the action at hand and also to complete future similar actions with less or no assistance. In this way, constraints on action lead to empowerment. Thus, constraining and empowerment are two perspectives on the same interdependent process necessary for development within social contexts. According to this perspective, the term "constraints" is more accurately read as implying potentials rather than limits. One advantage of describing social process in terms of differential constraining/progressive empowerment is that it provides a framework within which to consider social contexts of this developmental process.

However, it should be noted that this consideration of context in child development need not lead to a situationism which assumes that each social encounter is composed of a unique constellation of social and individual influences. Individuals bring to social interactions both knowledge of past experiences and preferred patterns of interaction. Social interactions occur within physically structured and socially organized environments that exhibit similarity across situations. Social events reflect underlying functional similarity across instances of social exchanges. Thus, consideration of context permits description and understanding of development without the need for a geometrically progressing specification of influences required by an extreme situationism.

This form of contextualism does not aim to predict the specific outcome of particular developmental paths. Rather, it explicitly recognizes that development, while dependent on social influences, is not determined solely by these social influences. Thus, the relationship between developing child and social environment has been described as one of "dependent independence" (Winegar, Renninger, & Valsiner, 1989).

The recognition that children are interdependent with their environment implies that while children may come to understand their world through interaction with others, their understanding of the world is not a veridical copy of the constraints provided by others during these interactions. Children's cognitive abilities organize their understanding. The influence of this organization is expressed in children's understanding of both the physical and social world. Further, children are not passive recipients who faithfully internalize the constraints provided by more expert others and blindly adhere to social structure in the form of rigid rules and goals that are temporally and causally organized by others. Rather, children actively negotiate the relative invariants of social exchanges and are willing and eager to modify social rules as circumstances require.

Thus, children's understanding of social events can be viewed as being constructed in two ways. First, children's understanding of events is an active construction arising from their current level of understanding and information provided by the environment. Children do not copy directly the information offered by their physical and social environment. More accurately, children construct understanding of an event using both information from their environment and understanding from previous experience. This intraindividual construction of understanding is presented elsewhere as a co-constructive metatheory (Wozniak, 1986).

There is a second way in which children's understanding of social events may be considered as constructed. Participation with others in an event entails the expression of understanding through language and action. The meaning and value of these expressions is co-constructed from the relation of one individual's actions to the actions of others. Thus, actions acquire meaning in relation to complementary actions of others. In this way, events are social interactions that are negotiated between participants as participants jointly construct the organization and social meaning of the activity. In this way, social events are interindividual co-constructions arising from the organization of social interaction (Winegar, 1988). Aspects of this interindividual co-construction are presented elsewhere as intersubjectivity (e.g., Newson & Newson, 1975; Rommetveit, 1979;) and social constructionism (e.g., Gergen, 1985, 1988).

My approach to the question of how children come to participate in social events and gradually come to understand the relatively invariant conventional procedures of social interactions has been to focus on the role that others play in facilitating this participation and understanding. This approach seems to be intuitively reasonable. After all, children do not learn to participate in social events by themselves, but rather, by definition, they learn within a social context.

Several observations of adult-child interaction during social events suggest that the approach outlined above is a meaningful and heuristic description of the nature and development of children's understanding of social events. In this chapter, I will report results from two studies of adult-child interaction during which children gain increasing experience with an event and correspondingly demonstrate, through their action, increased understanding of routine social exchanges. The first study to be reported is an experimental, repeated-measures study of adult-child interaction in a store setting. In this study, children's performance in the store was recorded and coded as children made repeated trips to this store. The second study to be reported is an observational, longitudinal study of teacher-child interaction during preschool snacktime. In this study, interactions between teachers and children during snacktime were recorded and coded during the first four weeks of a new school year. Taken together, the results of these two studies are interpreted as providing support for the theoretical claims made above and as suggesting that these claims have important implications for a more complete understanding of the development of children's performance in, and understanding of, social events.

ADULT–CHILD INTERACTION IN A STORE

In the first study, seventeen four-year-old children (eight females and nine males, $M = 51.00$ months. $SD = 5.23$ months) individually made repeated trips to purchase a toy in a store established under experimental conditions in their school. An adult storekeeper was instructed and rehearsed in a script prescribing the sequence and timing of permissible actions and vocalizations. Sequence and timing of actions and vocalizations of the storekeeper were specifically prescribed to provide the minimum amount of information necessary for children's successful negotiation of this event. According to the script, the storekeeper was to allow the child a set amount of time (15 secs.) to initiate each of five action components of the store transaction (i.e., choosing an item for purchase, establishing the price of the item, paying for the item, requesting a bag for the purchased item, and leaving the store). If a child did not initiate a given scripted action within the time limit, the storekeeper proceeded to the next utterance in the script. In this way, adult support in the transaction remained consistent across both children and across trips. although adjusted in relation to a given child's performance on a particular trip.

Children were given 12 cents and individually shown to the store. From the time the child reached the store entrance until the transaction was completed, the child interacted solely with the storekeeper. Children made five trips to the store over two weeks. One week after completion of these trips, children made a purchase in a novel store that was constructed in a different room and displayed different items for purchase than the store visited previously. The novel store was staffed by a storekeeper with whom children were unfamiliar, although this storekeeper followed the same scripted procedures as the storekeeper in the first store. Children's actions in both stores were recorded by a stationary video camera placed unobtrusively behind the storekeeper.

Judges coded the performance of children during their trips to the store by recording the number and sequence of event component actions initiated by each child on each trip. Judges also recorded changes in the direction of each child's eye gaze during each store transaction. In the following sections, summaries of findings and individual performances will be presented.

The mean proportion of children's eye gaze directed at the storekeeper and the mean number and sequence of child initiated actions by store trip are shown in Figure 3.1. As measured by the number and sequence of event component acts initiated, children's performance in the store continually improved during trips to the store and declined slightly on their trip to the novel store. Greatest improvement in both number and sequence of actions occurred between Trips 1 and 2. Overall, children's performance improved greatly from Trip 1 to Trip 2, continued to improve slightly on Trips 3–5, and decreased on the trip to the novel store, although decrease from Trip 5 to Novel Trips is significant for sequence of acts only.

Proportion of eye gaze directed at the storekeeper also changed over trips to the store. On the first trip to the store, the proportion of children's total eye gaze which was directed at the storekeeper was higher than on later trips. Again, greatest decrease in storekeeper-directed eye gaze occurred between Trip 1 and Trip 2. This proportion decreased significantly from Trip 1 to Trip 2, maintained this lower rate on Trips 3–5, and increased minimally on the trip to the novel store.

Thus, in this event in which the adult side of the transaction is controlled, children's use of an adult to provide information supporting successful performance can be observed. On their first trip to the store, children directed a large proportion of their attention toward the storekeeper. On later trips children's performance in the store improved and the proportion of their gazes directed at the storekeeper correspondingly declined.

Children's use of an adult to provide direction for their performance also can be seen by examining individual children's patterns of visual reference while within the store and changes in these patterns over trips to the store. In general, a child was more likely to direct his or her gaze toward the storekeeper after the child had completed one action component of the event and was waiting for a response from the storekeeper. For example, a child may enter the store and only make an initial glance toward the storekeeper. The child surveys the toys on the counter, chooses one, and then looks again at the storekeeper. If the storekeeper is slow to respond, the child will look from toy (in hand) to storekeeper and back again. If the storekeeper still has not responded (in this case with a price) the child will again look from toy to storekeeper, sometimes holding the gaze at the storekeeper. In this way, the child not only relied on the adult for information about the "correctness" of the previous action, but also apparently signaled and eventually demanded by his or her gaze, the next action in the event from the unresponsive storekeeper.

On early trips, this back-and-forth gaze from toy to storekeeper continued un-

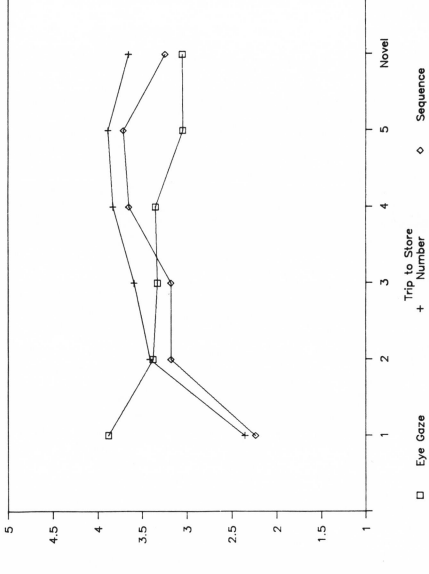

Figure 3.1. Proportion of eye gaze toward storekeeper, mean number and sequence of initiated acts by store trip.

53

til the storekeeper responded. In contrast, on later trips, when the child's understanding of the conventional procedures of the store had changed, the child often proceeded to the next action (in the current example, offering the money to pay for the toy) if the storekeeper did not respond to the initial series of eye gazes. In this case the lead in organizing the event was taken by the child and demanded a readjustment in procedure by the storekeeper.

This study illustrates the process of participatory interaction through which children's understanding of their social world develops and suggests that the social constraining provided by others during such interaction need not be explicit. By following her prescribed script, the storekeeper does not provide specific, explicit directions to the children regarding the next appropriate action in the store. Rather, the storekeeper provides a consistent condition under which children can begin to fill in the expected role activity. By consistently taking her turn in the dialogue of action that defines the store event, the storekeeper provides a structured framework into which the children can mesh their own actions. The finding that children so readily respond to this form of interaction suggests that they are either familiar with it or prepared to benefit from it.

This study, in which children participate in an experimental situation allowing structured adult support, but no direct tuition, also highlights one means by which children use their environment to provide information about social events. Children's improved performance in the event with experience and their corresponding decreased referencing of the expert adult suggests the increased responsibility for canonical performance assumed by the initially novice child in this social interaction. The improved performance of the child is enabled by the constraints on action initially provided by the adult storekeeper. On early trips to the store, the storekeeper sets boundary conditions on a child's performance by proceeding to the next action in the script if the child does not initiate the required action. In this way, the children are channeled toward successful performance in this social setting. With experience, children begin to initiate appropriate actions themselves without requiring the same level or type of adult guidance. During later trips to the store, children take the lead in initiating the actions required for successful participation in this event. However, the storekeeper's consistent responses to the correct event actions initiated by the children continue to serve as support for children's performance.

Thus, these observations of the changes in children's actions with experience in this event illustrate how the actions of an adult, which at one level might be considered as functioning to limit children's action, when considered at another level, actually can serve to empower children through supporting children's performance and eventually enabling children's increasing responsibility for the initiation of event actions. It is in this way that differential constraining is the complement to progressive empowerment and that constraints can be more properly characterized as potentials.

Finally, the procedures and results of this study can be used to illustrate the social/individual dialectic process out of which children's understanding emerges. During their trips to the store, children express their understanding of this event through their actions as they attempt to successfully complete the purchase of an object. On the first trip to the store, the expression of their understanding reflects their previous experiences with store events. On later trips to the store the expression of this understanding reflects children's previous experience with store events generally and their experience in this particular store gained on earlier trips.

During all experiences in the store, children use information provided by the environment to guide their actions. Some information is provided by the physical environment. The store counter serves as a physical barrier partially defining the space within which children can act. Paper bags on the counter provide visual cues that can serve to remind the children of previous actions. Additional information is also provided by the social environment. The statements and actions of the storekeeper provide direction for immediate action and cues for future performance in this event. Children's actions while within the store setting are thus expressions of an understanding that is intraindividually co-constructed. This understanding is co-constructed from understanding gained from previous experience with this event and information provided by the physical and social environment within which the event occurs.

Children's understanding of the store event is also an interindividual co-construction arising from a social interaction negotiated within a matrix of contextual constraints. This can be most clearly seen in the children's attempts to lead a slow-to-respond storekeeper to the next action of the event. On early trips to the store children's repeated looks to the storekeeper presumably are a means of acquiring information about the correctness of the children's actions or as a clue to the next appropriate action in the store transaction. However, after experience in the store, children no longer tend to look to the storekeeper for such direction. Rather, children hold their gaze toward the storekeeper or initiate the next action of the store event without waiting for the storekeeper's cue. In this way the store event can be viewed as an interindividual co-construction negotiated between the storekeeper and the child.

These interpretations of the results of this first study provide preliminary support for and illustration of the processes of participatory interaction and differential constraining/progressive empowerment which constitute the social/individual dialectic out of which children's understanding of social events emerges. However, the procedures of this study are one-sided in that they focus on changes in child actions while attempting to control the actions of the adult. The one-sidedness of these procedures presents two problems, one more related to the theoretical approach which guided this study, the other more practical and related to the methodology of this study.

From the theoretical perspective which guided this study, focusing on one member of an interaction while ignoring the other (even if claiming to ''control'' this other) creates an artificial situation and violates the assumed interdependence of social interaction. While such an approach has value under some conditions, by itself it cannot provide answers to questions about the influences of social interaction on developing understanding. Attempts to prescribe the actions of one member of a social interaction also have procedural limitations—in practice it proved very difficult to control the actions of the storekeeper. Negotiation of social interaction between participants also influences the storekeeper script. Thus, within the limits provided by the experimental script, the storekeeper constantly must readjust her actions to the actions of the children. For these reasons, a second study was undertaken which, rather than attempt to control the adult side of the interaction, abandoned attempts at control and moved to natural observation.

TEACHER-CHILD INTERACTION DURING SNACKTIME

In the second study, 18 children age 31 to 57 months, and their teachers were observed interacting as a group during a preschool event—"snacktime." Seventeen of the children had not attended preschool previously. The three teachers in this classroom were also new to this preschool, although one of the teachers had prior teaching experience. Teacher direction and child performance during this event was observed and recorded on videotape. Taping was done daily for the first three weeks of school, twice a week for the remainder of the year, and for the week immediately after Christmas break. Observations from the first four weeks of school will be presented here.

In order to appreciate the complexity of the child's social world, consider the following generalized description of snacktime after children have learned to participate in this event:

In the preschool observed, snacktime occurred each day after children had been in school for about an hour and a half. Snacktime followed a period of free play and children were required to put away the toys used in play before taking a seat at the snack table. Children usually chose their own seats in chairs at low tables of appropriate height for children of this age. At the beginning of snacktime a pitcher of water and a pitcher of juice were placed on the table. The pitcher containing juice was marked with a piece of red tape; the water pitcher was not marked. Children were provided with paper cups for their drink. Occasionally, children were provided with napkins that were used both for wiping faces and hands and as plates for food. Usually cups and napkins were distributed by children taking one of the items and passing the rest on to another child who in turn took an item and passed it on to the next child. Pitchers of drink were poured by each child and the pitcher passed on to other waiting children. Verbal requests for food, drink, napkins, and cups were to be accompanied by the use of the word "please."

The food available for snack varied from day to day. It included a variety of crackers and fruits and occasionally baked goods such as muffins, pancakes, or banana bread either made by the children at school or brought by a parent and child from home to share with the group. Sometimes items made by the children at school were consumed on the same day they were prepared; at other times the items were saved for snack on a subsequent day. Like cups and napkins, food items also were usually distributed by the children. While "seconds" on drink were almost always allowed, additional helpings of food were not always permissible. Children ate almost all foods using their fingers. However, eating utensils were observed twice, once when children spread peanut butter on bananas using a communal knife and once when children ate hot apple crisp with individual spoons. Occasionally a metal bowl was put on the table to be used to discard unwanted or inedible pieces of food such as orange rinds, seeds, and muffin papers. Children were responsible for cleaning up after themselves by discarding used cups and napkins in a large trash can on one side of the room. After snacktime children were encouraged to use the bathroom. Snacktime was usually followed by either outside play or circle time.

Obviously, there is a lot going on in this everyday event. Through many hours of watching children at snacktime and viewing and reviewing videotapes of this event, I have been repeatedly struck by the complexity of this apparently mundane event. It is so complex, in fact, that I continue to be amazed at how quickly and how well children apparently are able to cut through its complexity in order to learn just what are the social rules and conventional procedures of this and other social interactions.

As a first attempt at understanding the role played by others in the development of children's understanding of this event, all statements made by teachers toward children during snacktime were coded into one of the following four categories: directive statements, nondirective statements, informative statements, and social pleasantry statements. Here only the first two categories, directive and nondirective statements, will be discussed. Directive statements were those that made a direct request for children's action or change in action. Most of the statements in this category made an explicit request of the child (e.g., "Sit down in your chair.", "Just take one cracker.") Also included in this category were other statements that, while linguistically phrased as a question, did not offer the child a legitimate choice of action and were thus functionally directive (e.g., "Can you ask him to pass the juice?").

In contrast, nondirective statements were statements made by teachers that supported a child's performance but did not make a direct request for the performance (e.g., "Who remembers what we do after we finish our snack?", "I like the way you asked to have the juice passed."). This category also included statements that offered children legitimate choices of actions (e.g., "Can you pour your juice by yourself?", "Would you like more crackers or are you finished?", "When you're finished go sit on the rug unless you have to go to the bathroom.").

Proportion of type of teacher's statements during snacktime during the first four weeks of school are shown in Figure 3.2. As can be seen, the proportion of the total number of teacher statements that are directive declined over this period of time. During the first three days of school, about half of the teachers' statements were in this category. By the eleventh day directive statements made up less than a third of teachers' total statements.

In contrast, the proportion of teacher statements classified as nondirective showed an increase during this same time span. During the first six days of school nondirective statements comprised an average of 15 percent of total teacher statements. By the tenth day the proportion of nondirective statements approached 30 percent of total teacher statements. Comparison of mean proportion of statements for the first seven days of school and second seven days of school indicated that proportion of directive statements declined significantly while proportion of nondirective statements increased significantly.

Thus, here we see specific changes in the degree of directiveness of teacher statements during snacktime over the first four weeks of the new school year. Teachers began the year using a majority of statements that explicitly directed children's action and requested changes in children's action. Later, teachers used a greater proportion of statements that provided support for children's actions, but were not expressed by the same degree of directiveness that characterized teachers' statements earlier in the year.

This finding has an important implication for the present discussion. It suggests that the type of social constraining provided by social others changes as children gain experience in an event and presumably demonstrate increasing responsibility for guiding their own action. As with the results of the store study reported above, these results can be interpreted as reflecting changes in actions by experts as novices gain increased experience in an event that are predicted by a differential constraining/progressive empowerment model of socialization. Here again, we can see how constraints provided by experts, rather than being restrictive, can actually serve an enabling function by supporting potential actions on the part of the novice.

In the discussion above, change in the degree of the directiveness of teacher statements is interpreted as being complementary with children's increasing responsibility for guiding their own actions. That is, this interpretation assumes that, with experience, children are doing more in the event. However, this interpretation is based on the coding of the actions of only one participant in the event, the teacher. The force of this interpretation would be strengthened if this assumption could be verified through an interactive coding of both participants. In this way, relations between actions of teacher and action of children could be directly evaluated.

In order to assess relations between teacher action and child action during this event, all teacher actions and statements and all child actions and statements that pertained to the procedures of snacktime were coded. This included 11 teacher

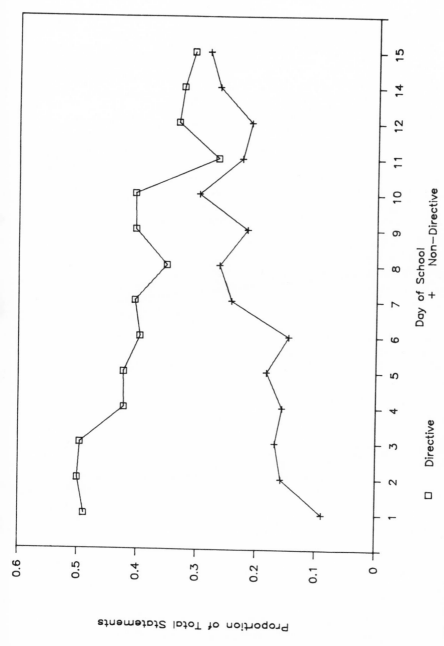

Figure 3.2. Proportion of teacher statement type by day of school.

actions and five child actions. Three teacher actions (command, offer option, and joint action) accounted for 91 percent of all teacher-initiated action. Three child actions (comply, noncomply, and request) accounted for 93 percent of all child-initiated actions.

The number of all teacher-initiated actions and all child-initiated actions by day is shown in Figure 3.3. As can be seen, the number of teacher-initiated actions declined over the first three weeks of school while the number of child-initiated actions increased during this same time period.

The relation between teacher-initiated actions and child-initiated actions is expressed as a ratio in Figure 3.4. Larger ratios indicate a higher proportion of teacher actions to child actions, while smaller ratios indicate a high proportion of child actions to teacher actions. This ratio decreased over the first three weeks of school indicating that over this time, children were initiating more actions while teachers were initiating less. Comparison of mean ratio of actions for the first seven days of school and the second seven days of school indicated that ratio of action is significantly lower during the second seven days of school.

This last finding provides empirical support for the claim made above that teachers change the degree and kind of direction they provide as children take increasing responsibility for initiating event actions in socially acceptable ways. With experience, children initiated a greater proportion of the actions required for successful completion of snacktime and teachers initiated a lower proportion of these actions. When taken in conjunction with the changes in teacher statements reported above, we can begin to see a clearer relationship between changes in the actions of the teacher and corresponding changes in the actions of the children.

Like the store study reported above, this study also illustrates the processes of participatory interaction, differential constraining/progressive empowerment, and intra- and interindividual co-construction. Since these processes have been discussed above in the context of the first study, here I will only outline how they apply specifically to this second study.

The procedures and results of this study illustrate the process of participatory interaction in which the teacher establishes general goals and structure of the event and children fill in expected activity. Unlike the structure provided by the scripted storekeeper, some of the structure provided by teachers during snacktime is in the form of direct instruction. This direct instruction may be either verbal, such as teacher commands, or nonverbal, such as teacher-child joint action. Additional structure provided by the teachers takes the form of a teacher offering options to a child. Whatever the specific nature of the constraining provided by the teachers, children are expected to respond with appropriate actions. In so doing, children demonstrate their understanding of this social event.

This study also illustrates the process of differential constraining/progressive empowerment as it occurs in the snacktime setting. As suggested by the changes in teacher statements used to organize this event, teachers change their manner of

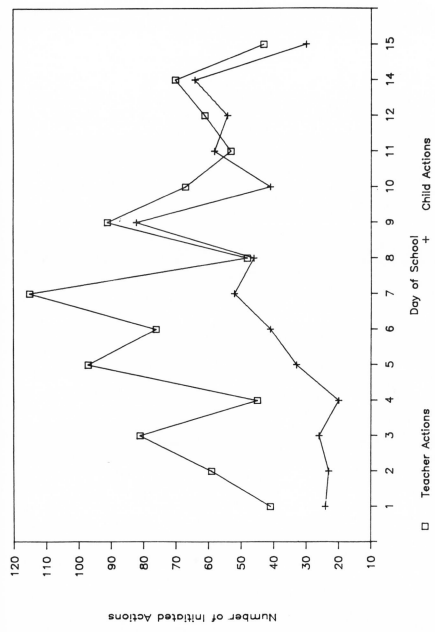

Figure 3.3. Number of teacher- and child-initiated actions by day of school.

61

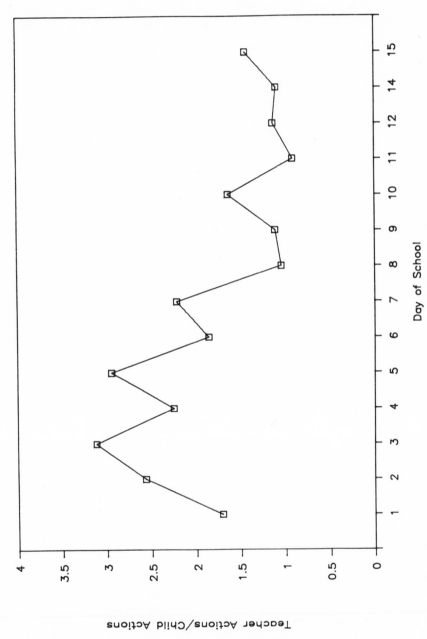

Figure 3.4.   Ratio of teacher initiated actions to child initiated actions by day of school.

direction as children gain experience with event procedures. Over time, children initiate a greater proportion of the actions necessary for appropriate functioning within this event.

Finally, this study illustrates both the intra-and interindividual co-constructive nature of children's understanding of social events. Children come to snacktime in the preschool with a variety of experiences with both mealtimes and interaction with others. Thus, teachers do not have to provide instruction on how to eat and drink and how to interact with others. Rather, teachers are faced with the task of supporting children's eating, drinking, and social interaction toward the actions that are preferred in this particular setting. Further, children do not always accept the goals and procedures of snacktime as reflected in the teachers' actions. Thus, children's understanding of the snacktime event is an intraindividual co-construction arising from children's understanding of mealtimes gained from previous experience and information provided by the physical and social environment of the snacktime setting. Children's understanding of the snacktime event is also an interindividual co-construction arising from the negotiation of snacktime goals and procedures between participants in this event.

SUMMARY AND CONCLUSIONS

With these two studies in mind, let us return to the process by which children come to understand social events generally, and the conventional procedures of stores and snacktime specifically. Social interaction during an event provides a forum in which (a) through their language and action social others make explicit their understanding of the conventional procedures of the event, and (b) through their language and action children express their understanding of conventional procedures. The expression of understanding by *either* participant reflects intraindividual co-construction of knowledge, while the *joint* negotiation of knowledge by both participants reflects interindividual co-construction of understanding. Thus, understanding of social events is represented as a process of active co-construction both within and between individuals.

Intraindividually, children's understanding of these transactions is a co-construction arising from their general level of understanding, previous experience in these and similar events, and information provided by the physical and social environment (Wozniak, 1986). Interindividually, children's and others' participation in these social interactions involves not only the joint co-construction of the actions in the immediate event, but also the negotiation of procedures and conventions as will be applied to future encounters (Winegar, 1988).

In this way, Vygotsky's (1978) claim that "every function in the child's cultural development appears twice: first, on the social level, and later, on the individual level" (p. 57) can be applied to the development of children's understanding of their social world. Further, through this application, both aspects of the dialectical relationship between social and individual are explicitly recognized and the nature of social understanding is brought full circle. This circle is completed with the recognition that understanding expressed on the social level reflects knowledge on the individual level, knowledge which in turn was first apparent in social interaction.

Integrating empirical findings from the two studies, it is concluded that children's understanding of the social world as reflected by their performance in it, need not be considered as following only from structural changes in their knowledge, but can also be fruitfully construed in terms of social transactions that characterize members of social groups. This suggests that the nature of children's action in, and understanding of, social interactions might not be best described in terms of preplanned, well-scripted sequences of procedures, but rather as co-constructed, interdependent transactions that occur within a matrix of social support and constraint.

In conclusion let me briefly restate the claims of this chapter. Interpersonal negotiation in social interaction constitutes a matrix of contextual constraints. These social constraints are interpreted, generalized, and internalized. Once internalized, such knowledge organizes future actions and negotiations. The implication of the theoretical approach outlined in this chapter is that if we want to know what children understand about conventional procedures of social events and how this understanding develops, one fruitful place to look is at the social interactions out of which their understanding emerges.

REFERENCES

Beilin, H. (1983). The new functionalism and Piaget's program. In E.K. Scholnick (Ed.), *New trends in conceptual representation: Challenges to Piaget's theory* (pp. 3–40). Hillsdale, NJ: Erlbaum.

Damon, W. (1977). *The social world of the child.* San Francisco: Jossey-Bass.

Fivush, R., & Fromhoff, F.A. (1988). Style and structure in mother-child conversations about the past. *Discourse Processes, 11,* 337–355.

Fivush, R., Hudson, J., & Nelson, K. (1984). Children's long-term memory for a novel event: An exploratory study. *Merrill-Palmer Quarterly, 30,* 303–316.

Gergen, K.J. (1985). The social constructionist movement in modern psychology. *American Psychologist, 40,* 266–275.

Gergen, K.J. (1988). If persons are texts. In S.B. Messeri, L.A. Sassi, & R.L. Wollfolk (Eds.), *Hermeneutics and psychological theory* (pp. 28–51). New Brunswick, NJ: Rutgers University Press.

Gray, J.T., & Fivush, R. (1987, April). *Memory in action: Contextual differences in two-year-old's memory performance.* Paper presented at the meeting of the Society for Research in Child Development, Baltimore, MD.

Kassin, S.M., & Ellis, S. A. (1988). On the acquisition of the discounting principle: An experimental text of a social-developmental model. *Child Development, 59,* 950–960.

Nelson, K. (1981). Social cognition in a script framework. In J.H. Flavell & L. Ross (Eds.), *Social-cognitive development: Frontiers and possible futures* (pp. 97–118). New York: Cambridge University Press.

Nelson, K. (1986). *Event knowledge: Structure and function in development.* Hillsdale, NJ: Erlbaum.

Nelson, K., & Gruendel, J.M. (1981). Generalized event representations: Basic building blocks of cognitive development. In A. Brown & M. Lamb (Eds.), *Advances in developmental psychology* Vol. 1 (pp. 131–155). Hillsdale, NJ: Erlbaum.

Newson, J., & Newson, E. (1975). Intersubjectivity and the transmission of culture: On the social origins of symbolic functioning. *Bulletin of British Psychology-Social, 28,* 437–446.

Renninger, K.A., & Winegar, L.T. (1985a). Emergent organization in expert-novice relationships. *The Genetic Epistemologist, 14,* 14–20.

Renninger, K.A., & Winegar, L.T. (1985b, August). *Teacher-student interaction: Differential constraining/progressive empowerment.* Paper presented at the 93rd Annual Convention, American Psychological Association, Los Angeles, CA.

Rommetveit, R. (1979). On the architecture of intersubjectivity. In R Rommetveit & R. Blakar (Eds.), *Studies of language, thought and verbal communication* (pp. 93–108). New York: Academic Press.

Valsiner, J. (1984). Construction of the zone of proximal development in adult-child joint action: The socialization of meals. In B. Rogoff & J.V. Wertsch (Eds.), *Children's learning in the "zone of proximal development"* (pp. 65–76). San Francisco: Jossey-Bass.

Valsiner, J. (1987). *Culture and the development of children's action: A cultural-historical theory of developmental psychology.* New York: Wiley & Sons.

Vygotsky, L. S. (1978). *Mind in society: The development of higher psychological processes.* Cambridge: Harvard University Press.

Winegar, L.T. (1988). Children's emerging understanding of social events: Co-construction and social process. In J. Valsiner (Ed.), *Child development within culturally structured environments: Vol. 2. Social co-construction and environmental guidance in development* (pp. 3–27). Norwood, NJ: Ablex.

Winegar, L.T., & Renninger, K.A. (1985, April). *Social influence on knowledge: Structural constraints and procedural constraining.* Paper presented at the meeting of the Society for Research in Child Development, Toronto, Canada.

Winegar, L.T., Renninger, K.A., and Valsiner, J. (1989). Dependent-independence in adult-child relationships. In D.A. Kramer & M. Bopp (Eds.), *Transformation in clinical and developmental psychology* (pp. 157–168). New York: Springer-Verlag.

Wood, D.J. (1980). Teaching the young child: Some relations between social interaction, language, and thought. In D.R. Olson (Ed.), *The social foundations of language and thought* (pp. 280–296). New York: Norton.

Wozniak, R.H. (1986). Notes toward a co-constructive theory of the emotion/cognition relationship. In D. Bearison & H. Zimiles, (Eds.), *Thought and emotion: Developmental perspectives* (pp. 40–64). Hillsdale, NJ: Erlbaum.

CHAPTER 4

The Development of Practical Social Understanding in Elementary School-Age Children*

Martin J. Packer and John R. Mergendoller

Many developmental psychologists have turned their attention to the ways in which social exchanges and communicative interactions have a developmental influence. Both social and cognitive development are no longer viewed solely as the result of epistemological construction by individuals, but also as consequences of negotiated social construction among family and peers. This change parallels an increased appreciation that knowledge itself is best not considered an atemporal, acontextual accomplishment, and that forms of understanding have power and relevance in a particular historical epoch, for a specific social group (Gellatly, 1987). Knowledge has its origins in situated social practices, not in formal theories and logical principles (Packer, 1985a, Packer, 1987; Gergen, 1985; Shweder, 1982). Our culture's accumulated knowledge is to be found as much in the ways in which our social institutions are organized, in our forms of entertainment, in our interpersonal practices and customs, as in any repository of facts or principles, whether scientific, legal, or political. It is most appropriate, then, that we study the forms of understanding children evince in their everyday practical activity, rather than their reasoning when they reflect upon hypothetical situations.

* The authors wish to acknowledge the support of the Office of Educational Research and Improvement, Department of Education, under OERI Contract 400-86-0009 to the Far West Laboratory for Educational Research and Development, San Francisco, California. The opinions expressed herein do not necessarily reflect the position or policy of OERI and no official endorsement by the Office of Educational Research and Improvement or the Department of Education should be inferred. We wish to take this opportunity to extend our thanks to the teachers and principals of Bountiful and Knowlton Elementary Schools, to Bonnie Middleton of the Davis County School District, Utah, and to the Office of Educational Research and Instruction, U.S. Department of Education.

It has become apparent that the social and moral development of the young child involves the construction, in and through coordinated activity with others— both peers and adults—of skillful, effective, and meaningful ways of acting. Following the tradition of a number of philosophers (e.g., Heidegger, 1962; Fingarette, 1967; MacIntyre, 1984), we call these meaningful ways of acting and interacting in the world *practices*. Practices are meaningful, concerned, patterned activities recognized by members of a culture. Children learn practices that provide ways to be effective members of their various social worlds before they learn abstract systems of knowledge like grammar and logic. Some, perhaps most, will never learn the latter. But it is one thing to recognize the developmental significance of social interaction, quite another to find an appropriate way to study this influence. We can now see that Piaget, while recognizing the importance of social factors in development (Piaget, 1932), was unable to find a fully adequate way of characterizing these factors and integrating them into his epistemological framework. He once commented at a Geneva seminar, ''Je me suis cassè la tête'' (I broke my head on that one), referring to his investigation of moral development.

THE HERMENEUTIC APPROACH TO SOCIAL INTERACTION

We consider the hermeneutic or interpretive approach the most appropriate form of investigation of social interaction (cf. Bernstein, 1983; Bleicher, 1980; Packer, 1985b; Palmer, 1969). From the hermeneutic perspective interaction has unique and special characteristics that require a method of research investigation and an understanding of the research enterprise that are radically different from the empiricist and experimentalist approaches usually employed, that are also distinct from the formalist program that characterizes cognitive science, and from the structuralist analyses employed in cognitive-developmental research. Children's practical activity is subtly organized and difficult to study. In the face of the need to study action and interaction, researchers must avoid a return to reductionist analyses of human behavior that regard it as in essence physical movement, as organized by impulsive responses to stimulus situations. Social learning theory, placing emphasis on modeling, imitation, and reinforcement, identifies the barest few details of social influence. But nor should we reduce human interchange to a simple matter of rule-following, assuming that underlying systems of competence that resemble formal axiomatic systems dictate the choice and character of our actions by means of a combinatorial generativity (Chomsky, 1965; Cicourel, 1973). Our view is rather that action has what, at first cut, one might call a textual organization (Ricoeur, 1976; 1979; Freeman, 1985). Unlike biological processes like growth, digestion, and reproduction, social interaction has a *semantic* level of organization (Packer, 1985b). Social events and actions have influence and significance by virtue of their meaning, not as a result of simple material causation or logical necessity. Action is found to be meaningful, and meaning—in both scientific and everyday knowledge—is grounded in action. Researchers, unless unduly constrained by methodological proscriptions, interpret a person's characteristic style of interaction and engagement in a particular project or course of activity in semantic terms, and find that meaning shaped both by mood and emotion.

Given these considerations our approach to the study of social interaction and the development of social understanding is a hermeneutic one. Working within what Taylor (1985) has called post-Heideggerian hermeneutics, we make the assumption that everyday practices—the social and instrumental activities found meaningful by participants and researchers—are the origin of our knowledge. Engagement in these practices constitutes who and what we are, and structures our being-in-the-world, and this is the reason that social interaction has a significant role in social and cognitive development. But in order to understand this influence we need to look at the *details* of social interchanges that children engage in with peers and adults, and there are serious reasons for thinking that coding scheme approaches to the study of these interactions are inadequate; there are no "facts" to social interaction that can be recorded and reported in an interpretation-free manner. The facts of a social encounter are always embedded in a structure of values, interests, and assumptions; a structure that participants and researchers swim in unthinkingly. A naive descriptive approach misses this constitutive framework (precisely because it both assumes it and at the same time maintains a naive realism), but this framework is just what the child must pick up or construct for him- or herself. We thus begin our research with the ready-to-hand mode of engagement in the world (Heidegger, 1962), not the detached contemplation of philosopher or theorist.

One central consequence of the semantic character of practical activity is the intrinsic polysemy or ambiguity of action. Every social act can be understood in a variety of ways, depending on the perspective from which one views it and the context in which one encounters it. This is not to say that *any* interpretation can be made of an action; there are limits to the semantic range of a specific act (c.f. Taylor, 1979). We argue for pluralism, not total relativism. But this central characteristic is denied or ignored by the majority of methodologies currently employed in psychological research, which insist on the tacit assumption that there are value-free and interest-free "facts" to human behavior (Smith & Heshusias, 1986).

Examination of the actions and interactions of individuals suggests that action has further important characteristics, in addition to its polysemy. Action has an intrinsic temporal organization. As agents, we move *through* a series of coordinated acts rather in the way a reader moves through a good book, never quite sure what is ahead of us, understanding what turns up in the frame of what has gone before (Ricoeur, 1981). This kind of temporality is lost by analytic approaches to social interchange that merely correlate frequency of occurrence of kinds of event, no matter in what sequence they occurred, or that treat the sequence as simple associative chaining.

Much action and interaction is unmediated by reflection, deliberation, or calculation. Consider for example a carpenter's involvement in using a hammer, a student's request to borrow a pencil, a professor's introductory lecture, or the banter of good friends playing a game of darts. When engaged in practical activity our awareness is holistic. Our action is guided by implicit social know-how, not by explicit knowing-that.

Finally, practical activity always takes place against a background, or horizon, of possible projects and forms of life, and the meaning of action makes reference to this context or social setting. Action is situated within networks of interrelated possibilities as well as thwarted potentialities. The form and importance of setting is ignored or assumed rather than examined when researchers employ operationalized coding schemes. We would maintain that to examine and explain the action of a child is to *articulate* what is being done, to talk about it and give an account of it, as it stands out from its setting in the way a visual figure stands out from a ground.

In the current post-positivist era much of this sounds, we suppose, uncontroversial and straightforward, but the methodological consequences that follow from adopting a hermeneutic perspective on action are complex, and it is for this reason that we pursue these points here. For this view of action implies that most of what we do, and what the children we study do, is—so to speak—just *done* without reflective or explicit examination. Although researchers make a lot of assumptions about the character of action, few of them look at action in an appropriate manner.

Second, our concerns and interests as researchers play a part in establishing what we see when we investigate action—and this is both good and bad news. Good, because it could never be otherwise, and to be frustrated by this lack of impartiality would be to refuse to accept something basic about being human. Our preunderstandings and prejudices make it possible for things to "count" for us in a social episode. But it is bad news too because there will inevitably be an extent to which we *mis*understand the activities of the children we study: we comprehend only part of what they do, assimilating what we see to mechanistic or formalistic models, and denying those aspects of children's lives we find troublesome, as individuals or as a culture.

What should be done? We must allow that, as psychologists, our ability to understand other people's action is only human. We comprehend only part of what we study, and inevitably begin by assimilating it to our preconceptions and assumptions. Many factors that influence our interpretations are, at least initially, outside explicit awareness and any claim to observe and analyze social action in a fully objective manner, some way that isn't filled with judgments and interpretations, must be viewed with skepticism. Acknowledging these intrinsic constraints on the study of human action is the first step towards employing a more adequate method of investigation. We must incorporate a reflexive component into our research; we must recognize our partiality, and do justice to the interpretation-loaded character of action. We must uncover and recognize our misunderstandings, perhaps even succeed in correcting some of them. A hermeneutic investigation takes its starting point in the fact that, despite the ambiguities of action, we always have a preliminary practical understanding of what the children we study are "up to."

There are kinds of developmental influence that make sense only within a hermeneutic framework; a stronger claim would be that they become *apparent* only within this framework, when one examines interaction hermeneutically. One such influence is the way engagement in social practices can *precede* development of skill in these practices. Children, when motivated by the practical problems of interacting with others, look back at, reflect on, and interpret what they have done. In doing so they begin to recognize the interests that played a structuring role in their initial understanding of events, and begin to appreciate that there are other possible ways of understanding things. Unlike reflection upon instrumental action with physical objects, reflection on social action always involves the possibility of reinterpretation, of reascribing agency for events that have taken place. In fact, the term "reflection" is misleading when we discuss this examination of action, because it suggests that we can accurately "mirror" something when we turn to look at it. With a semantic domain such as practical social activity this can never be done; every description, every new look at a social episode is an interpretation that can never mirror or match some original uninterpreted version of events; no such version exists. In this way social episodes can be opened up to new frames of understanding, and this semantic phenomenon would not be possible if social exchanges were simply sequences of objectively describable events (Packer, 1987).

The major contribution which a hermeneutic approach makes to the study of child development is a new perspective on the direction or telos to development. Such an approach suggests that we should view children in the first place as skilled practitioners, constructing practical skills and concerns in collaboration with peers and adults. Children don't need to think like scientists in order to manipulate objects, like psychologists to interact with their peers, or like philosophers to act morally.

We would propose that "social fluency" is an important telos to social development. Viewed this way, social development is a matter of increasingly broadened fluency: becoming skilled in the social practices of a wide range of situations or subworlds—the family, the school, and so on. By this we do not mean children develop an underlying, acontextual competence—a set of rules, procedures, or scripts—but rather that they come to have, and be aware of having, interests and concerns that make action rational and coherent. Young children develop forms of expert conduct not in a deliberate and planned manner but "on the fly" as they find themselves involved in meaningful social practices that accomplish everyday social tasks. Children ultimately take up and acquire control over practical activities they find themselves already doing. With practice in practices, the child becomes a "reflective practitioner" (Schön, 1983). It is such a change in the manner of children's engagement in their social activities that we wish to discuss in this chapter.

STUDENT'S UNDERSTANDING IN PRACTICAL ACTIVITY

This chapter focuses on our attempt to study and understand children's conduct and accounts of their conduct in school classrooms. We shall describe children's social understanding in elementary school classrooms where the teachers deliberately aimed to bring about change and development in social skills, attitudes, and self-image, in addition to fostering academic goals. These classrooms provided us with the opportunity to study social development in a real setting; one that emphasized, valued, and actively tried to alter the understanding children had of themselves, their peers, and their academic and social practices. When we say that changes occurred in children's "understanding" we mean not their cognitive appreciation of social events, but the manner of their engagement in key practical activities. These practical activities were ones with both social and moral relevance, as we shall illustrate.

The Classes

The classes that we visited were in two elementary schools situated to the north of Salt Lake City, Utah. These classes were not taught with what has become the traditional reliance on frontal instruction by a teacher who adopts an authoritarian stance (even if one of benevolent authority), with frequent evaluation by means of graded individual seatwork (Goodlad, 1984). Instead, teachers used an instructional approach known as "Workshop Way."[1] Teachers at several grade levels in these two schools had adopted this curriculum because of its emphasis on students' social and moral development. The teachers were impressed by the link the curriculum made between academic performance and students' social capacities and self-understanding. A central premise of the Workshop Way curriculum is that the social structure of the traditional classroom, with its emphasis on rote work and frequent competition, and the character of traditional instruction, with its emphasis on correct answers rather than on effort, lead in combination to the majority of students developing negative perceptions of their own academic ability and their worth as individuals. A major belief expressed in the design of the Workshop Way curriculum is that if an effort is made to provide an educational environment where students can feel effective and valued, then their

---

[1] The name "Workshop Way" is copyrighted and owned by The Workshop Way, Inc.

self-image will become more positive and, as a consequence, their academic performance will improve.

Our interest has been to understand how this curriculum works on a daily basis: what its specific aims are, what the means are by which it pursues them, and whether it does indeed bring about the changes it intends. We think our report will be of interest to both educators and researchers interested in social development, though the fact that our analyses and discussion are embedded in the particularities of elementary school classroom life may seem unusual to the latter. As our introduction suggests, we think that in the study of social development we must abandon the attempt to describe universal stages, and recognize that cultural and individual variation are inherent in development. Here, our discussion of development pivots around the particular telos emphasized in the Workshop Way classes, one among many possible developmental paths.

On visiting the Workshop Way classes, our initial impression was that instruction and interaction between teacher and students established a particular kind of community, one that involved a specific way of accomplishing and interpreting academic events during the day. In large part this appeared to be due to the introduction of a set of practical activities that many students became progressively engaged in over the year, and came to understand in new ways. As some students' engagement in these activities changed so did their self-understanding. We also became increasingly aware of the centrality of a moral aspect to these practices and to the developmental outcomes they were linked to. The teachers deliberately organized their instruction and students' classroom tasks in an effort to "grow," as they put it, students' moral character and sense of moral worth.

In order to build upon these initial impressions and learn more, we talked in some depth and detail with three teachers and perhaps one third of the students in their classes (24 in all). We conducted three sets of interviews with students, in the fall, winter and spring of one school year. We also visited and observed classes, at the teachers' and their principals' invitation. The three teachers taught grades 1, 2, and 5 respectively; the students we talked with were approximately 6, 7, and 10 years of age.

Since the reader is probably not familiar with the Workshop Way curriculum, we shall describe its general makeup before examining some of the details of classroom interaction. Knowledge of the context the curriculum provides, and of the practical activities that make up a large part of what was done each day, will help the reader understand the way students responded to our questions and the changes we noted over the year. In brief, the curriculum operates as follows. A "Workshop" comprising up to 20 tasks, in fixed order, is the major academic work that students attempt each day. The Workshop includes drawing and numbering tasks, pattern-completion tasks, book research, puzzles of various kinds, vocabulary, and sensorimotor exercises. Each of these is taught, one or two each day, at the start of the school year. The teacher will occasionally add a new task until there may be as many as 30 toward the end of the year in fifth grade. Each day the tasks are varied in their content, though the format and order remain the same. The starting and ending numbers in a counting task, for example, will be changed. The task titles and instructions are pinned up on a "task board" on the wall, and each afternoon after the children have gone home the teacher puts up directions for the next day. In this way it is not the teacher who "bosses" the children, as they put it, but the task board. The children do not have to finish all the tasks, nor remember where they left off the day before. When a student completes a task they put their work products in a file tray, but this work is not graded. Instead, the teacher checks it after school (though many of the children don't realize this) and notes any tasks and skills that a child is having difficulty with. Emphasis is placed on the pleasure of working and of getting work done rather than on correct answers, and the teachers try to avoid grading or even making comparative evaluations of students' work in the classroom. This is not to say that mistakes go uncorrected, but that children are not criticized or reprimanded for their errors.

Students work on the Workshop tasks at their own pace, moving independently about the classroom and interacting freely with peers, save that they must maintain a reasonable noise level, and not stop working altogether. They can request assistance from the teacher, but are encouraged instead to ask each other for help. While students are busy with the Workshop the teacher calls small groups together for individualized instruction. Two types of small-group session are employed: "Six groups" are occasions where the teacher reteaches a specific skill to those students who seem to require this assistance, from inspection of their work. More interesting to us were the "Reading Groups," which are regularly scheduled occasions where the teacher calls together students who she has grouped on the basis of their academic work-related behavior.

These Reading Groups are organized not by ability level but on the basis of students' learning-relevant behavior (what the teachers term their "personality type"). The teacher introduces activities designed to improve their behavior and their self-image. There are three groups, though students are not told that they are grouped on any criterion. The "A" students are those who have good study habits, enjoy learning, and show self-confidence. The "B" students also evince these characteristics but work at a much slower pace. The students who make up the "C" group have a particularly poor academic and social self-image, are frequently off-task in the classroom and are generally academically at-risk. They are given special attention in the Workshop Way program: for example, they are given specially designed group and individual tasks in their Reading Groups, and they have Reading Group more frequently during the day than students in the other two groups. The teacher keeps the pacing of tasks high with "C" students, because on their own they tend to work slowly and irregularly, and she works hard to keep their attention, since their academic motivation is low.

TEACHER–STUDENT INTERACTION IN THE CLASSROOM

We visited classes in order to observe and tape-record interaction among students and teacher, and our aim in this section is to illustrate the ways in which interactions foster change and development in students' social understanding. To anticipate, our argument will be that the teachers interact with children to ensure that they are drawn into a set of practical social activities. The activities reflect valued forms of social interaction and engagement and include helping others and seeking help from them, expressing tolerance towards others' faults and errors, taking academic and social risks such as answering a question even though unsure about the correctness of the answer, working quietly and industriously and so on. The significance of the practical activities lies in the fact that each encompasses both an immediate practical aim and at the same time a developmental telos. Next, we shall argue that the teacher works so that *she* is not the "reason" the children are doing these things; instead the teacher uses an interpretive framework that ascribes "responsibility" in the practices to the students in a way that emphasizes their effectiveness, their initiative, and their value as individuals. The children differ in the extent to which they "take up" this perspective on their own agency, and in the extent to which they accept the social practices of the classroom as legitimate and meaningful. Consequently they differ in the *manner* in which they are engaged in the practices, and they differ in the kind of account they give of them.

In short, the teachers' organization of the social and instructional structure of their classes, and the detailed form of their interaction with students, accomplish three goals. First, the children become engaged in the academic and social activities of the classroom. Second, many of the children begin to adopt new ways of understanding and talking about their ability, their own successes and failures, and their academic and personal worth. Third, at least some begin to discover an intrinsic value to these classroom activities, coming to understand them as legitimate and holding themselves responsible for carrying on the activities. We want to illustrate these three aspects of teacher-student interaction and then discuss precisely where we think their significance lies for an understanding of social development.

The Practical Social Activities of the Workshop Way Classroom

The practical activities of the Workshop Way classrooms cannot be described without reference to two evaluative aspects. The developmental significance of these practices lies in the fact that each involves both an immediate goal and a developmental telos. First, each activity involves an end or purpose that is socially and personally meritorious or virtuous; for instance, providing another child with assistance in a Workshop task. And second, each activity is designed to help the children develop a "skill" that entails conduct or concern that one would consider virtuous, for instance, sincere interest over others' learning and academic progress in class. Though the teachers and the curriculum guide spoke not of virtues but of "human skills [that] are human powers for living and surviving" (Pilon, 1980, p. 241), these skills were clearly interpreted by the teachers as exemplary of virtuous conduct. Once we recognized the importance of the value-laden character of these activities, we tried to discover how the children understood and valued their participation in them. In describing the activities here we shall draw attention to the moral end each entails. We shall also explain briefly something of the role each plays in the classroom. The following are the eight practical activities we came to focus our attention on, and question the children about:

Doing homework. Homework assignment in Workshop Way classes is routine and straightforward in its content, but unusual in its social setting and evaluation. Every evening each child must read aloud a short list of words, in a fluent and expressive manner. "Homework Checking" is the first class activity each morning, and the teacher hears each child read their words individually, encouraging them to make eye contact and speak forcefully. If the homework hasn't been done, or if the list is left at home, the child must take a new list and recite the words immediately, but there is no sanction, punishment, or even any disapproval expressed by the teacher. The end that the Workshop Way curriculum aims to foster by means of the ritualized practical activity of Homework Checking is "responsibility," in the sense of "independence of work habits" (Pilon, 1980, p. 77). This is both the virtue that the activity embodies and the end toward which it is oriented.

Getting help and advice from others. The second practical activity we came to recognize does not take place at a particular time in the school day, but runs through all the time the children are in the class. Students are discouraged from asking the teacher for advice, though many of them continue to do so, particularly in first grade. Instead, they are supposed to "ask a friend" if they can't figure something out. Here the aim is to encourage cooperation among peers. This activity is interrelated with the following two.

Giving help and advice to others. If students are to ask their friends how to do things, they will of course be asked for advice and help in turn. Although they are encouraged to provide assistance, there are no sanctions from the teacher or pupils for a child refusing to do so. As with the previous activity, the aim is to encourage cooperative activity as an instructional means and a social end.

Working together on Workshop tasks. Students are given the opportunity to work together on Workshop tasks if they wish, though only one or two of the tasks actually require cooperative work. The aim is to give children the freedom to choose whether to work together or alone, and who to work with.

Tolerating other students' mistakes. The teachers make a point of not blaming students for their mistakes, and they encourage the students themselves to be tolerant of their own and others' errors. Their view is that mistakes are an inevitable and necessary part of learning. This is an area that the students we talked to have some difficulty with: many were very aware of their own mistakes, and some told us that peers made fun of them when they erred. The end this activity is directed towards is an "acceptance of limitations of human nature as the reasons for their mistakes" (Pilon, 1983, p. 155).

Taking risks. Students are encouraged to "take a risk": to take on tasks where they are not certain what to do, to risk making mistakes, to accept academic and social challenges. This activity begins with the regular use of a worksheet called the "Risk Sheet," on which students must try to interpret directions on their own, and try to do their best without (in this case) help from others. Their understanding of what "risking" means changes. A first grade boy told us, early in the year, that a risk meant "it's not important if we get the answers all right." Steven, a fifth grade boy whose interviews we shall return to in more detail later, told us risking was when "You're not sure of something, so you do it, so you have a try." At the end of the year his illustration of risking was significantly changed. He told us of an occasion when:

> Tom asked me to do Workshop with him, my friend, and I said, "I'm going to do it by myself," and then he asked Jim, and Jim said, "I'm going to do it by myself," and so we just took that risk that he might hate us. But we just had to do our work.
>
> Int: What makes that a risk, exactly?
>
> Uhm, you're doing something and then taking the consequence of what could happen. The consequence would be that he'd get mad at us but we'd rather work and learn.

The telos in this activity is for students to "grow in courage." The teachers' manual proposes explaining this to the children in the following terms: "We are not willing to risk unless we are willing to be wrong, even if it turns out that we are right" (Pilon, 1983, p. 110). Courage is the counterpoint of the tolerance expressed in not criticizing others' mistakes.

Maintaining quiet while working. Students are supposed to keep their noise at a level where others are not disturbed, though they are free to talk to one another about work, and socialize in moderation. If they get too noisy a bell may be rung by the teacher, who then waits for the students to stand in silence. It is important that "a thing is used to give directions instead of the human voice" (Pilon, 1983, p. 106). "The teacher's voice could make policy feel like punishment and negative responses could be expected" (Pilon, 1980, p. 232). The telos here is that children recognize and tolerate each others' right to a comfortable work environment, and act to create that environment. But each child also has a right to speak in the classroom, and should come to be confident of this right.

Keeping busy. Students are expected to continue working on the Workshop tasks when they are not otherwise engaged. There is, however, no sanction from the teacher if they choose not to work. The aim is for students to develop initiative: "willingness to start a task" (Pilon, 1983, p. 155), and self-confidence: "awareness of one's power to finish tasks" (Pilon, 1983).

We interviewed a selection of students in each of the three grades to see how they understood these practical activities. Were they aware of the activities that we felt were of central interest? Did *we* make sense to *them* when talking about these activities? We found that even the youngest children were able to describe in accurate detail the character of each of the eight activities, including what they should do and what sanctions, if any, were involved. The children differed, though, in their explanation of the reasons or justifications for each of the activities, and we shall return to these differences later.

Development of Responsibility in Practical Activity

Our interest became directed towards *responsibility* because its development is an explicit focus of the Workshop Way curriculum. A number of conceptual and empirical problems arise, however, when one tries to study responsibility. In its everyday usage the term refers to an aspect of action that it is particularly tricky to put one's investigative finger on. Responsibility and its role in action have been viewed in a variety of ways by researchers. Social psychologists have treated responsibility as a matter of conforming to social role expectations as a consequence of socially and personally administered rewards and sanctions. In this view responsibility is a situational matter, a reaction to a normative force that impels an individual to act in a certain manner, generally prosocially, and that can be "focused" or "diffused" (like a light beam) by various means, to bring greater or lesser pressure to bear. Thus the "norm of responsibility" (Berkowitz & Daniels, 1963) is the expectation that we should help those who are in one way or another dependent upon us. Staub (1978) discusses the focusing of responsibility on a child by parents and other adults through more and less structured "assignment." In these analyses responsibility is identified in terms of behaviors with a particular content, that satisfies a consensual criterion, and the responsible individual is one who produces such behaviors. In the same line Wentzel, Siesfeld, Wood, Stevens and Ford (1987) assess adolescent responsibility in terms of the tendency to choose correctly between "a socially responsible and irresponsible course of action . . . (E.g., going to work vs. calling in sick to go to a concert)" (p. 8).

This emphasis on discrete acts categorized as responsible is not an unreasonable one, but it leads to difficulties. The danger is that by identifying being responsible with actions of a particular kind, or with picking a specific course of behavior, we may assume that *how* one acts or picks an act is unimportant. But this is a move we are unwilling to make. We know from everyday experience that simply making an inventory of the kinds of actions someone produces is not sufficient for us to judge whether they are responsible or not, because they may have acted grudgingly, out of a desire to avoid punishment or to please others, or in order to *appear* responsible. An adolescent can tell friends who have arrived with hard liquor that they cannot enter a party (an example from Wentzel et al., 1987) because an adult orders her to, because she fears punishment, from unwillingness to face the consequences of guests drinking, or from a sense that drinking is wicked. Wentzel et al. are comfortable talking of occasions "when being responsible is related to the avoidance of negative consequences," (p. 11), but one might reasonably argue that this is not responsibility but obedience. Such distinctions must be borne in mind when considering ethical matters in adults, and they must not be abandoned when we walk into an elementary school.

On the other hand, one can go too far in emphasizing the role of individual reasoning and judgment in rendering an action responsible. In Kohlberg's cognitive-developmental account, responsibility is a judgment that mediates between the stage-determined judgment of the appropriate action in a moral dilemma, and actual performance of that action. Kohlberg, Levine, and Hewer (1983, p. 49) suggest that "moral stage influences moral action in two ways: (a) through differences in deontic choice and (b) through judgments of responsibility." "Responsibility" here is solely a matter of the judgment a person makes of their accountability in a situation: the extent to which they judge they could be justly blamed or criticized for not acting. This leads to a judgment of the necessity of carrying out the action. In a similar manner, Higgins, Power and Kohlberg (1984) consider responsibility a judgment an individual makes by assessing their degree of personal involvement in a situation. Here again the claim is made that such a judgment provides "a mediating bridge from a deontic judgment of rightness and justice to moral action" (p. 74). Responsibility, then, is defined not by the content of the action, but in terms of the individual's assessment of their own liability, accountability, and personal obligation, attending to such considerations as others' welfare, self's moral worth, blame or guilt, and intrinsic values of social relationships such as friendship and community.

There are several problems with this cognitivist account of responsibility. First, the account assumes that the action under consideration is either exhibited or inhibited, so that the judgment of responsibility is an all-or-nothing matter, a "yes" or "no" binary decision. There is no recognition that engagement in an act can take various forms, while "content" is unchanged. Second, in total contrast with the behavioral view that responsibility is a matter of external correspondence to social norms, no matter what the motives, the cognitivist view of responsibility considers it an entirely private, individually determined decision, no matter what action one is judging ones responsibility for.

We came to adopt a perspective on responsibility that differed from both the behavioral and the cognitive accounts we have sketched; one that owes much to Fingarette (1967) and to MacIntyre (1984). Both these writers pay close attention to the fact that one can carry out a single course of activity in a variety of different manners, with a variety of ends in mind. Each tries to characterize and distinguish responsible or virtuous conduct from that starting point. Fingarette does this by identifying what he considers three "essential dimensions of responsibility." The first is the "forms of life," the social givens, that give form and content to responsible action. The second is an individual's acceptance of these life-forms as valid, and consequent care or concern about them. "Responsibility emerges where the individual accepts as a matter of personal concern something which society offers to his concern" (Fingarette, 1967). The third dimension is obligation, which Fingarette views as the mediating link between the practices proffered by a social group and their acceptance by a member of that group. Acceptance of a social practice involves understanding that the practice is legitimately obligatory in some respect. Such a view of responsibility contrasts on the one hand with the intellectualism of Kohlberg and Higgins, and on the other with the behaviorism of Staub and Wentzel et al.. In Fingarette's account responsibility plays a broader role than merely mediating between moral competence and performance, and a more constitutive role than does a social norm or expectation. Responsible action is a concerned engagement in a course of action that a social group habitually participates in. This account captures what strike us as the apposite concerns of the behaviorist and cognitivist views. The social normative aspect is found in the notion that practices are always socially-given, while the role of individual choice and involvement is found in the notion of concerned engagement in these practices.

MacIntyre presents an account of moral development that stresses, in a return to an Aristotelian view of conduct and character, virtues such as truthfulness, courage, and justice. MacIntyre views the development of virtues as resulting from participation in the various social practices that are institutionalized in a society. MacIntyre's definition of "practice" is somewhat specialized, complex, and deliberately circular, but it is worth quoting. "By 'practice' I [. . .] mean any coherent and complex form of socially established cooperative human activity through which goods internal to that form of activity are realized in the course of trying to achieve those standards of excellence which are appropriate to, and partially definitive of, that form of activity, with the result that human powers to achieve excellence, and human conceptions of the ends and goods involved, are systematically extended" (MacIntyre, 1984, p. 187). Architecture, farming, the games of football and chess, arts, sciences, and friendship are all practices; bricklaying and tic-tac-toe are not.

Next, MacIntyre distinguishes between two kinds of goods or outcomes that can be gained from participation in a practice. The first are those goods that are specific to the practice, that have an "internal" relation to it—for instance, chess playing can lead to "the achievement of a certain highly particular analytical skill, strategic imagination and competitive intensity" (p. 188) and so on. The second are those goods that are contingently related to the practice, whose relationship is an "external" one; goods such as prestige, status, and money. There are always alternative ways of achieving such goods. MacIntyre argues that virtues are acquired when a person participates in a practice in such a manner that they strive for the goods that are internal rather than external to that practice. Conversely, only virtuous (courageous, truthful, just) participation in a practice will result in achieving internal goods. "A virtue is an acquired human quality the possession and exercise of which tends to enable us to achieve those goods which are internal to practices and the lack of which effectively prevents us from achieving any such goods" (p. 121). For instance, a doctor who practices medicine for financial gain will not, in all probability, be a good doctor. MacIntyre argues that, in addition, he will not be a good *person*, for it could only be by acting with concern for patients' well-being, with a curiosity and interest in the working of the human body, and with a commitment to others' welfare, that a person would, by practicing medicine, develop virtues such as honesty and dedication. MacIntyre goes on to provide an explanation of which set of activities constitute a practice, the way that institutions and practices coexist, and the way practices make up a life, but we cannot discuss these here. What we wish to point out is that in MacIntyre's account—like Fingarette's—being virtuous is not a matter of carrying out particular actions so much as acting in a particular *manner* in ones practices. When we ask ourself if a person is virtuous we ask, then, not *what* they do so much as *how* they do it. (The respect in which MacIntyre rejects both deontological and consequentialist ethics in favor of a teleological approach may now be clearer.)

What relevance do these philosophical analyses have to the classroom? We were struck, first, by the fact that both the Workshop Way curriculum manuals and the teachers spoke of traditional virtues such as honesty, courage, and responsibility as "skills" children could and should acquire in Workshop Way classes. We came to appreciate that the practical activities of Workshop Way classes, at least taken as a whole, accorded well with MacIntyre's preliminary definition of practices as "ongoing modes of human activity within which ends have to be discovered and rediscovered" (p. 273), as well as with the more precise definition cited above. When we reflected on the ends that children referred to in their accounts of the classroom practical activities, it seemed that we could reasonably distinguish between internal and external ends. We shall describe these accounts shortly, but first we need to examine the way teachers tried to bring about changes in the manner in which students engaged in these activities.

PROVIDING STUDENTS WITH A FRAMEWORK
OF INTERPRETATION

In comparison with other classes we have studied, these teachers strove to engage children in the classroom activities in a particular way and encourage a distinctive kind of involvement. What, we asked ourselves, was the form of engagement they were trying to encourage? The teachers told us that they believed they must remove emotional and conceptual blocks that prevented the children from free engagement (both academic and social) in classroom practical activities. Their view was that many of the children engaged ambivalently in classroom activities because they had become afraid of taking risks; they would not cooperate with others, or ask a peer for help, because they feared appearing ignorant. In short, they brought to the classroom ways of understanding themselves that interfered with a genuine engagement in the classroom's social practices. Consequently part of the teachers' job, as they described it to us, was to provide the children with a new way of understanding their success and failures. One of the teachers' most important jobs was to help students construct a new interpretive framework.

Parenthetically, we found it interesting that the teachers' accounts of the changes they were trying to expedite in their instruction referred not only to facilitating more advanced, mature, or moral ways of acting and thinking, but also to undoing and replacing previous patterns of understanding and interpreting self and others that were understandable, but considered defensive and ultimately maladaptive. In other words, social development was not seen as proceeding with inevitable progress, but as involving dead ends and distortions that called for remediation.

In our first interviews with the students we wanted to discover whether they (in particular the "C Strategy" students; those with maladaptive learning styles) expressed the concern over academic failure that the teachers understood them to have, and whether they did indeed tend to understand themselves as inadequate when they made mistakes. We found that this was indeed frequently the case. Consider the example of Peter. Peter was a friendly but shy fifth grader, heavily built and somewhat awkward in his movements. He soon became relaxed in our discussions with him, and talked easily about his class. In our first interview he talked about his sense of frustration when he didn't get correct answers. His account was a clear example of the kind of attitude and self-understanding the teachers were trying to change:

Interviewer: If you don't get all the right answers in the yes/no cards, how do you feel when that happens?

Peter: I don't know, sometimes frustrated.

Int: What do you do if that happens?

Peter: Well, I just, I don't know. (I just) get mad and stuff, sometimes. Sometimes it stops me from doing my work and stuff. Just get really frustrated probably ( ).

Int: What does the teacher do when that happens? If you don't get all the right answers.

Peter: Oh nothing, she just says, "That's OK, as long as you tried," and stuff.

Int: How does that make you feel?

Peter: Better.

Int: Do the other guys in class say anything if you get answers wrong on the yes/no cards?

Peter: Yes, some of them do. Some of them don't.

Int: What kinds of things do they say?

Peter: They laugh.

The teachers confronted assumptions like Peter's that one should not make errors on assignments by introducing the children to a new way of talking about and understanding interactions with peers, and their successes and failures in classroom tasks. This new perspective must be established at both the practical level and the articulated level (Packer [1985b] follows Heidegger [1962] in calling these the "ready-to-hand" and "unready-to-hand" levels). So what the teachers say and the way they say it (to oversimplify) reflect and sustain this new framework or perspective.

To appreciate the teachers' motivation here it is necessary to return to the contrast they see between the Workshop Way curriculum and traditional instructional techniques. As we mentioned earlier, the Workshop Way curriculum reflects a conviction that traditional elementary school classes have a detrimental effect on children's development, largely as a consequence of the social organization they employ to minimize management problems and reduce the teaching load. Traditional instructional techniques require that students work individually on academic material that places low demands on them (the ubiquitous "worksheet"), and assign them an "official" social and academic standing among their peers largely on the basis of their grades. The overall effects of this have been documented by educational researchers: a discouragement of open-ended thinking and intellectual risk taking, disenchantment with school, and persistent, stable poor self-image that is overly dependent on their academic performance, among many including the most able students.

Traditional classes, it is believed, then, create a divisive atmosphere, a lack of community because students are prevented from interacting meaningfully over academic material, and because they are differentially labeled on the basis of performance. We might say that traditional classes encourage students to study and work for goods and outcomes that are largely external ones: grades and prizes, intellectual status, and reputation. The Workshop Way teachers aim, in contrast, to encourage students to discover the goods that are internal to learning and working. They do this by changing the nature of students' accountability for classroom work, by encouraging initiative, and altering the criteria by which students' worth is judged. To pick three from the many ways in which the teachers try to change the way things are done, students are treated as equal to one another, given the freedom to work together, and allowed to schedule their work at their own pace.

These are not just changes in instructional practice; they also involve a new interpretive framework, a new way of talking about the world. For example, "Cushioning" and "Risking" are two terms the teachers use that index a new way of talking and thinking about classroom work. Cushioning is what teachers do to reduce the danger students experience in academic work. They shift emphasis from achieving success to making an effort; frequently reminding their students that "No one knows everything"; that "It's okay to make mistakes." Risking is what students do in their work when they try something new, and advance into academic areas where they lack self-confidence.

Perspective on Accountability

So we can characterize the interpretive framework teachers use in terms of the perspectives it provides concerning students' accountability, their initiative and their worth as people. In each case, the new perspective can be readily contrasted with a perspective which is operative in more traditionally organized classrooms. We shall not try to demonstrate the existence or prevalence of the traditional perspective; it has been amply documented elsewhere (Goodlad, 1984; Morgan, 1977; Silberman, 1970).

Old perspective. Incorrect answers are a sign of inadequacy, at the least, of inadequate understanding, and possibly of incompetence: they show lack of ability or effort, or both. Incorrect answers are justly repaid by low grades, and good grades are the end that students should work for in school.

New perspectives. It is "okay to fail." Mistakes, lapses of memory, errors, and failures are due not to stupidity or social background, but are an inevitable part of being human, of attempting a project and taking risks. Such mistakes are often necessary if learning is to take place, and so they should not cause embarrassment, guilt, or distress. Mistakes do not lead to poor grades; effort, rather than ability or achievement, is what will be praised, but effort is also its own reward. One does not study and work to get correct answers, let alone good grades; studying is done for the pleasure of discovery, for the excitement of risking, and in order to learn.

Teacher:	[Speaking to the whole class.] . . . . Now does it mean you're dumb if you make a mistake? No, it doesn't! OK, we're growing courage today. Right answers are not the most important thing. Next one.

Teacher: Eight! Is it OK if we make a mistake? We're just learning. So you
                                  have to think through what I'm saying.

Student [2nd grade]:   I haven't got it finished.

Teacher: That's all right, just say it out loud. [Several answer.]

Teacher: Now this is really using your brain, isn't it? Is it okay if you don't
                         know everything? [Students respond affirmatively.]

Perspective on Initiative

Old perspective. Students should do what the teacher tells them to. The
teacher gives directions that determine the pacing and order of tasks, and children are expected to wait for these directions. Children who do not wait are
misbehaving, and should be disciplined and punished.

New perspective. "Do what you think." In the Workshop, children should
take the initiative in selecting and attempting tasks and making contact with one
another. They have responsibility for pacing their work and completing tasks,
and should not depend on the teacher to tell them what to do. The teacher still has
authority in the class, but she encourages students to take initiative for what they
do, and the Workshop tasks require student initiative.

Student: Mrs. Smith. What, uh, do you circle this line, or X it?

Teacher: What do you think?

Student: Circle.

Teacher: You do what you think, if you're not sure, you can ask a friend.

Student: OK.

Teacher: Okay, is there any part of you that tells you that? What do you use to know
             that?

Student: My brain.

Teacher: Your brain, right! Needs a lot of initiative, doesn't it. You get a Thinker [a
             type of learning activity in the Workshop]. And what do you do after you do
             the Thinker?

Student: Put it away.

Teacher: Yep. That's responsibility, great!

Perspective on Status

Old perspective. Respect is contingent upon classroom performance; students receiving good grades are "Honor students," while those with poor academic performance have less worth.

New perspective. All students are of equal worth, no matter how they perform academically. People have an intrinsic worth, irrespective of how competent they are or what they do. Studying should not be motivated by status, any more than by grades.

Teacher:	Is it okay if you don't know this word?
Students:	Yes.
Teacher:	If someone knows this word and you don't know it does that mean they're smarter than you?
Students:	No!
Teacher:	No. No one knows everything.

Teacher:	OK, now, I'm going to open my paper up, and I'm going to write—what's the most important thing we always put on our papers?
Students:	Our name!
Teacher:	That's right, because we're important people, aren't we? So, we have to know who that paper belongs to, so we're going to put our name on our paper. I'm going to put mine on my paper.

Teacher:	[As the students work:] . . . Now, we want to draw *powerful* lines that show that we're concentrating. If you make them too small, you're working too hard; if you make them too long, we don't have good concentration. So, we've got to find the just right size for ourselves. If everybody's hands are different, and everybody's powers different . . . That is great concentration!

Notice how in this last example the teacher strives to make the children feel proud of their work. She emphasizes that everyone is unique and special: this is why the children put their names on their work. Each person must find their own, individual balance between working too hard and not concentrating. Notice also that "concentration" is talked about as a skill: something that is a result of effort and practice, not ability. Concentration is something one learns "how to do." The task is described as one of learning how to concentrate, and success is interpreted as achieving "good concentration."

ENGAGEMENT

We've discussed the importance of the students' engagement in an integrated set of practical activities. The teachers seemed to be working hard to find ways that every student could become engaged in these activities, in the hope and expectation that they would come to find internal goods and ends in what they were doing. Responsible or virtuous conduct would be a matter, for example, of responding to a peer's request for assistance out of a concern for the peer's learning and progress through the Workshop rather than to please peers or the teacher, which are both external ends. It is hoped students will come to have this concern with an internal end as a result of engaging in the practical activity of giving help, even if they initially became engaged to achieve an external outcome.

We were left with the question of whether the children changed in the manner of their engagement in the classroom activities over the course of the year, and set out to explore this issue.

Changes in Engagement

We again interviewed the students in each of the three classes who had been identified by the teacher as "Strategy A" or "Strategy C" students. Our second and third sets of interviews with these children were intended to ascertain whether their accounts of engagement in each of the focal practical activities changed over the course of the school year. With each child we tried to get a sense of the kind of obligation they felt each activity had, probing to undercover the kind of purpose or end they felt they acted in terms of when engaged in each of the eight activities.

Two Students' Stories

We have insufficient space here to discuss in depth the responses the 24 children gave to our questions. Instead we shall depict just two children, both fifth-grade boys, whose descriptions of key classroom activities were distinctly different. (We have quoted from each of them earlier in this chapter.) Both Steven and Peter were identified by the teacher as "C" strategy students at the beginning of the year, but by the time of our final interviews Steven had been moved to the "A" strategy Reading Group, while his teacher said Peter was being difficult in class. It became apparent as we talked with them that Peter had come to lose any sense that Workshop Way was a sensible way to run a classroom. For reasons that we could not be entirely clear about, he felt alienated and resentful of his participation in classroom activities. Steven's understanding of the activities, on the other hand, had changed in almost the opposite direction.

We quoted Steven earlier to illustrate a changed understanding of "risking." By the end of the year his example of risking was not a Workshop task but an exchange with a friend where he risked losing the friendship. Asked about homework in the earlier interview, Steven said it was okay to do because "it's fun." In the final interview his account was different, as he explained the activity in terms of its challenge and the responsibility involved:

> Yeah. 'Cause it's nice to . . . when you get really high [i.e., progress through the numbered Homework assignments] and everything and you get the challenge and you get up there . . . then, you can finish all the sheets, and that gives you . . . know that you've done something that's hard.

Int: And the homework helps you do that?

> Yeah. Helps you be responsible too 'cause you have to bring the same paper everyday.

In the earlier interview Steven said he kept working in the Workshop " 'Cause I like to get far enough 'cause there's fun tasks up there," referring to "Physical fitness, like you get to go outside and shoot a basket or something." In our last conversation, Steven explained that:

> One of my goals this term was to try to do my best in Workshop, do my very best work and then try to get as far as I can, but do my best work. It might seem that I'm going slower but that's the purpose of the Workshop, is to do the tasks how they're supposed to.

We again see a shift from a focus on a goal external to the activity—getting to a "fun task"—to recognition of an internal goal: doing his best, doing tasks "how they're supposed to." He talks explicitly of his own "goals" and of "the purpose of the Workshop," and the two seem in concord.

Peter is the fifth grader whose description of frustration we used earlier to illustrate a self-condemnatory understanding of academic work. In our earlier interview with Peter he said that he felt the Workshop tasks were too hard, but that he liked and respected his teacher, who he said was the best thing about the class: "I've had a lot of crabby teachers, and she's nice and understanding and everything." "Mrs. X she really likes us, wants us to do Workshop for the brain power stuff." But, "She *changes* some tasks. She makes us do them harder."

In the first interview Peter talked about homework in terms of having "to be responsible for taking it home and studying it," though his main motivation is the external goal of keeping up with his peers:

Int: OK, have you ever not done your homework?

> Huh, well, yeah, sometimes. Sometimes you forget and she gives you a new one, but, but you can't read it [to the teacher immediately]. If you lose yours, she'll give you a new one but you have to do it tomorrow.

Int: How do you feel about that?

Oh, I get, I'm kind of mad that . . . Very mad. 'Cause she has homework for responsibility. You have to be responsible for taking it home and studying it, bringing it back.

Int: When you get mad, what do you get mad about?

I don't know. I like to just, I like to stay up with the rest of the people and not get behind.

And in the last interview his accounts of the classroom activities were still in terms of external goals:

Oh, I don't know. I just don't really practice it [Homework], it's kind of easy. Just go up there and say.

Int: So what do you do? You take a look at it in the morning?

Yeah, just before I read it to her. Like if there's a couple of people before me, I just read it through.

His accounts of risking showed a similar lack of change. In first interview, "Well if you have no idea what it is, then you just write something down what you think it is." In the second, "Sometimes you don't know the answer so you just have to guess and risk the answer." And an additional element becomes apparent: Peter now talks of avoiding punishment and justifying an activity. Asked if it would be bad not to take a risk he responded:

Yeah. 'Cause she'll get mad at you and send you over, like if you sit by your friend, at your desk, she'll send you over somewhere else all by yourself.

In general, by the time of our last conversation Peter apparently saw nothing of value coming from his participation in the classroom activities. In particular he strongly disliked the teacher's role in the Workshop:

Int: What's the reason that you're working on the workshop?

I guess to develop your brain, that's what she says.

Int: You don't think that's true?

I don't know, I guess it is. I just, I really don't know. Just the way *she* does it that I don't like. I just don't like the way she does it.

We picked these two students as extreme examples: of a clear shift from external to internal goals, and of an absence of any change in the goals found in the practices. These two patterns are linked to acceptance and rejection respectively of the teacher's role in the classroom. The other children we talked with showed similar though less dramatic changes.

CONCLUSIONS

A word may be needed to prevent any confusion between our examination of internal and external ends, and the notions of internal and external motivation. The latter concepts in social learning theory reflect a belief that socialization (and specifically socialization as a responsible citizen) consists in the "internal" control of behavior, in contrast to constraints and elicitors applied "externally" in the form of punishments, rewards, and threats, where "internal" and "external" refer now to the child and the environment respectively. "Internal" control has been achieved, it is argued, if a behavior occurs or persists in the absence of such elicitors and constraints. In our view this notion of progressive transfer of agency and initiation of action to the child is overly individualistic in the developmental norms to which it makes tacit reference. While such a transfer may occur, the attempt to explain responsibility in such terms leaves unanswered the question of the goals towards which conduct is directed. Guilt and anxiety may replace punishment and rebuke as motivators of an action such as helping another, but in both cases the end sought is extrinsic to the action. In the first case the end sought is reduction of a painful emotion, in the second it is the avoidance of a painful sanction by an adult.

Conversely, if the child's interest in helping peers shifts from a desire to please the teacher to a concern with others' working and helping, it is by no means obvious that the locus of agency has moved from an "external" to an "internal" source. In both cases the social milieu of the classroom is inextricably involved. What *has* changed is the manner of the child's engagement in the practice of helping; the change is from an extrinsic end (pleasing the teacher) that has no essential connection to the practice, to an intrinsic end (others' performance) that is intimately connected to the activity of helping as it is established, discussed, and justified in the Workshop Way classrooms.

And a related matter: when we have talked of engagement, we don't refer simply to the idea that children learn prosocial behaviors by taking part in them and then internalizing relevant cues, as has been suggested by social learning theorists. For example, Staub describes "natural socialization" in terms of "participation" in positive behavior, the "focusing" of responsibility by adults, and subsequent "internalization" by the child. "[A]n important influence on children learning to behave prosocially is the focusing of responsibility on them by parents and other socializing agents to engage in behavior that enhances others' welfare. Focusing responsibility refers to the demand by the parent that the child engage in social behavior. . . . [This] refers to a particular content area, to a particular type of behavior the parents wish to promote" (Staub, 1979, p. 189). But the Workshop Way teachers would balk at the suggestion that they are "demanding" that students engage in the classroom practices. Of course not all students commit themselves to the Workshop Way regimen (as Peter demonstrates), and the teachers use a variety of techniques to cope with inappropriate behavior.

And some students will not move beyond acting in ways they expect will please the teacher. What seems important, however, is the potential for movement, and, as we have begun to document in our interviews, this movement does occur for some children.

Having clarified these points, let us summarize the ground we have covered. We've taken an interpretive stance in this chapter. Our conversations with the children were an opportunity for them to give accounts of the practical activities in their classroom, and for us to try to characterize their understanding of these activities (Honey, 1987). Especially, we listened to whether they spoke of their engagement in terms of goals or ends that were *internal* to each activity, or in terms of goals that were *external*. For there is a theme common to both MacIntyre and Fingarette: that virtue (for MacIntyre) and responsibility (for Fingarette) consists in (and arises from) accepting the internal ends, the intrinsic concerns, of a particular way of life as ones own. Recognizing that all of us can just "go through the motions" in our lives, they both emphasize the manner in which a person acts; and the form of engagement in a project.

This distinction mirrors a concern among educators today: that students are being educated into what Wiggins (1987) refers to as "thoughtless mastery": a superficial acquisition of curriculum content in pursuit of grades, rather than a deeper concern with and appreciation of the *intrinsic* satisfactions to be derived from study and learning. This worry can be found expressed in the writings of those who find that academic tasks typically entail only the mastery of the trivial and neglect the meaningful (Mergendoller, Marchman, Mitman, & Packer, 1987).

We came, then, to understand the Workshop Way curriculum as an integrated set of activities that made up what it was for the children in those classes to be "students." From this perspective, teaching was not a matter of imparting knowledge by means of lecturing or assigning academic exercises, but of finding ways to engage students in those practical activities, in the hope and expectation that they would come to discover internal ends and goods in what they were doing. This interpretation is supported by the description of the curriculum in teachers' manuals, by the teachers' accounts to us of what they were trying to accomplish, and what we observed of daily classroom life. When the teachers talked of the "skills" students were developing—initiative, independence in their work, responsibility, courage, honesty, self-confidence, willingness to ask for help, and creativity—these pointed to a view of education as a matter of development of personal powers (cf. Harré, 1984), of a child coming to value intelligent and assiduous work, and attaining responsibility and virtue in the process. One aim of this chapter has been to take this rather homely notion and grant that it may have credence.

Another aim has been to illustrate one approach to the study of children's social understanding—interpreting students' accounts of their activities with an ear to the kinds of goal they attend to and are motivated by. The distinction between goods that are internal and external to practices provides, we think, one index or sign of children's changing sense of their own responsibility and agency. And this development is not one relevant only to the moral periphery of developmental psychology; an understanding of ones agency must play a role throughout social development. We view moral development not as a matter of increased autonomy through articulation of ethical principles, but of an increased interdependence and sensitivity to social concerns that develops through participation in social activities.

And, while curriculum evaluation is not our major interest, if we grant that Workshop Way classes exemplify the kind of education of the virtues in and through social practices about which MacIntyre and Fingarette talk, then attending to the kinds of ends in terms of which students act can provide a means to assess such a curriculum.

REFERENCES

Berkowitz, L., & Daniels, L.R. (1963). Responsibility and dependency. *Journal of Abnormal and Social Psychology, 66*, 429–436.

Bernstein, R. (1983). *Beyond objectivism and relativism*. Philadelphia: University of Pennsylvania Press.

Bleicher, J. (1980). *Contemporary hermeneutics: Hermeneutics as method, philosophy and critique*. London: Routledge & Kegan Paul.

Chomsky, N. (1965). *Aspects of the theory of syntax*. Cambridge, MA: MIT Press.

Cicourel, A.V. (1973). *Cognitive sociology: Language and meaning in social interaction*. Harmondsworth, England: Penguin.

Fingarette, H. (1967). *On responsibility*. New York: Basic Books.

Freeman, M. (1985). Paul Ricoeur on interpretation: The model of the text and the idea of development. *Human Development, 28*, 295–312.

Gellatly, A.R.H. (1987). Acquisition of a concept of logical necessity. *Human Development, 30*, 32–47.

Gergen, K.J. (1985). The social constructionist movement in modern psychology. *American Psychologist, 40*, 266–275.

Goodlad, J.I. (1984). *A place called school: Prospects for the Future*. New York: McGraw-Hill.

Harré, R. (1984). *Personal being: A theory for individual psychology*. Cambridge, MA: Harvard University Press.

Heidegger, M. (1962). *Being and time*. (J. Macquarrie and E. Robinson, Trans.). New York: Harper & Row.

Higgins, A., Power, C., & Kohlberg, L. (1984). The relationship of moral atmosphere to judgments of responsibility. In W. Kurtines & J. Gewirtz (Eds.), *Morality, moral behavior, and moral development*. New York: John Wiley & Sons.

Honey, M.A. (1987). The interview as text: Hermeneutics considered as a model for analyzing the clinically informed research interview. *Human Development, 30*, 69–82.

Kohlberg, L., Levine, C., & Hewer, A. (1983). Moral stages: A current formulation and a response to critics. *Contributions to Human Development, 10.*

MacIntyre, A. (1984). *After virtue: A study in moral theory.* South Bend, IN: University of Notre Dame Press.

Mergendoller, J.R., Marchman, V.A., Mitman, A.L., & Packer, M.J. (1987). Task demand and accountability emphasis in middle grade science classes. *Elementary School Journal, 88,* 251–265.

Morgan, E.P. (1977). *Inequality in classroom learning: Schooling and democratic citizenship.* New York: Praeger.

Packer, M.J. (1985a). *The structure of moral action: A hermeneutic study of moral conflict.* Basel: Karger.

Packer, M.J. (1985b). Hermeneutic inquiry in the study of human conduct. *American Psychologist, 40,* 1081–1093.

Packer, M.J. (1987). Social interaction as practical activity: Implications for the study of social and moral development. In W. Kurtines & J. Gewirtz (Eds.), *Moral development through social interaction.* New York: Wiley.

Palmer, R.E. (1969). *Hermeneutics: Interpretation theory in Schleiermacher, Dilthey, Heidegger and Gadamer.* Evanston, IL: Northwestern University Press.

Piaget, J. (1932). *The moral judgment of the child.* London: Routledge and Kegan Paul.

Pilon, G.H. (1980). *The Workshop Way.* New Orleans: The Workshop Way, Inc.

Pilon, G.H. (1983). *Self concept and reading the Workshop Way.* New Orleans: The Workshop Way, Inc.

Ricoeur, P. (1976). *Interpretation theory: Discourse and the surplus of meaning.* Fort Worth: Texas Christian University Press.

Ricoeur, P. (1979). The model of the text: Meaningful action considered as a text. In P. Rabinow and W.M. Sullivan (Eds.), *Interpretive social science: A reader.* Berkeley: University of California Press.

Ricoeur, P. (1981). *Hermeneutics and the human sciences: Essays on language, action and interpretation.* J.B. Thompson, (Ed.). New York: Cambridge University Press.

Schön, D.A. (1983). *The reflective practitioner: How professionals think in action.* New York: Basic Books.

Shweder, R.A. (1982). Beyond self-constructed knowledge: The study of culture and morality. *Merrill-Palmer Quarterly, 28,* 41–70.

Silberman, C.E. (1970). *Crisis in the classroom: The remaking of American education.* New York: Random House.

Smith, J.K., & Heshusius, L. (1986). Closing down the conversation: The end of the quantitative-qualitative debate among educational inquirers. *Educational Researcher, 15,* 4–12.

Staub, E. (1978). *Positive social behavior and morality. Vol. 1. Social and personal influences.* New York: Academic Press.

Staub, E. (1979). *Positive social behavior and morality. Vol. 2. Socialization and development.* New York: Academic Press.

Taylor, C. (1979). Interpretation and the science of man. In P. Rabinow and W. Sullivan (Eds.), *Interpretive social science: A reader.* Berkeley: University of California Press.

Taylor, C. (1985). Philosophy and the human sciences: Philosophical papers volume 2. Cambridge: Cambridge University Press.

Wentzel, K.R., Siesfeld, G.A., Wood, D., Stevens, E., & Ford, M.E. (1987, April). *Does being good make the grade? Adolescent social responsibility and classroom achievement.* Paper presented at the annual meeting of the American Educational Research Association, Washington, DC.

Wiggins, G. (1987, June). *Intellectual and moral education.* Paper presented at the colloquium, *Adolescence and adulthood: The development of self and the experience of moral conflict.* Harvard University, Cambridge, MA.

CHAPTER 5

Children's Planning in Social Contexts: An Observational Study of Kindergarteners' Planning in the Classroom*

Mary Gauvain

Much of daily cognitive activity occurs within social situations. This is particularly the case for young children in that their cognitive performances are often accomplished in the company of or under the supervision of others. Understanding how children establish, organize, and benefit from cognitive opportunities available in social contexts, as well as how social organization may influence the cognitive opportunities children have available to them, is crucial for unraveling the influence of social experience on cognitive growth. Our understanding of this process is limited, however, in that there are few studies in which children have been observed as they coordinate their own individual cognitive activities with the behaviors of others in everyday situations. The research reported in this chapter was an effort to increase understanding of young children's skill at defining individual acts and coordinating these actions with those of others by observing kindergarten children as they constructed and implemented plans for classroom activities over 10 class sessions.

In addition to the influence that social experience may have on children's developing knowledge base, children's metacognitive skills may benefit from so-

* Without the support of the children who allowed me to participate in and observe their kindergarten year, and Carol Skillman, a teacher *par excellance*, this research would not have been possible. I extend my deepest gratitude to them. I also appreciate the help of Donald Rizzo and the other administrators at the Maurice Hawk School in Princeton, New Jersey; Grace Mest for her invaluable assistance as a reliability coder; and Judy DeLoache, Shari Ellis, Barbara Rogoff, Jon Tudge, Jaan Valsiner, and Terry Winegar, for their helpful comments on the manuscript. A postdoctoral fellowship # T32 MH 17126, from the National Institute of Health awarded to the Oregon Social Learning Center provided financial support for completing the research.

cial interchange. Conducting activities in social contexts requires working with and around the activities of the other people present, and may therefore draw heavily on metacognitive skills like planning, as children define, monitor, and coordinate their activities with the activities of others. While an individual acting on his or her own may be able to execute a plan devised largely in terms of the next immediate move or set of moves, planning and executing plans in social contexts often requires merging cognitive with social concerns. This is especially true when other people are instrumental for accomplishing an individual's goals (Gearhart, 1979).

Competence at coordinating individual and social activities may be an important characteristic of skilled planning, and the development of children's skill at doing this may be facilitated as children try to execute individually formulated plans in the company of others. Observations of children as they construct and execute plans for an activity performed in social contexts may reveal personal and social considerations young children have as they plan, such as an individual's goals and awareness of other's plans, as well as reveal opportunities children may have for developing planning skills in social situations.

This chapter is concerned with the role of social organization in the development of young children's planning skills. First, the development of planning skills in social contexts is discussed. This is followed by presentation of an observational study of kindergarteners' planning in the classroom. The chapter concludes with a discussion of social and individual considerations children may have as they practice and develop their planning skills in the company of others.

THE DEVELOPMENT OF PLANNING SKILLS IN SOCIAL CONTEXTS

Interest in children's planning skills stems from recent trends in cognitive developmental research to understand the development of metacognitive skills (Brown, Bransford, Ferrara, & Campione, 1983). Awareness and regulation of one's own cognitive processes is considered central to learning and cognitive growth (Brown & DeLoache, 1978; Flavell & Wellman, 1977). Planning, which includes devising actions prior to engaging in them and monitoring the effectiveness of the plan as it is executed, is an exemplary metacognitive activity.

Planning is the deliberate organization of a sequence of actions oriented toward accomplishing a specific goal (Hayes-Roth & Hayes-Roth, 1979). Much of the research on the development of children's planning skills has focused on plan formulation. This research, the aim of which has been to increase understanding of the development of children's skill at formulating relatively complex plans, has yielded insight into the aspects of a task that children consider when predetermining a course of action (Forbes & Greenberg, 1983; Klahr, 1978; Gauvain & Rogoff, 1985, 1989; Rogoff & Radzisewska, 1985; Pea, 1982). The development of plan execution skills, and the relation between plans and action, has seldom been studied, however. As Pea (1982) points out, most models of the planning process are top-heavy, relying too much on individual mental activity prior to engaging in action, whereas most everyday planning appears to be bottom-heavy in that it is strongly influenced by circumstances of a situation. Thus, models based solely on plan formulation cannot explain how plans are monitored and controlled or what a planner does if the plan poses difficulty during execution. By examining how a plan is implemented, monitored, and revised during plan execution, we may learn how plans direct action. In addition, aspects of the planning process that may become known to the planner during execution of a plan, and thereby have the potential for affecting subsequent planning behavior, may be revealed.

In a paper on children's planing, Glick (1983) points out that most approaches to studying the development of planning skills emphasize the importance of endogenous factors, such as the acquisition of expertise or structural changes in the organization of the child's thought. While acknowledging the importance of these factors in the development of children's planning skills, Glick stresses the need to investigate exogenous factors—such as features of the physical and social environment and their relationship to endogenous changes—to understand the development of skills which are as complex, and as action-tied, as those involved in planning. Examination of the influence of exogenous factors on plan development and execution may indicate how situational circumstances affect planning.

It would appear that a planner's sensitivity to exogenous factors that could affect future action is a central feature of skilled planning. Hayes-Roth and Hayes-Roth (1979) propose a model of planning which characterizes expert planning as the skill of opportunistically and flexibly identifying and using resources in the environment to support the development and execution of a plan. Rogoff, Gauvain, and Gardner (1987) extended this idea into a developmental framework by proposing that, with development, children increase in sensitivity to the resources and constraints available in a setting that may facilitate or hinder action. An important task of development is increasing skill and flexibility in fitting the action being planned with the context in which the action will occur (Gardner & Rogoff, 1985).

Planning in social situations may facilitate the development of planning skills, in particular, the development of contextual sensitivity while planning. By planning and executing plans in social contexts children may have opportunities to observe or participate in the planning behaviors of others when organizing actions in advance. This experience may provide children with opportunities to reflect on a process that is difficult for them to do on their own, thereby influencing their developing planning skills. In coordinating plans children seem to learn about their own and each other's cognitive activities (Forbes & Lubin, 1979; Gearhart & Newman, 1980; Goldman & Ross, 1978; Lomov, 1978). Gearhart (1979) found that even pairs of 3-year-olds publicly prearranged all play episodes in a pretend-store situation, but each child's plan lacked a model of the other person's perspective. The younger planner needed her companion in the play, so she told her what to do ahead of time, using her like a tool for the accomplishment of the plan. Gearhart pointed out that the fact that the companion does not serve as an effective tool (as she generally has a plan of her own) is a condition for learning to coordinate plans. That even the 3-year-olds were learning to plan more effectively was evidenced by their attempts to prearrange elements of the plan which caused difficulty in earlier episodes.

Planning and executing actions in social contexts may also encourage children's awareness of aspects of social situations that may impinge on the planning process. Social relationships and organization, particularly in ongoing social situations, may facilitate or restrict an individual's opportunities for formulating or implementing a plan in that context. In addition, compromises involved in coordinating activity interests with preferences for social companionship may be important considerations when planning individual activities in social contexts. Thus, examination of plan development and use within social contexts may reveal opportunities children have for developing planning skills as they plan in the company of others, as well as elucidate children's awareness of and sensitivity to social factors that govern the planning process.

KINDERGARTENERS' PLANNING IN THE CLASSROOM

The present study examined kindergarten children's planning in the classroom. A kindergarten class was observed over 10 occasions prior to, during, and following a classroom intervention in which the children were asked to plan their activities for a daily open activity period in advance. Following the 10 observational sessions each child was interviewed about his or her favorite class activities and classmates, as well as their reactions to planning their activities in advance. The classroom was chosen as the observational setting because it is one of the primary habitats of young children, contains a continuous social grouping, and provides children with opportunities to organize their own activities within a social context. What young children choose to do during an open activity period, and what they do when they are asked to plan this time in advance of action, may reveal considerations young children have as they organize activities in social contexts, as well as suggest some important characteristics of the nature of young children's planning.

Although the classroom is not a context in which extensive planning, at least on the part of the children, naturally occurs, the focus of this study was on the process of children's planning in an ongoing social situation. As such, this research was concerned with the social and environmental factors of the class environment that may influence children's activity goals in that setting and thereby affect children's plan development and execution in that context. The influence of peer relations and children's individual activity interests on plan development and execution was the focus of the investigation. Exogenous factors, like social relations and activity interests, may influence how an individual organizes his or her behavior in a social situation. In this way exogenous factors may function as superordinate goal structures that guide the development and execution of a plan.

Among the many components of the planning process, the goal is central in guiding the development and implementation of a plan. As critical as the goal is, however, it is difficult to study within usual experimental paradigms since a characteristic of most experimental designs is the imposition by the experimenter of task constraints—in particular, a task goal—on the participants (Newman, Griffin, & Cole, 1984). But in most everyday settings, the planner is not only developing, orchestrating, and executing means to a goal, he or she is often defining the goal as well. Thus, the present method of investigation was devised as an attempt to understand the goals that may be guiding young children as they organize and plan activities within a social context.

The Class Setting

I became involved with this class at the beginning of the school year when the teacher agreed to allow her students to participate in a study of young children's planning skills. In order to become familiar with the children prior to conducting the study, I acted as participant-observer in the class one morning a week, an involvement which continued throughout the school year. In the course of being in the classroom, I became interested in the children's skill at organizing their activities during a daily open activity period. The middle hour of each class session was designated as Free Choice. During this time the teacher met with small groups of children in work groups. When not in work groups, the children were free to participate in any of 11 classroom activities: art, blocks, chalkboard, climber, construction toys, housekeeping, library, listening, puppets, sandbox, and table games.

In order to facilitate classroom organization while the teacher was occupied with small work groups, a freestanding pegboard positioned in the middle of the room was used. Each child was provided with a personalized name tag for hanging on the Free Choice pegboard and was expected to identify the activity in which he or she was engaged. The children identified only one activity at a time, immediately preceeding engagement in that activity, and moved their personal label between activities. Although this procedure did not require extensive planning on the children's part, it seemed that it might be providing the children with some opportunity to practice planning, or at least to consider some of the practical aspects of planning and organizing individual activities within a social context.

By allotting a limited number of pegs at each activity, the teacher hoped to control the number of children who congregated in each area. Behavioral expectations for the children during the Free Choice period, as well as the rules for the use of the Free Choice pegboard, appeared to be understood by the children and no child was observed having difficulty using the Free Choice board. The teacher intervened in the children's behavior during the Free Choice period only in cases when her assistance was solicited or if children became raucous, both of which occurred infrequently. Thus, Free Choice activity period was predominantly a child-constructed event within teacher-established conventions or guidelines.

Observational Procedure and Planning Intervention

A short-term longitudinal study involving systematic observations of children's activity patterns during the Free Choice period and the effect of planning Free Choice activities in advance of the period on their activity patterns was conducted. The investigation combined naturalistic observation with a classroom intervention in an attempt to trace the influence of individual interests and social relations on children's activity plans and plan executions during this period. The planning intervention was designed to present the children with a situation that interfered with their normal behavioral patterns. The children's responses to this interference were used as indices of the children's cognitive and social concerns as they organized their activities during the free activity period. It was hoped that this approach would permit examination of the goals that guided the children's Free Choice behavior and help determine how these goals interacted with children's planning in this context.

Twenty-two children ($\bar{X}$ age = 5:8 years, sd = 3 months), nine of whom were girls and 13 of whom were boys, were observed. Observations were conducted one day a week over a 10-week period, resulting in 10 observational sessions overall. The observation schedule included two sessions prior to the intervention as a baseline assessment of the children's behavior during the Free Choice period, followed by seven sessions during which the children were asked to plan their Free Choice activities in advance, and concluded with one observational session following cessation of the planning intervention.

A "scan sampling" technique (Altmann, 1974) was used to assess children's selection of activities on the Free Choice pegboard, as well as the children's actual activities. Activity selection and engagement were recorded at five-minute intervals throughout each of the 10 observed Free Choice periods using a pencil and paper recording procedure. The author, acting as observer, sat adjacent to the Free Choice pegboard to have access to conversations and behaviors as the children selected activities. The observer also noted behaviors that occurred at the pegboard during Free Choice activity selection, such as discussions or disagreements. By the time the observations were conducted, the children were accustomed to my presence in the classroom, and an explanation that I was doing some work while they engaged in Free Choice was uniformly accepted.

A five-minute interval was chosen as the observational unit on the basis of experience in the class during the fall and winter when the children were observed to spend an average of 11.5 minutes (sd = 8.3 minutes) at each activity and, for practical reasons, following piloting intervals of closer measure. To assess observer agreement, 20 percent of the observations were also coded by a second observer. Observer agreement for Free Choice selection was Cohen's kappa .90, and for Free Choice activity engagement was Cohen's kappa .88.

During the seven advance planning sessions, the children were asked to complete a form itemizing an activity plan for the Free Choice period for that day. (See Figure 5.1 for an example of the planning form.) The form was developed by the observer in collaboration with the teacher. It was modeled after ideas presented in an in-service workshop attended by the classroom teacher which advocated such a procedure as a method for teaching young children about planning. Each child was asked at the beginning of each of the seven advance planning sessions to circle on the planning form the activities he or she wanted to do during Free Choice that day. The children were then asked to enumerate the order in which he or she planned to do these activities.

At the conclusion of the 10-week observational period, the children were interviewed about their favorite Free Choice activities and their favorite classmates, their reactions to planning Free Choice activities in advance, and their understanding of the planning process in general. Free Choice activities were ranked according to the frequencies with which they were identified by the children as their favorite. Information about the children's favorite activities was used to analyze whether activity preference influenced planning and organizing Free Choice activities. Peer nominations of favorite classmates were used to determine each child's social ranking or popularity in the class. Each child received a score based on the number of times he or she was nominated as one of three best friends identified by classmates during the interview. This information was used to examine whether social relations played a role in the activity patterns children displayed during the Free Choice period.

Free Choice Activity Pattern Prior to Planning Activities in Advance

The initial two observational sessions were used to establish a baseline for comparing the children's Free Choice behavior prior to and during the planning intervention. The proportion of Free Choice time children spent in activities of their own choosing during these first two sessions suggested that it was reasonable to assume that the children were provided with a substantial amount of classroom time that they could organize on their own. During these sessions most of the children's time was spent in activities of their own choosing (53 percent), rather than working in small groups (32 percent), eating snack (8 percent), or out of the room (6 percent).

Observations also indicated that the children did change activity involvement during the Free Choice period. Over the course of these two sessions, children were observed participating, on the average, in three different activities during the Free Choice period ($\bar{X} = 3.2, sd = .4$), with no difference between boys and

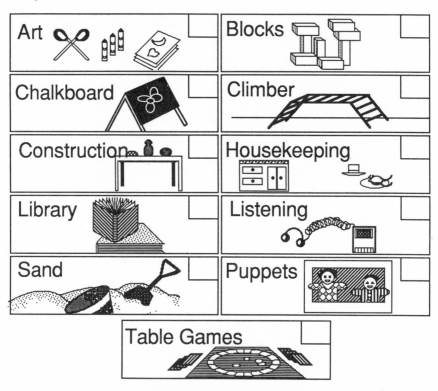

My Name is _____

My have-to is: Group Work

My want-to's are:

Art

Blocks

Chalkboard

Climber

Construction

Housekeeping

Library

Listening

Sand

Puppets

Table Games

Figure 5.1.   Example of the planning form completed by the children at the beginning of the seven class sessions involving advance planning of Free Choice activities.

girls. Since children ordinarily participated in several activities over the course of the Free Choice period, asking the children to schedule several activities in advance was consistent with their usual Free Choice pattern.

Of particular interest during the first two sessions was whether the children actually identified on the pegboard the activities in which they intended to engage prior to action. To determine this, the rate of congruence between the activity identified on the Free Choice pegboard and the activity in which each child was engaged for each of the five-minute observation intervals was calculated.

Results suggest that the children were competent at identifying an action immediately prior to engaging in it. For sixty-five percent (sd = 20 percent) of the observation intervals, the activity the child designated on the Free Choice pegboard corresponded with the activity in which the child was engaged, with no difference for males and females (females, 67 percent, sd = 19 percent; males, 64 percent, sd = 21 percent). Skill at identifying and then engaging in a certain activity may provide opportunity for developing planning skills in that it may constitute a rudimentary form of planning or be a prerequisite to planning longer sequences of actions. The relationship between identifying activities using the Free Choice pegboard and skill at planning and then executing a sequence of activities during the Free Choice period is examined in the next section where children's plans and action patterns during the seven advance planning sessions are discussed.

Free Choice Activity Patterns During Advance Planning

Plans for what the children intended to do during Free Choice were made during the third to ninth observational sessions. Like adult planners (Hayes-Roth, 1980), children tended to overplan their activities. Although they engaged in an average of three activities per session, they planned to do about six ($\bar{X} = 5.8$, sd = 1.7) different activities per session, $t(21) = 4.5, p < .01$. Interestingly, the number of activities planned did decrease over the course of the advance planning sessions (mean number of activities planned for the final advance planning session was 4.6; with a consistently decreasing pattern across the seven advance planning sessions, Repeated Measures ANOVA, $F(3,60) = 3.10, p = .03$). Although the children's estimates of the number of activities in which they intended to engage remained inflated, over the course of the seven advance planning sessions it appeared that children were becoming more realistic in their planning. Perhaps practice devising and executing activity plans made children aware of some of the practical parameters of planning actions in advance.

At least initially, planning activities in advance did appear to affect the children's activity pattern during the Free Choice period. For the initial session in which activities were planned in advance, children engaged in significantly more activities than in the previous two sessions when they did not plan in advance, $t(19) = 3.8, p < .01$. The average number of activities in which the children participated during the first two baseline observational sessions was 2.7 (sd = .9). But during the initial planning session the average number of activities was 3.9 (sd = 1.1). The effect of planning activities in advance on increasing the number of activities in which children engaged was short-lived, however. By the second advance planning session, and for the five remaining planning sessions, the number of activities in which children engaged dropped to the range observed in the two observational sessions before planning was introduced to the class.

At first encounter, planning activities in advance may have reminded the children of the breadth of activities available in the classroom. By providing the children with a "shopping list" of these activates prior to Free Choice, the children may have been encouraged to plan and engage in more and different activities than usual. In support of this, children participated in several activities at the first planning session that children did not participate in during either of the previous two observational sessions. For the girls, art and blocks appeared for the first time in the initial planning session, and for the boys, construction, listening, and housekeeping made their first appearance at this session. This pattern highlights the activity-based nature of the plans developed in this situation. Perhaps children viewed planning activities in advance as a reservation of sorts, thereby making activities in which they rarely engaged, yet enjoyed, available to them.

The notion of the plans as providing the children with advance reservations at class activities seemed to be adopted by the children, at least according to the types of discussions and disagreements which occurred at the Free Choice pegboard during the planning sessions. Over the course of these sessions, children were frequently observed at the Free Choice pegboard asserting that an activity that was planned in advance guaranteed the planner the right to participate in that activity. These assertions were particularly evident when an activity was identified as fully occupied according to the identification labels hung beneath the activity on the pegboard. In a few cases, children used this tactic to defend the right for large groups of children to be congregated at certain activities. These behaviors hint at an interesting relationship between plans and social activities, or any activity for that matter—the use of a plan as an authoritative structure for regulating an event.

But it may also be the case that planning activities in advance facilitated engaging in a greater number of activities in that by carrying out their plans the children did not require as much time during the Free Choice period as they usually did to determine subsequent activities. This suggestion relies on the assumption that the children were executing their plans fairly successfully. We can examine this possibility further by assessing the rate of congruence between the children's plans and their actual activities.

The Relation Between Plans and Plan Execution

To assess congruence between the children's plans and their actual activities during Free Choice, children's plans for the first three activities were compared with their actual activity sequence during the Free Choice period. For each child the rate of congruence was the ratio of the number of times an activity was executed in the planned sequence for the first three activities planned. Analysis was restricted to plans for the initial three activities since the children engaged in about three activities per session. Incidentally, there were no instances of congruence between plans and activities sequenced beyond the first three activities of the day. When children did not adhere to their plans they were engaged in one of the other 10 activities in the class, or they wandered around the classroom, or stood at the Free Choice pegboard. Participation in small work groups and time spent out of the classroom were controlled in the analysis.

Fifty-six percent (77) of children's plans over the seven advance planning sessions identified a behavioral sequence that was, at least in part, congruent with the child's actual behaviors during the Free Choice period. Of these 77 instances, 52 of them were congruent for the first activity planned only, 21 were congruent for the first two activities planned, and just four were congruent for the first three activities planned.

This pattern indicates that the children were most competent at planning and executing their plans for the initial activity of the day. This process is similar to what the children had been doing in the classroom all along while using the Free Choice pegboard. Comparison of the children's rank orderings, based on their congruence scores for these two activities, supports this assertion. Children who displayed greater congruence between identifying activities on the pegboard and then engaging in them also displayed greater congruence between activities planned in advance and the execution of these plans, Spearman's rho = .99, $p < .01$. It may be that experience selecting Free Choice activities using the pegboard gave children practice thinking about activities in advance of action, a consideration central to planning.

Although children were capable of planning a sequence of activities in advance, it appeared that some children were more skilled than others at identifying activities prior to action. It is unclear why individual differences occurred, however, in that all the children were familiar with the activities in the class and displayed some skill at identifying actions immediately prior to engagement by using the Free Choice pegboard. To investigate individual differences further two exogeneous factors, children's activity interests and social relationships in the classroom, were considered as mediating influences on children's planning and plan execution during Free Choice.

Influence of Activity Interests and Social Relationships on Planning

There was more congruence between plans and activities when the activities planned were popular, that is, identified as favorite activities by the majority of children. When children planned to participate in one of the three class activities identified as most favored by the children (climber, sand, library), there was a 42 percent congruence rate between plans and actual activities. Whereas when children planned to engage in one of the three least favored activities (chalkboard, construction, puppets), there were no instances of congruence between plans and actual activities. Congruence between plans and actual activities may indicate that children were executing their plans successfully. But it may be that congruence reflects a coincidence between planning a favorite activity in which the child was then likely to engage, independent of whether it was planned.

The rate of congruence between plans developed by boys and their actual activities was greater than the rate of congruence between plans and activities for girls, $F(1,20) = 6.37, p = .02$. Closer examination of this difference suggests that activity interests may play an important role in determining whether children's plans were congruent with their actual activities. In general, congruence between plans and actual activities was related to the frequency of including the child's favorite activity in the plan, $r(22) = .39, p = .03$. And boys, more so than girls, were likely to engage in their favorite activity during the Free Choice period, $t(20) = 3.11, p < .01$. In this situation, advance planning favored an activity-based plan of action. In other words, children who engaged in activities for reasons other than solely activity preference may have had greater difficulty planning Free Choice activities in advance. Girls, whose activity interests may be more socially driven than boys (Hartup, 1983), may have had greater difficulty than boys in planning Free Choice activities in advance. Therefore, what appears as a sex difference in planning skill per se may actually be a difference in a tendency to engage in an activity pattern governed more by activity than social interests. This suggests that congruence between plans and execution is affected by consistency between the goals that organize and guide behavior and the goals proscribed in the plan.

Further evidence of the role of exogenous factors in mediating children's planning and plan execution appears when the relation of plans, plan execution, and social relations in the class are examined. Greater congruence between plans and plan execution was related to social relations in the class, based on children's peer nominations collected in a postobservational interview. Each child was assigned a social ranking based on the frequency with which the child was identified as one of three best friends by the other 21 children in the class. An independent assessment by the teacher of the children's social rank provided support that the children's nominations were an accurate reflection of the class social relations. Teacher ratings of each child's friendship status, based on a five-point scale (lots of friends, many friends, some friends, few friends, and no friends) were significantly related to the social rankings based on the children's peer nominations, $r(20) = .64, p < .01$.

On the basis of these calculations, the children were divided into two groups. Eight children (four girls and four boys) were nominated an average of 5.5 times (range 3 - 12, sd = 2.9) as one of their classmates' three best friends. For the present analysis, these children were considered the more popular children in the class. Fourteen children (five girls and nine boys) were nominated an average of .7 times (range 0 - 2, sd = .7), and were considered the less popular children in the class. This grouping seemed to be the most rational way of clustering the children on social rank. The two groups clustered at either the high or low end of the rank ordering, with the difference between the two groups being the largest gap in the rankings.

The mean rate of congruence between plans and actual activities across the seven planning sessions for the less popular group was 25 percent. Only one-quarter of the time did these children engage in activities in the sequence in which they planned to do them. This rate changed little across the seven advance planning sessions. The pattern of congruence between plans and activities across the seven advance planning sessions for the more popular children was, at least initially, quite different. For the group designated as more popular, the average rate of congruence between plans and execution during the initial advance planning session was 42 percent. This was significantly greater than that of the less popular children who had a congruence rate of 19 percent during the initial session, $t(20) = 2.09, p < .05,$. However, the rate of congruence for the more popular children declined significantly from the initial to the second advance planning session, from 42% to 10%, $t(6) = 17.0, p < .001$. For the five subsequent advance planning sessions the mean rate of congruence for this group stabilized at an average rate of 23% (sd = 3%), which was roughly equivalent to that of the less popular children.

Analysis of the rates of congruence between plans and plan execution across the first two planning sessions indicates that, by the second session, there was an appreciable decrease in the rates for some of the children, those who were more popular among their classmates. More popular children, who initially showed a high rate of congruence between plans and plan execution, showed little congruence during the second advance planning session. The more popular children may have been socially oriented, and thus were constrained by having to decide activities in advance of the Free Choice period. Planning in advance may have also established too rigid a plan of action for the less popular children, but these children may have been less willing or confident in their ability to join other children who were converged at an activity site. Although the explanation for these patterns is far from clear, the observations suggest that the children's activities during Free Choice, and their ability to plan their activities in advance, may not be independent of social relations in the class.

In sum, these data provide some evidence that children as young as 5 years of age can plan activities in advance of action and can follow through on these plans to some degree. Most of the children were able to identify a single activity prior to action with some success. However, there was little evidence of the children planning a sequence of activities in advance and then executing the plan successfully. The instances when this did occur may be as easily explained by some coincidental factors, such as planning routine or favorite activities, as evidence of planning per se. Examination of the children's planning appeared to be related to peer relations in the class, suggesting that social relationships may influence children's experience with planning in social contexts.

In order to understand children's planning in this context, further examination of what planning Free Choice activities in advance afforded children in this situation and what factors may have impeded successful plan execution is needed. It may be that children were dissatisfied with the plans because they were too rigid and did not support the children's goals for the activity period. Therefore, the low rate of congruence between plans and plan execution may reflect, at least in part, willful plan violation and not simply lack of competency.

Children's Efforts to Revise the Planning Process

Observations suggest that the children were dissatisfied with planning Free Choice activities in advance, presumably because the plans specified courses of action that interfered with achieving the children's goals. Even during the initial advance planning session, children were observed revising their plans and the planning process. During the initial planning session, two children requested permission of the observer to revise his or her plan during plan execution. Other revisions began to appear during the third advance planning session, and revision attempts appeared consistently throughout the remaining advance planning sessions.

Children revised the planning process in a number of ways. They altered their plans during the Free Choice period. They refused to enumerate the activities as they planned. They sometimes refused to develop advance plans entirely. In several instances they developed plans in collaboration with friends. And in one case a child revised her plan at the conclusion of the period in order to coordinate it with her actual activities. There were 36 observed instances of children revising the planning process prior to or during plan execution. Eighteen of the class of 22 children were observed participating in one or more of these revisions (see Table 5.1). These efforts indicate that the children were monitoring their plans during plan execution. Thus, for these children, the written plans did have some linkage to reality, although this link may have been tenuous or easily broken.

Devising and executing advance plans posed difficulty for the children in organizing their Free Choice time. This could be a consequence of the bias inherent in the plans which favored those who organized their Free Choice time on the basis of preferred activities only. Since the majority of children evidenced some difficulty executing activity-based plans, it must be that these children were

Table 5.1. Number of Children Displaying the Various Types of Revisions of the Planning Process Across the Seven Advance Planning Sessions

Planning Session	3	4	5	6	7	8	9
Changes own plan	0	0	0	0	2	12	1
Dyads collaborate on plan	0	0	0	0	2	0	1
Montiors other's plan execution	1	0	0	1	0	0	0
Refuses to develop plan	0	0	2	1	1	1	0
Refuses to enumerate acts	0	0	0	1	0	0	0
Requests permission of observer to change plan	2	4	2	0	1	0	0
Revises plan at end of period	0	0	0	0	1	0	0

guided by other considerations while organizing their activities. Other important considerations, like social participation or spontaneous games at an activity site, are not easy to plan in advance since they arise during the Free Choice period. Such considerations may have made planning Free Choice activities in advance a difficult task indeed. And this difficulty may have been exacerbated by social relations in the class.

Plan revisions and children's social relations in the class. Comparison of child-regulated versus adult-regulated revisions suggests a relationship between the social relations of children in the class and the manner in which children revised their plans. Children who were less popular among classmates appeared to treat their advance plans differently than more popular children in that they were more reticent to revise their plans on their own. When plans were revised during plan execution, less popular children were more likely to ask permission of the observer to change their plans. For all nine instances in which children asked permission to change their plans, it was children who were less popular among classmates who were involved, $t(20) = 1.66, p < .10$. More popular children tended to regulate their own revisions.

There was some additional evidence that less popular children treated plan violation differently from more popular children. On two occasions one child was observed chastising another child for violating his or her plans. In both cases a less popular child criticized a more popular child for violating the plans without receiving permission from the observer. It seemed that these two children were treating plan violation as a form of social transgression, implying that plans carry a behavioral commitment which is important to maintain.

It may be that less popular children viewed plans as less under their control due to their having or perceiving they have fewer activity opportunities. The classroom social environment may have afforded more popular children greater opportunity for activity engagement as a consequence of social resources and support, and thereby affected the manner in which they executed their plans. Thus, movement across activities for more popular children may have presented more real possibilities that it did for the less popular children. In other words, greater social mobility in the class, which may be a consequence of being favored by classmates, afforded more activity opportunities for the popular children which affected how these children executed and revised plans during Free Choice.

These differing approaches for dealing with unsatisfactory plans diminished by the fifth advance planning session when children began to revise their plans openly during the Free Choice period. At the beginning of the fifth advance planning session, a child asked, during large group activity, if the plans could be hung on the chalkboard adjacent to the Free Choice pegboard for better visibility. Upon suggesting this, the children voiced unanimous agreement and the plans were displayed accordingly. This made the plans, as well as the capability of watching other children as they altered their plans, more accessible to the entire class. At the beginning of the Free Choice period during this session, four of the children made public statements at the Free Choice pegboard that they intended to change their plans if needed during the Free Choice period. During this period, children were observed watching others as they revised their plans, and in one case two children were observed revising their plans collaboratively nearby to where the plans were posted. By the sixth advance planning session more than one-half of the children (12, or 54 percent) revised their plans during the course of the Free Choice period, with both more and less popular children participating.

By engaging in behaviors that actively violated the planning process, yet may have afforded greater access to goal attainment, the children provided evidence that they were monitoring their plans during execution. In the next section, these strategies are discussed in conjunction with factors that may have influenced how children planned and executed their plans during the Free Choice period.

FACTORS INFLUENCING PLANNING AND PLAN EXECUTION OF FREE CHOICE ACTIVITIES

Why is it that the children were unable or not very successful at planning and executing actions much beyond the first activity of the day even though, with each session, children experienced more practice planning and executing their plans? What do the planning behaviors children exhibited reveal about young children's activity goals in a social setting? And, finally, what were the children plans about planning as a consequence of planning Free Choice activities in advance? To address these questions, this section focuses on children's knowledge of the planning process, the demands of the planning task itself, and children's satisfaction with planning Free Choice activities in advance.

Children's Knowledge of the Planning Process

Interviews with the children following the 10-week observational period revealed that most of the children had a rough idea of what a plan is. When asked to describe what a plan is, 70 percent of the children indicated that a plan identifies something a person wants to do or places a person wants to go. Some children even acknowledged the importance of planning, as evident in one child's comment that "if plans weren't invented, you couldn't even invite a friend over." But few of the children understood a plan as embodying a sequence of activities. Only two children described a plan as including steps to accomplish a task. Both of these children offered examples of an activity requiring planning a sequence of steps, with one describing how to get ready to go to a swimming pool and the other describing the steps he would take to rob a bank. The remaining 30 percent of the children said they did not know what a plan is.

Given this vague understanding of planning, it is not surprising that several of the children appeared to confuse the process of planning, per se, with the actual planning exercise employed in the class. This was apparent in the children's responses to whether they considered planning Free Choice activities an easy or a difficult task. Sixty-five percent of the children said they felt planning was easy, with about three-quarters of these children stating that it was easy to circle and enumerate activities on the planning sheets. The remaining children felt planning was easy because they knew what they wanted to do before they came to class. For the 35 percent of the children who viewed planning as difficult, most (86 percent) stated that it was hard to decide what to do before Free Choice time. The few remaining children who felt planning was difficult said this was due to their hand getting tired from circling and numbering activities on the planning sheet.

Regardless of whether children felt planning was easy or difficult, almost half (45 percent) responded by evaluating the superficial aspects of the planning exercise completed in the class, that of circling and enumerating activities on a sheet of paper. This suggests that for many of the children the process of planning as a general cognitive activity was not separate from the physical exercise of planning as it appeared in this setting, indicating a rudimentary understanding, at best, of what planning is.

Despite confusion about what planning is, 65 percent of the children did indicate that they thought about what they wanted to do during Free Choice prior to coming to school. About three-quarters of these children mentioned they thought about particular activities they wanted to do and the remainder (all of whom were girls) indicated they thought about who they wanted to play with during Free Choice. Although the children possessed a somewhat limited understanding of the planning process, children's emerging planning skills may be evident in their interest in predetermining actions for the Free Choice period prior to coming to school. The vague quality of these behavioral intentions may be due to the primitive nature of the children's planning skills. But they may also reflect difficulties in planning Free Choice activities in advance, difficulties which are inherent to the task itself.

Task Demands

Planning may be affected by features of a task or the context of performance. Two task demands, memory and the nature of the Free Choice activity period, may have affected how children planned and executed their plans during the seven advance planning sessions.

In order to execute a plan successfully, the planner needs to remember the plan. Since plan execution relies heavily on memory, understanding how children's developing memorial competencies integrate with their developing planning skills is central for understanding the development of planning skills. The children observed in this study may not have been very skilled at executing plans developed prior to Free Choice due to an inability to remember the plans they devised. After the children made their plans, they stored them in individually labeled bins located in one corner of the room. Five children were observed going to these bins during the initial planning session to check on their plans, with three of these children deciding to carry their plans with them throughout the entire Free Choice period. As the planning sessions proceeded, most of the children, at one time or another, were observed checking their plans. Over the seven advance planning sessions, six children were observed carrying their plans with them during the Free Choice period. By the fifth advance planning session, children seemed weary of checking their plans in the storage bins, and when one child requested that plans be displayed in a more accessible location, the class expressed unanimous support.

These behaviors suggest that children as young as 5 years of age are aware that an important aspect of plan execution is remembering plan details. The children appeared sensitive to the importance of monitoring plans during execution, as well as aware that plans are often difficult to remember without some reminders. Not all of the children displayed active efforts to remember their plans, however. Individual differences in memory may play an important role in children's ability to execute planned actions. Further investigation of the role of memory in children's plan execution seems important for determining how these cognitive processes operate together as children attempt to implement their plans.

The nature of the Free Choice period may also account for children's limited success at planning and executing Free Choice activities. Wellman, Fabricius, and Sophian (1985) found children of the same age capable of sequencing searches and retrieving a small number of hidden items. However, sequencing and performing activities in a social context may impose great difficulty and perhaps, as may have been the case during the Free Choice period, little benefit for children in attaining their own activity goals. Mature planners are probably aware of potential problems and limitations in planning activities to be performed in social contexts. In developing planning skills, children need to learn that individual planning may not be the best way to negotiate joint action. Processes available in social interaction, such as conflict and collaboration, may support the development of this planning knowledge (Rogoff, Gauvain, & Gardner, 1987).

Children's Satisfaction with Planning Free Choice Activities in Advance

Children appeared to understand some of the benefits and limitations of planning Free Choice activities in advance, as reported in the postobservational interviews. When the children were interviewed about whether they liked to plan Free Choice activities in advance, the majority (70 percent) indicated that they found it useful. Half of these children mentioned reasons that suggested they viewed the plans as helpful for structuring their activities; for example, one child, who was observed by both coders to be rather shy, commented that it helped her start the day so she "wouldn't just have to walk around." And another child, also somewhat of a loner, commented that the plans were good because "you get to play on whatever you want," apparently viewing the plan as a type of advance reservation. Four of the children remarked that planning helped them remember what they wanted to do that day, implying that they come to class with some idea of what they would like to do during Free Choice. The remainder of children who said they liked to plan Free Choice activities in advance said that they thought it was fun.

All but one of the less popular children viewed planning in advance as useful. It may be that the children nominated less often by classmates as best friends are less social, with their Free Choice behavior mainly guided by activity preference. Therefore, these children may have liked planning Free Choice in advance in that it organized their Free Choice time in accordance with their activity goals. Some of the children's comments, such as those quoted above, suggest that the less popular children may have perceived the plans as providing them with access to activities from which they ordinarily felt excluded.

For some of the children (30 percent), advance planning was burdensome, either due to task difficulty, as expressed in one girl's statement that she "had some trouble deciding what to do," or due to problems with the rigidity of advance plans, as exemplified by one boy's remarks, "I don't like it cause I want to go on everything and you can only go on things you circle. If you make a mistake in your plans, you still have to go on it." A similar view was expressed by several children. Along this line one girl raised an interesting concern, stating that she didn't know if she liked to plan in advance because on "the first day, I thought, I don't like to do this because we aren't getting enough free choice." Dissatisfaction with planning Free Choice activities in advance was expressed predominantly by the more popular children, perhaps indicating their preference to remain more opportunistic in terms of Free Choice behavior. What is important to note is that satisfaction with planning did not stand in isolation of social relations in the class.

SUMMARY AND CONCLUSIONS

The kindergarten children observed in this research displayed competence at constructing written plans, monitoring their plans during execution, and following through on their plans—at least when they wanted. The weak relationship between the children's plans and plan executions may have been due, in large part, to the difficulty of planning Free Choice activities in advance, and not merely to an inability to remember and/or execute a plan.

Having children construct activity-based plans may have interfered with acting on social concerns during plan execution. It may be that in social situations, social concerns often override activity concerns as children organize and engage in activities. This consideration makes planning activities to be performed in a social context a difficult task. It is surprising, therefore, that the children did not try to discover other children's plans or collaborate with other children during planning more frequently. This may hint at a limitation young children have as they plan. Although young children may be capable of modifying their plans when a social opportunity arises, they may not be able to anticipate the importance or likelihood of social opportunities in advance.

The children's efforts to revise the planning process or the plans themselves underscores the difficulty in planning individual actions to be performed in social contexts. Cognitive performances in social settings are not just caused by knowledge structures in the actors' heads. They are also supported by social processes within the environment. For many of the children in this class, the social realities of the Free Choice period influenced their planning. Our desire to interact socially (or to avoid social interaction) interferes with our individual plans since we never or very rarely have complete knowledge about others' plans. Coordinating one's own actions with those of others may not, in most instances, be very easy to plan in advance since the best strategy may be to have a flexible schedule which is easy to adjust to the behavior of others. However, a flexible schedule in and of itself may not necessarily yield access to opportunities as they arise in an ongoing social situation. The ability to take advantage of opportunities may depend upon social relations within the group.

Both more and less popular children were dissatisfied with their advance plans, as indicated by their efforts to revise them during the Free Choice period. Less popular children were more likely to request assistance from the observer in revising their plans during plan execution. These may have been attempts by these children to override social relations within the class which they may have perceived as restricting their access to activities during the Free Choice period. Children's reports of their satisfaction with planning Free Choice activities in advance supports this interpretation. Less popular children reported more satisfaction than the more popular children with planning activities in advance, stating that planning helped them organize their time and allowed them to engage in a wider range of activities in the class. In contrast, more popular children reported less satisfaction with planning Free Choice activities in advance, perhaps reflecting, at least in part, the social limitations imposed by planning individual activities in advance of social engagement. This suggests that cognitive opportunities in the classroom during child-orchestrated activity periods are interrelated with children's social relationships in that setting.

It is important to note that observations of plan formulation and plan execution were vital for understanding children's planning skills in this context. To understand the development of planning skills we need to look beyond plan formulation on problem-solving tasks and see how plans are developed and executed in individual and social contexts. In plan execution the goals that organize individual's actions may be revealed as the planner takes advantage of opportunities available in the setting for attaining these goals. For the children observed in this study it seemed that the plan became "real" when they tried to execute it. And it was executing their plans that the children appeared to be learning about planning.

One purpose in conducting these observations was to investigate children's goals in planning and executing activities in ongoing social situations. Although in many instances we may be only tacitly aware of the process (Langer, 1978), defining goals and organizing means to achieve these goals are central to planning, and as such are requisite features of children's emerging planning skills. Observations suggest that studying children's goals is important for understanding children's planning skills. In addition, consideration of exogenous factors that may influence the development of competence at establishing and achieving goals is important for understanding the development of planning.

Methods such as the one employed here may be useful in developing a better understanding of the types of goals young children have as they formulate plans, as well as the role of the environment in facilitating or impeding plan execution. Charlesworth (1983) proposes a similar method for studying cognitive behavior in natural contexts. He suggests that researchers pose blocks or hindrances to ongoing behavior that may elicit responses that an observer has reason to believe is motivated by some form of cognitive process. The range of responses employed to remove the blocks may reveal individual modes of intelligently responding to restricted circumstances. Although a researcher loses experimental control in this type of investigation, and hence cannot answer some questions, other questions can be asked.

The observations presented here were inductive in nature and pertained to a single group of children. Nonetheless, they permitted a glimpse of some of the cognitive and social processes involved when young children attempted to coordinate individual activities in a social context. Careful observation of children in ongoing social situations may yield important insight into the integration of cognitive and social opportunities as children develop, and may reveal previously neglected but important aspects of human behavior and development (Blurton Jones, 1967). It is surprising that only about eight percent of all psychological research is based on any kind of observation (Bakeman & Gottman, 1986). If empirical assessments of psychological phenomena remain unaccompanied by careful and systematic observations of behavior as it is structured and unfolds in social contexts, our understanding of the complexity of human functioning, and particularly of development, will be incomplete. These observations may prove particularly fruitful for those studying the development of metacognitive skills since the coordination of social and cognitive means and goals may rely heavily on skills at monitoring, regulating, and revising action plans.

In the course of arranging and negotiating joint action, children may be learning about the process of planning and executing actions in social contexts. But what children learn from performing cognitive activities in social contexts may be mediated by other factors, such as social and activity preferences, operating in the setting. When researchers examine children's learning and cognitive competence in social contexts it is important to remember that children in ongoing social environments bring to the situation unique interpersonal experiences and relationships. These experiences and relationships may, in turn, affect the intellectual performances children display and the cognitive opportunities they have or perceive they have in that setting. It seems that the social organization of children's environments during the early school years may have important cognitive as well as social implications.

REFERENCES

Altmann, J. (1974). Observational study of behavior: Sampling methods. *Behavior, 49,* 227–265.

Bakeman, R., & Gottman, J.M. (1986). *Observing interaction: An introduction to sequential analysis.* Cambridge: Cambridge University Press.

Blurton Jones, N.G. (1967). An ethological study of some aspects of social behaviour in children in nursery school. In D. Morris (Ed.), *Primate ethology* (pp. 347–368). Chicago: Aldine.

Brown, A.L., Bransford, J.D., Ferrara, R.A., & Campione, J.C. (1983). Learning, remembering, and understanding. In J.H. Flavell & E.M. Markman (Eds.), *Carmichael's manual of child psychology* (Vol. 3, pp. 77–166). New York: Wiley.

Brown, A.L., & DeLoache, J.S. (1978). Skills, plans, and self-regulation. In R.S. Siegler (Ed.), *Children's thinking: What develops?* (pp 3–35). Hillsdale, NJ: Lawrence Erlbaum.

Charlesworth, W.R. (1983). An ethological approach to cognitive development. In C.J. Brainerd (Ed.), *Recent advances in cognitive-developmental research* (pp. 237–258). New York: Springer-Verlag.

Flavell, J.H., & Wellman, H.M. Metamemory. (1977). In R.V. Kail & J. Hagen (Eds.), *Perspectives on the development of memory and cognition* (pp. 3–33). Hillsdale, NJ: Lawrence Erlbaum.

Forbes, D., & Greenberg, M. (1982). *Children's planning strategies: New directions for child development* (Vol. 18). San Francisco: Jossey-Bass.

Forbes, D., & Lubin, D. (1979, August). *Reasoning and behavior in children's friendly interactions.* Paper presented at the meetings of the American Psychological Association, New York.

Gardner, W., & Rogoff, B. (1985, August). *The development of flexibility in children's improvisational and advance planning.* Paper presented at the meetings of the American Psychological Association, Anaheim, CA.

Gauvain, M., & Rogoff, B. (1985, April). *The development of planning skills in individuals and dyads.* Paper presented at the biennial meetings of the Society for Research in Child Development, Toronto, Canada.

Gauvain, M., & Rogoff, B. (1989). Collaborative problem solving and children's planning skills. *Developmental Psychology, 25.*

Gearhart, M. (1979). *Social planning: Role play in a novel situation.* Paper presented at the biennial meetings of the Society of Research for Child Development, San Francisco, CA.

Gearhart, M., & Newman, D. (1980). Learning to draw a picture: The social context of an individual activity. *Discourse Processes, 3,* 169–184.

Glick, J. (1983). *Planning and environmental constraints.* Unpublished manuscript, City University of New York, Graduate Center, New York.

Goldman, B.D., & Ross, H.S. (1978). Social skills in action: An analysis of early peer games. In J. Glick & A.K. Clarke-Stewart (Eds.), *The development of social understanding* (pp. 177–212). New York: Gardner.

Hartup, W.W. (1984). Peer relations. In E.M. Hetherington (Ed.), *Carmichael's manual of child psychology* (Vol. 4, pp. 104–196). New York: Wiley.

Hayes-Roth, B. (1980). *Estimation of time requirements during planning: Interactions between motivation and cognition.* (Rand Note: N-1581-ONR). Santa Monica, CA: Rand Corporation.

Hayes-Roth, B., & Hayes-Roth, F. (1979). A cognitive model of planning. *Cognitive Science, 3,* 275–310.

Klahr, D. (1978). Goal formation, planning, and learning by pre-school problem solvers or: "My socks are in the dryer." In R.S. Siegler (Ed.), *Children's thinking: What develops?* (pp. 181–212). Hillsdale, NJ: Lawrence Erlbaum.

Langer, E. (1978). Rethinking the role of thought in social interactions. In J. Harvey, W. Ickes, & R. Kidd (Eds.), *New directions in attribution research* (Vol. 2, pp. 35–58). Hillsdale, NJ: Lawrence Erlbaum.

Lomov, B.F. (1978). Psychological processes and communication. *Soviet Psychology, 17,* 3–22.

Newman, D., Griffin, P., & Cole, M. (1984). Social constraints in laboratory and classroom tasks. In B. Rogoff & J. Lave (Eds.), *Everyday cognition: Its development in social context* (pp. 172–193). Cambridge: Harvard University Press.

Pea, R.D. (1982). What is planning development the development of? In D.L. Forbes & M.T. Greenberg (Eds.), *Children's planning strategies. New Directions for Child Development* (Vol. 18, pp. 5–27). San Francisco: Jossey-Bass.

Rogoff, B., Gauvain, M., & Gardner, W. (1987). The development of children's skills in adjusting plans to circumstances. In S.L. Friedman, E.K. Scholnick & R.R. Cocking (Eds.), *Blueprints for thinking: The role of planning in psychological development* (pp. 303–320). New York: Cambridge University Press.

Rogoff, B., & Radzisewska, B. (1985, April). *The influence of collaboration with parents versus peers in learning to plan.* Paper presented at the biennial meetings of the Society for Research in Child Development, Toronto, Canada.

Wellman, H.M., Fabricius, W.V., & Sophian, C. (1985). The early development of planning. In H.M. Wellman (Ed.), *Chilldren's searching: The development of search skill and spatial representation* (pp. 123–150). Hillsdale, NJ: Lawrence Erlbaum Associates.

CHAPTER 6

Context, Conflict, and Coordination in Social Development*

Melanie Killen

The predominate view of toddler's and preschooler's social orientation has been interpreted from the psychoanalytic and socialization perspectives as primarily selfish or premoral. These views argue that the basic process for the acquisition of moral concepts is the transmission of values by parents to children; adults are the moral agents of society. Piagetian and social cognitive perspectives do not postulate that the young child is selfish or asocial. Rather, it is theorized that children are socially oriented and actively seek to understand their social world. In addition, adults are not viewed as the primary transmitters of social values but are theorized to be one source of information and experience from which the child constructs social and moral categories. In fact, equal, if not greater, importance is given to experience with peers rather than with adults for developing a moral awareness. Thus Piagetian views differ from socialization views in their characterization of early social orientations in development and in the role of adults for accounting for the acquisition of social and moral understanding (see Shantz, 1987, and Turiel, 1983, for a more extensive comparison of these perspectives).

Consistent with the Piagetian view, this chapter proposes that social development involves active processes of interpretation, evaluation, and coordination of issues by individuals and that these processes are evident in early development. Furthermore, we will propose that in order to examine these processes in action or in judgment, several steps are necessary. First, analyses of the context must be made in order to tap the full range of children's social competencies. The context

* The research reported in this chapter was supported, in part, by a Project Grant and a Biomedical Start-up Grant from Wesleyan University awarded to the author. Jennifer Cahill, Richard Rende, and Cheryl Slomkowski assisted in the data collection and analysis of the preschool study. Thanks are extended to Judith G. Smetana, Elliot Turiel, and Lucien T. Winegar for their helpful comments on the manuscript.

includes who one interacts with, the history of that interaction, and how that interaction bears on the type of social exchange taking place. Children observed in settings with adults behave differently from those with peers. There are other dimensions as well, such as the social structure (at home or at school), the types of activities available, and the goal of an exchange that bear on the type of social experience. We propose that children demonstrate different social abilities in a range of contexts and that this is an important dimension which should be considered in analyses of social development.

Second, it will be proposed that a classification system for interpreting the social nature of the different components from both the researcher's and the subject's viewpoint is essential. In the social cognitive area, a classification system has been proposed by Turiel (1983) which outlines three domains of social knowledge: moral, social-conventional, and psychological. This scheme serves as a heuristic by setting up criteria for how to classify patterns of interaction as well as how to interpret conceptual evaluations of social problems. Behavioral exchanges are often assumed to be positive or negative without detailed analyses of the patterns of interaction. For example, conflicts are often defined as negative social encounters. Yet, as Shantz (1987) has recently pointed out, research has shown that conflicts are not necessarily negative and are often constructive means by which children work out problems. Thus conflicts may be positive as well as negative and reveal children's social orientations. Detailed analyses of behavioral exchanges need to be made before attributing a positive or negative quality to the interaction.

Third, it is proposed that processes of behavioral exchanges need to be investigated. In most social encounters, individuals have different perspectives about the goals of the interaction. For example, when three children are playing with blocks at a table, each participant has a specific aim in the interaction which is usually not explicitly communicated, such as using the toys to establish a new friendship or using the toys to experiment with properties of solid objects. These diverse goals may produce conflicts. As one child wants to trade toys as a mark of friendship, the other child wants to hold onto them in order to figure out how they work. When these interactions result in conflicts, a common interpretation is that one child is selfish or asocial in ignoring the other child's requests. An alternative interpretation is that a lack of coordination and communication of the goals by the participants results in the conflict, rather than that one child is selfish or asocial. This alternative interpretation does not rule out the possibility that a selfish orientation by one child fuels the conflict. Instead it claims that conflicts may also be a product of a lack of coordination and weighing of perspectives by the participants. Investigating how children coordinate different considerations is an important part of understanding early social orientations.

These three themes, (a) the role of context in analyses of development; (b) the nature of social conflicts in early adult-child and child-child exchanges; and (c) processes of cognitive and social coordination, are central to analyses of social behavior and judgment and will provide the organizational framework for this chapter.

ISSUES OF CONTEXT

Studying social interaction necessarily involves looking at behavior in a context. This context may be the laboratory or the field but in either case there is a context in which individuals interact. As Rogoff and Lave (1985) and others (Brownell, 1987) have argued, even the laboratory is a context within which aspects of the setting constrain social exchanges. One of the important aspects of examining behavior in different contexts is that the range of behaviors observed demonstrate a heterogeneity of experience, especially in early development. The diversity of experience encountered by young children within given cultural settings and contexts is, in itself, a testament to the complexities of the social world. Documenting this variability and the type of knowledge abstracted from these experiences is a necessary part of understanding the range of concepts evident in early social development.

For the most part, contextual influences on children's social behaviors have not been systematically examined in research on early social development, especially during the preschool years (Hartup, 1983). (An exception is the Vygotskyan work by Renninger, Valsiner and Winegar—Chapters 7, 1, and 3, respectively—discussed in this volume). Yet contextual influences may be quite profound and bear on the extent to which a child displays certain social abilities. In order to investigate this, a system for examining context variables, based on a theory about what is important or relevant to look at, has to be established and then incorporated into the research program.

The ethological approach has been most systematic in its analysis of the context on social interaction. Traditional ethology has specified three levels of the context: (a) the physical habitat; (b) social ecology, and (c) the individual (Strayer, 1980). This has been translated by Strayer (1980) to include three levels of context: (a) the physical environment, (b) the social structure of the setting, and (c) the pattern of social interactions. Much of the work on early social interaction has directly or indirectly examined at least one of these three levels in analyzing social behavior. In a review by Hartup (1983) on peer relations, setting conditions included the effects of toys, space, adults, group size, and familiarity on children's social behavior. Research on toys and space pertains to the physical environment and are, in effect, nonsocial context variables. Work on "toy involvement" has shown individual differences in toy use (Smith & Connolly, 1977). For the most part, however, few studies have examined the effects of the physical environment on social behavior other than showing that the types of exchanges that children engage in are constrained by the toys and space in their environment. One exception is the work by Renninger (1987); she has conducted detailed analyses of children's play with toys of "interest" and those of "noninterest.'' She has found that children's play with toys of interest is more varied and of longer duration than toys of noninterest, suggesting that social and affective components of play influence the richness of the experience. Thus, the role of adults, group size, and familiarity represent two levels of context which have received a lot of attention in the literature: the social structure and the history of interactions.

Social Structure

The social structure of the context includes the activities, roles, and rules established by some or all of the participants in the setting. For the most part, studies on preschool social relations have concentrated on peer interaction and have excluded adult-child interactions from analyses, even though adults are clearly present. Studies with preschoolers have typically looked at helping behaviors (Bar-Tal, Raviv, & Goldberg, 1982), sharing (Barton & Ascione, 1979), use of space and social behaviors (Eisenberg-Berg, Haake, & Bartlett, 1981), peer popularity (Krantz, 1982; Masters & Furman, 1981) and types of conflict resolutions (Sackin & Thelen, 1984). In addition, most of the observations in these studies were conducted during school-time free play. Thus, the two aspects of the social structure that are relatively constant in the research are the particular setting and the individuals included in analyses.

Yet, as proposed earlier, the nursery school environment is a diverse social structure with many established rituals and procedures that potentially bear on the type of interactions observed in such settings. Activities at the preschool vary in the degree of adult supervision and structure. Teachers designate different play areas (such as the truck or block area), arrange daily schedules, and establish sets of rules. The specific structure of many activities at preschool are a product of teacher-child interaction, such as the particular routines around the general activity of ''snacktime,'' which are subject to negotiation (Winegar, 1986). The determination of the types of activities, however, lies with the teacher.

Several studies with preschoolers during free play have shown that children treat adults and peers differently depending on the gender of the peer and whether the interaction occurs indoors or outdoors (Hinde, Easton, Meller, & Tamplin, 1983; Killen & Turiel, 1985). Free-play time itself is quite varied in that it allows children the opportunity to change activities at a high rate (Killen & Turiel, 1985) or become engaged in a singular activity for 15–20 minutes (Renninger, 1987). Most likely, these differences in the social structure influence the types of social competencies and abilities observed in different settings.

One of the important differences between free-play and adult-structured activities is that children tend to form peer groups during free play. In fact, much of the research on early social development has investigated these peer networks. Yet, as Hartup (1983) points out, only a few studies have examined how the context influences the structure of peer exchanges. Peer networks are often examined either within the free-play nursery school context or in semistructured settings organized by the researcher. Studies that have looked at the structure of peer groups in free play have documented how children enter peer groups and inclusion and exclusion strategies (Corsaro, 1979; 1985). Corsaro's ethnographic work has shown that preschoolers' justifications for exclusion of others are tied to friendship and interpersonal relations. Inclusion and exclusion strategies vary depending on the social structure of the setting. Children who exclude others in free play may resist exclusion strategies in semistructured peer group settings. Interestingly, a recent study (Hartup & Laursen, 1987) has found that friendship alliances play an important role in the types of conflicts and conflict resolutions observed in preschool.

Studies on children's social abilities in peer groups apart from the preschool context have shown that the types of conflicts that arise differ, just as the types of conflict resolutions differ from free play (Killen & Turiel, 1985). Further, the number of playmates in a peer group influences the degree of social exchanges. In a study by Vandell and Mueller (1980), male toddlers displayed more socially mature behavior in dyadic than polyadic situations. This pattern is also shown in a study by McLoyd, Thomas, & Warren (1984) with three-, four-, and five-year-olds who were videotaped in triadic and dyadic play groups. Five-year-old children were more successful at maintaining triadic states than three-year olds, who frequently shifted to dyadic states and thereby excluded one of the participants. Children who are not capable of coordinating polyadic states often end up excluding others. This exclusion may be due to the relative ease of dyadic over polyadic interactions. If this is the case, then exclusion among young preschoolers may be due to something other than selfishness, such as the lack of the ability to coordinate interactions among more than one playmate. This is an important distinction and raises a series of issues which will be discussed in the next section. The results of the McLoyd et al. study also suggest that group compositions are influential on the social nature of the exchanges and that seminaturalistic peer group sessions provide information about social development not observed during schooltime free play, when adults are present.

The differences between peer and adult-child exchanges in preschool with three-, four-and five-year-olds are reversed from the pattern shown in the home with toddlers between one-half and three years of age. In the home context, parents play a positive role. In fact, toddlers share with their parents more often than with their peers (Bronson, 1981; Hay, 1984; Rheingold, Hay, & West, 1976). Further, children are more social in their own homes than in strange environments (Jeffers & Lore, 1979). In addition, children show more positive behavior to parents than siblings (Baskett & Johnson, 1982) and play with mothers involves fewer moral transgressions than with unfamiliar peers (Smetana, 1986). Interactions pertaining to sharing and hitting occur more often between toddler dyads than between toddler-parent exchanges (Smetana, 1986). During preschool this pattern shifts. Studies with preschool children have shown that during the course of the first year at nursery school children develop rituals and routines with adult teachers that differ from those established with their parents (Winegar, 1986). In addition, children negotiate and work out social problems with peers in the absence of adults.

Most likely, this shift is due to the history of interactions established between the parent and toddler which is only just beginning between toddler peer mates. By the first and second years of preschool, children have developed established patterns of play with peers and thus are more able to communicate and engage in prosocial behavior. Clearly, the child's history of interaction with a playmate (child or adult) is influential in the type of reciprocity demonstrated in a particular social exchange. In the next section, the role of the history of interaction in social development will be discussed.

History of Interactions

Studies on familiarity and acquaintance show that the history of social interactions influences social behavior. Acquaintance among infants and toddlers enhances the degree of social reciprocity in peer interaction (Becker, 1977; Brenner & Mueller, 1982). In one study (Becker, 1977) pairs of children at ages 9–10 months were observed in homes for two to four weeks and compared with pairs (controls) who only met for the first and last observation times. Reciprocal interactions increased for the pairs who met over time but not for the control pairs. These results show that the ability to engage in mutual exchanges, but not to share objects, has been documented in longitudinal studies on toddlers' social interactions. This indicates that aspects of the context, such as acquaintance and the establishment of a common interactive history, facilitate social reciprocity in toddlers. This also suggests that social reciprocity is not a general orientation, but is dependent on the context of interactive exchanges.

Other research has also shown ways in which the relation between the interactants influences the type of social exchange. Doyle, Connolly, & Rivest (1980) found that children engage in more positive and neutral behaviors with friends than with nonfriends. Some children may appear to be more socially competent than other children depending on their interaction partner at the time of observation. It has also been shown that children tend to respond to peers that they associate with differently from peers with whom they do not associate (Hinde et al., 1983).

In the nursery school context, children begin to negotiate social reciprocity in their peer play. For example, in one study it was shown that children develop an array of rituals for gaining entry into ongoing peer group interactions (Corsaro, 1979, 1985). When examining young children's play in settings outside of free-play time, it has been shown that children develop strategies to maintain group interaction (McLoyd et al. 1984). Thus, there is some evidence that children structure their own interactions in peer contexts. These experiences have not been examined in relation to children's abilities to resolve moral disputes, such as sharing objects. Assessing preschoolers' social behavior in situations where adults do not intervene and where children determine the rules for interaction provides a setting for investigating young children's social reciprocity that differs from schooltime free play.

Detailed information on peer interaction processes in relation to social reciprocity has been documented in research with older children (Camras, 1984; Putallaz & Gottman, 1981; Renshaw & Asher, 1983). Beginning with Piaget's (1932) classic work, studies have shown that peer interactions differ qualitatively from children's interactions with adults and authority. Interestingly, findings from recent research has led to a diverse picture of the role of peer interaction in development. Some have proposed that peer interaction is important due to the cognitive conflict it creates in children's understanding of social issues (Blatt & Kohlberg, 1975; Berkowitz, 1985), while others have proposed that it is the cooperative aspect of peer interaction that is important in facilitating social understanding (Damon & Killen, 1982; Damon, 1983; Youniss, 1980). In either case, it has been shown that peer interaction plays an important role in the facilitation of social development. What it is about social interaction that facilitates social knowledge needs further study. In fact, the relation between social interaction and social judgment requires systematic attention, especially with younger children.

Recent work in social cognition has also shown that children's interactions with others differ depending on the type of issue involved in an exchange (Smetana, 1988; Turiel, 1983). For instance, in toddlerhood, moral and social-conventional conflicts are characteristic of parent-child interaction, whereas only moral conflicts are observed in early peer exchanges. In addition, children and adults respond differently to these types of conflicts in the context of their exchanges.

Thus, the pattern of findings from studies described above on the role of context indicates that investigations of preschool social orientations would be informed by examining (a) the history of social interactions with peers and adults and (b) the types of issues around which such interactions occur. In contrast with these concerns, social reciprocity with preschoolers generally has been studied as a specific ability (e.g., its absence or presence) and without regard to its antecedents in peer interactions. One of the most common measures of social reciprocity is its absence, and this is often measured in terms of conflicts and antagonistic exchanges. These exchanges are also subject to contextual influences. In the next section, the role of conflicts in research on early social development will be discussed. In particular, it will be argued that our understanding of social conflicts is better informed when the existing social structure and history of interactions is taken into account in our analyses.

CONFLICTS

It has recently been pointed out by Shantz (1987) that, while conflicts serve an important role in developmental theory, little has been done on the structure of conflicts in interpersonal exchanges. In developmental theory, conflict plays an important role in the facilitation of knowledge and understanding. Research has been conducted on whether and the extent to which conflict, as a source of disequilibrium, impels individuals to move to higher levels of social cognitive development (Berkowitz, 1985; Bearison, Magzamen, & Filardo, 1986; Blatt & Kohlberg, 1975; Piaget, 1932). In this framework, conflict refers to intrapsychic or cognitive conflict. Recently there has been a lot of work on behavioral or interpersonal conflicts (see Shantz, 1987). Behavioral conflicts in early development may also provide opportunities for social cognitive growth. In addition, children's methods of conflict resolutions reveal early social cognitive abilities. In the following sections, research on behavioral conflicts and the relation between interpersonal conflicts and reflective judgment are discussed.

Behavioral Conflicts

As with other indices of social behavior, many aspects of the social and physical environment are relevant to the types of conflicts that occur and to the acts that initiate them, and yet little research has taken the context into account when analyzing behavioral conflicts. Much research has shown that not all conflicts are necessarily aggressive (Hay, 1984; Shantz & Shantz, 1985) even though most aggressive acts involve conflicts. Analyses of the setting of conflicts may help to explain this diversity and to demonstrate the various roles that conflicts play in social exchanges. Analyses of conflicts typically include the issues that instigate them, their outcomes, and types of resolutions. Conflicts about the physical environment decrease with age while conflicts about the social structure increase (Shantz & Shantz, 1985). The most frequent event that creates conflicts in early development is the possession and use of objects (Brenner & Mueller, 1982; Bronson, 1981; Shantz, 1987). Interestingly, few studies have reported on ways in which children resolve conflicts. This may be a result of the paucity of studies that have examined children's responses to conflicts in settings in which adults do not intervene. This points to the need to examine behavior in different environments.

As mentioned above, some of the most detailed work on context stems from ethologically-inspired work by Strayer and others. In particular there has been an emphasis on examining ways in which conflicts are resolved. This has been examined by looking at dominance hierarchies and their relation to stable social units among preschoolers (Strayer, 1980). It is hypothesized that dominance hierarchies provide stability in a social unit by dispersing conflicts. In this research children are typically observed in the preschool environment and dominance is indexed by charting the aggressive and competitive exchanges in free-play social interaction. This index reflects the set of asymmetrical social relationships at the school that conform to a model of dominance.

Several researchers have challenged the theory that aggressive and competitive aspects of dominance are the major stabilizing force in children's preschool social exchanges and serve to resolve conflicts (Hartup, 1983; La Freniere & Charlesworth, 1983; Sackin & Thelen, 1984). Some have argued that since research with nonhuman primates has shown that nonaggressive variables, such as cognitive and social factors, often account for dominant positions, nonaggressive variables are even more likely to account for stability in human interactions (see Hartup, 1983). In addition, since aggressive acts are fairly infrequent among young children it is postulated that it is unlikely that this feature of their network is the guiding and organizing principle (see La Freniere & Charlesworth, 1983). It may be that children take leadership roles in their peer groups and that these roles are not established through dominance but through agreement among the members in the group. This interpretation is based on a view that young children are capable of working out their problems without resorting to biologically-based roles of submission and dominance.

More recently Strayer and others have shifted the attention to factors other than dominance—such as group cohesiveness—to account for methods of conflict resolutions (Camras, 1984; Sackin & Thelen, 1984; Strayer, 1980). Group cohesiveness is defined in terms of social proximity and attention. Social proximity is measured by the physical distance between a target child and others, and attention is assessed as the number of looks given by one child to another. Interestingly, Strayer and Strayer (1976) found that knowledge of a child's role in the social dominance hierarchy does not predict his or her role in the group cohesiveness network.

While the behaviors recently measured by Strayer—social proximity and attention—are nonaggressive, they are also noncognitive (and stem from the mother-child attachment literature). What seems to be missing from this type of analysis is the child's cognitive interpretation of the setting and of his or her peers, that is, to the way in which the child conceptualizes the context and the social relations within that context. This orientation leads to an analysis of the types of strategies and methods of conflict resolutions that children construct for structuring their interactions. Recent evidence from an ethological approach, in fact, suggests that children construct means of resolving conflicts in ways other than through dominance hierarchies (Bakeman & Brownlee, 1982; Sackin & Thelen, 1984).

Sackin and Thelen (1984) examined ways in which conflicts ended that were not aggressive or competitive but were conciliatory. Conciliatory behaviors included cooperative propositions, apologies, symbolic offers, object offer/share, and grooming responses (pg. 1099). Their results differ from the ones found by the more traditional ethological studies in that children generated methods for resolving conflicts that were independent from dominance-type behaviors. Further, they demonstrate that cognitively-based categories are informative about the ways in which young children structure their social interactions.

Thus, this review of the literature suggests that the strengths of the ethological work include the detailed analyses of the environment and the emphasis on analyses of dyadic exchanges as opposed to the traditional analyses of individual rates of activities. The limitations have to do with the lack of attention to the social-cognitive dimension of development. A social-cognitive view of dominance hierarchies would raise questions such as: How do children interpret dominance? What do children perceive to be the basis of dominance? An even more central issue is the relationship between dominance and authority. What is the perceived jurisdiction of a dominant child? What is the basis and rationale for his or her authority? These questions address relations between social interaction (e.g., patterns of dominance) and social knowledge (e.g., conceptions of authority). In the next section, relations between social interaction and cognition will be discussed.

Social Interaction and Social Knowledge

As mentioned earlier, few of the studies on peer interaction in preschoolers explicitly study relations between social behavior and social understanding. The aim of these studies has been to document the emergence of social abilities and social competence in young children without investigating children's interpretation of their behavior and the development of social concepts (Shantz, 1987). In addition, most of the studies on early peer relations have been atheoretical (Brownell, 1986). The aim has been to document the emergence of specific social abilities without a commitment to a particular theoretical perspective.

The paucity of studies on social judgment during preschool is also due, in part, to the difficulty of assessing social reasoning at this stage. Hypothetical interviews, which are often used in social cognitive research, are usually too difficult for young children. The language alone is often too abstract (Eisenberg & Hand, 1979; Smetana & Braeges, 1987). Yet, some studies have shown that children as young as two and a half distinguish between different types of rules (Smetana, 1986), thus indicating that rudimentary social knowledge is evident at this early stage.

One view has postulated that the diversity of social experiences necessarily leads to the development of different conceptual categories (Turiel, 1983). These categories—referred to as domains of social knowledge—are the moral, societal, and psychological realms of thinking. Research on the moral domain has included examining children's concepts of justice (Colby & Kohlberg, 1987; Damon, 1977; Killen, 1985; Nucci, 1984; Smetana, 1986; Turiel, 1983), harm (Helwig, 1985; Killen, 1987), and rights (Moshman, 1986; Turiel & Hildebrandt, in preparation). Studies on the societal domain include children's concepts of authority (Damon, 1977; Laupa & Turiel, 1986; Tisak, 1986), societal institutions (Furth, 1978), and conventions (Damon, 1977; Turiel, 1983). In addition, work has been conducted on children's concepts of self and personal relations (Broughton, 1978; Nucci, 1981; Selman, 1980) which would be reflective of the "psychological" domain. These studies have shown that individuals form conceptual categories of justice, social convention, and psychology as early as six or seven years of age.

Some of the research has been devoted to determining the criteria individuals use to evaluate various types of social rules and norms. These criteria stem from developmental and philosophical theories and include whether a rule is universalized, believed to be unalterable and impersonal, or a matter of group consensus (see Nagel, 1982; Gewirth, 1978; Rawls, 1971). It has been shown that individuals consider moral rules to be generalizable whereas social conventional rules are a matter of group consensus. Psychological issues are shown to be different from moral and societal rules since they are not considered to be codifiable rules, but are decisions which fall under the purview of the individual's jurisdiction (Nucci, 1981).

Four types of data have been collected in order to investigate the way in which these categories enter into individuals' conceptual and behavioral orientations: (a) observations of behavior in naturalistic settings (Killen & Turiel, 1985; Nucci & Turiel, 1978; Smetana, 1981, 1988); (b) judgments expressed during actual events (Turiel, in preparation); (c) judgments about events witnessed or heard (Damon, 1977; Laupa & Turiel, 1986; Nucci & Turiel, 1978), and (d) evaluation of hypothetical problems (Arsenio & Ford, 1985; Davidson, Turiel, & Black, 1983; Killen, 1985; Tisak and Turiel, 1984). In these studies, children are asked to evaluate rules, conflicts, dilemmas, or events. In one study (Nucci & Turiel, 1978), preschool children were asked to evaluate an event in which a bully pushed two children off a swing to get a turn (a violation of a rule about hitting) and to compare it to one in which a child calls the teacher by her first name (a violation of a rule about calling teachers by their surname). The results show that children as young as four years of age differentiate these acts on the basis of welfare (in the former case) and societal conventions (in the latter case) (Nucci & Turiel, 1978).

In an investigation by Turiel (in preparation) on the relation between judgment and action, elementary school-aged children have been interviewed about moral and social transgressions that they participated in or witnessed that occurred on the playground or in the classroom. Children are asked to recapitulate events on the same day or the following day as they saw them and to evaluate them in moral, conventional, psychological, or pragmatic terms. In addition to the interviews, detailed ethnographic records were made at the school to document general indices of social behavior such as the nature of authority relations and friendship alliances in different settings as well as when, where, and how rule transgressions typically occur. Recording the nature of authority relations involved noting who (teachers, monitors, or students) is responsible for structuring activities, making decisions, and enforcing rules in various settings. Thus the methodology is designed to compare relations between judgment and action and to understand how children weigh different considerations when evaluating a range of social conflicts.

Preliminary results show age and context effects on the types of moral and conventional violations that occur in elementary school. As an example, among first graders, moral and conventional violations occur more often in nonclassroom settings than in classroom settings. This changes in the higher grades, when such violations occur in both nonclassroom and classroom settings. The context of transgressions has a bearing on children's evaluations of the jurisdiction of the violation. An important part of the analyses will be on how children weigh different social organizational and moral concerns when evaluating transgressions in different settings. This process of weighing choices has been referred to as coordination (Killen, 1985; Smetana, 1981; Turiel & Smetana, 1984). As discussed in the first section of this chapter, coordination of ideas and of action share some similar properties, and analyses of both may help explain problems that generate cognitive and behavioral conflicts. In the next section, this issue of coordination will be discussed in further detail.

COORDINATION

In the cognitive developmental area, coordination has referred to ways in which two or more actions, ideas, or principles are integrated as elements into a new structure or scheme. As a behavioral illustration, infants coordinate visual and motoric actions in order to reach an object: two separate actions are integrated into a new scheme. As a conceptual example, children coordinate dimensions like height and weight to form a rule about the conservation of liquid or mass. Keil (1985) has discussed ways in which information from one domain of thinking may be applied to or coordinated with another domain.

In the social area, coordination takes on particular importance due to the multifaceted aspect of almost all social experiences and encounters. In order to study this process, a scheme for classifying social issues is crucial; so is an analysis of the context within which an event or problem occurs. Studies have investigated how individuals weigh considerations reflective of moral, conventional, or psychological issues (Killen, 1985; Smetana, Killen, and Turiel, 1987) and relate their judgment to their behavior in interpreting social transgressions (Turiel, in preparation).

In one study (Killen, 1985), children at 6, 8, 10, and 12 years of age were told stories in which choices involving preventing harm competed with helping a peer club, or giving preference to interpersonal relations. Children's ability to give priority to moral considerations was found to be related to their ability to coordinate different considerations. For example, when children were told about conflicts involving an act to prevent harm or an act to save a club, the youngest and oldest children—the six-and 12-year-olds, respectively—gave priority to preventing harm more often than the middle group—the eight-and 10-year-olds. The eight-and 10-year-olds were quite conflicted about the decision and often gave priority to saving a peer club. The 12-year-olds, however, weighed both choices and gave priority to preventing harm. Thus while the six-year-olds gave priority to preventing harm, they did not weigh both decisions to the same extent as the older children. In this study, children's ability to discuss and coordinate different aspects of the conflict influenced their moral judgments.

In another study on conceptual coordination, Smetana (1986) interviewed adolescents and their parents about interpersonal conflicts experienced at home. She asked individuals to classify a variety of issues, as to whether they were independent of authority's jurisdiction, dependent on authority, or under personal jurisdiction, criteria reflective of the moral, conventional, and psychological domains, respectively. Smetana found that the issues which generate the most conflicts were the ones in which adolescents and parents differed in their explanation of the reason for their position about the conflict. Hence, conflicts arose over those issues in which different categories of knowledge formed the basis of evaluation of the issue. The classification of issues into domains allows for analyses of how individuals weigh different considerations, a crucial part of how individuals make moral and social judgments.

The reason that analyses of the way individuals weigh social concepts is crucial to understanding the development of moral and social judgment is that most social problems involve more than one issue, and the way in which an individual gives priority to these issues provides information about the hierarchy of norms an individual has constructed. If individuals' judgments were analyzed without examining how they weigh different issues, then it would not be clear whether their judgment about the right course of action involved an explicit subordination of issues not discussed or an ability to weigh different considerations (and not an explicit subordination of particular concepts).

Investigating the way individuals coordinate their behavior in action involves some of the same issues raised by an examination of how individuals evaluate conceptual problems. Successful polyadic exchanges involve communication with others and this usually requires that individuals weigh different perspectives. The lack of perspective taking may be a function of an explicit subordination of another's perspective (that it's unimportant or secondary, etc.) or a lack of an ability to coordinate other views (without a statement about the merit of such perspectives).

Behavioral conflicts among preschoolers may also be understood in terms of a lack of coordination of goals and domain orientations. Social conflicts among preschoolers are usually thought of as struggles between the self and other or between selfish and moral orientations. Recent data has shown, however, that conflicts often involve nonselfish social considerations (Hay, 1984; Shantz, 1987). Sometimes these conflicts involve social rules, regulations, or friendship alliances, matters that are neither purely selfish or strictly moral. Coordinating these concerns may be difficult for young children and result in seemingly selfish behavioral response. Yet conflicts may, in fact, reflect struggles between competing nonselfish social goals, rather than between selfish and nonselfish desires. Work that addresses these issues will be discussed in the next section.

Current Research

A research program, designed to examine the way in which preschoolers structure their interactions and resolve conflicts in different settings, addresses some of the issues of context, conflict, and coordination just described (Killen & Turiel, 1985; Killen, Rende & Slomkowski, in preparation). The aim of this program has been to investigate the way in which features of the context bear on children's modes of interaction, methods of conflict resolution, and evaluations of social rules. The ways in which children structure their social interactions has been examined through analyses of how children relate to each other and resolve conflicts in peer group sessions and in nursery school free-play settings. In this project, context variables include the presence or absence of adults and school rules, the types of activities that children engage in, and the types of rituals and regularities children establish through the course of their interaction.

While there is a fair amount of documentation in the literature regarding young children's social exchanges, little is known about the role that contextual variables play on different types of social competencies, as described above. For instance, methods of conflict resolution experienced by children differ depending on whether adults are present or absent, whether the setting is familiar or unfamiliar, and whether the types of activities are structured or free play. In previous research, the role of these variables in different types of social exchanges has not been systematically examined. One way of examining this is to observe social behavioral patterns in different setting with a focus on how children resolve conflicts and negotiate the exchange of desired objects.

The conceptual framework and assessment methods of this program are based on findings from recent research on how children respond to moral, social-organizational, pragmatic, and interpersonal aspects of their social exchanges (Turiel, 1983). In addition, extensive pilot work has produced several measures for analyzing social interaction in diverse contexts. This includes measures for coding types of conflicts and methods of conflict resolutions in nursery school free play and peer group sessions.

Three sets of assessments with children at three, four, and five years of age (half male and half female) have been conducted: (a) Behavioral measures of conflicts and conflict resolutions that arise in peer group play and free-play sessions; (b) measures of how children structure their interactions, including rituals, patterns of friendship alliances, and the coordination of group interaction; and (c) measures of children's judgments about conflict resolutions, rituals, and norms. Comparisons have been made regarding the types of conflicts and conflict resolutions that arise in each setting for children at these ages.

Children are observed in two settings: peer group sessions and nursery school free play. In peer group sessions, triads meet in a room with a table and are instructed to play with the toys at the table. The toys consist of Fisher-Price people, blocks, and toy cars; there are about 20 toys in all. An adult sits in a corner of the room reading a book and remains uninvolved. When children appeal to the adult to solve problems the adult tells the children that he or she is busy. After the first session, the adult is generally ignored by the children in the groups. These sessions meet at regular intervals over the course of a month or more (the time varies with the specific study). These same children are observed during nursery school free-play time, when adults are present and often intervene in children's play. An observer records all conflicts that occur for each subject during specific observation periods.

In the free-play environment, adults are present and children often interact with older children (four- and five-year-olds) who are present during free play but not during the peer groups. Thus there are two major differences in the social structure of these settings: (a) the presence of adults and older age mates and (b) the types of activities available for children. The design allows for analyses of how children structure their interactions in settings in which adults do and do not, respectively, intervene in their ongoing interactions.

In Study I (Killen & Turiel, 1985), three-year-olds were videotaped in triads that met over the course of five months and observed during free play. This was done to analyze ways in which children develop rituals for organizing themselves as a group and how this pattern bears on their methods of conflict resolution.

In Study II (Killen, Rende & Slomkowski, in preparation), four- and five-year-olds were videotaped in triads for two months. The design of Study II differed from Study I in that observations were made of four- and five-year-olds rather than three-year-olds (as in Study I) and all subjects were observed in each setting (group and free play). In addition, subjects were first videotaped for four sessions in which there were new members at each meeting and then for four sessions with the same members. Altering the make-up of the triads allowed for measuring inclusion and exclusion patterns not observable in a fixed-group design (as used in Study I). For example, a child who is included in one particular group may be excluded in another.

Preliminary Results of Study I.

The results for the project with three-year-olds will be briefly described in two parts. First, analyses of children's behavior during the peer group sessions will be discussed and compared with their behavior during free play, and then how children at the three preschools dealt with conflicts will be portrayed. Two hundred and one conflicts were recorded for six triads over eight group sessions at Preschool A (for a total of 48 sessions). The mean number of conflicts for any given session was 4.19 (mean range, .5 - 9.75). The data presented in Table 6.1 show that a greater range of conflicts occur during the free play than the peer group. The types of issues that created conflicts during the free-play setting were physical harm (29 percent), psychological harm (e.g. teasing) (13 percent), distribution of resources (e.g., sharing) (33 percent), rights (e.g., giving someone the same opportunity to play) (7 percent) and social order (e.g., school rules) (18 percent). The types of issues that created conflicts during the peer groups were sharing the toys (76 percent), rights (e.g., use of the space) (15 percent) and the remainder were over teasing, hitting, and social order (10 percent). Thus one of the differences between the two settings has to do with the variation in conflicts and activities.

Analyses pertaining to gender (i.e., differences between groups with all girls, all boys, and mixtures of boys and girls) were not conducted due to the small number of each group type in the pilot study. Instead, analyses were conducted for gender differences (males compared with females) across all groups in the

Table 6.1. Percentage of Sources of Conflicts, Outcomes, and Resolutions for Children in Two Settings

	Settings	
	Peer Group[a]	Free-Play[b]
Sources of Conflicts*		
Physical harm	3	29
Psychological harm	5	13
Distribution of toys	76	33
Rights	15	7
Social Order	2	18
Outcomes**		
Instigator responds	38	37
Instigator ignores	42	13
Adult intervenes	5	38
Vic/Obs responds	15	12
Resolutions***		
None	60	23
Child-generated	36	19
Adult-generated	3	58

NOTE: There were 201 conflicts for the peer-group sessions and 61 conflicts for free-play.
[a]$N = 18$
[b]$N = 18$
*$X^2 = 82.7$, df = 4, p < .0001
**$X^2 = 54.5$, df = 3, p < .0001
***$X^2 = 103$, df = 2, p < .0001

peer sessions. Significant sex differences were found for conflicts that stemmed from the violation of school rules; males were involved in these conflicts at a higher rate than females. Across all types of conflicts, females were victims more often than males. There were no sex differences for the other roles or for outcomes and types of resolutions.

Table 6.1 also shows the results for the types of outcomes to conflicts for each setting. Instigators changed their behavior to adhere to the protests of the victims an average of 37.5 percent of the time in peer group and free-play settings. The instigator ignored the victim's protest 42 percent of the time during the peer group sessions and 13 percent of the time during the free-play sessions. This low occurrence of the instigator ignoring the victim's protest during free play was probably a result of the finding that adults intervened before instigators had a chance to respond in 38 percent of the free-play conflicts. Observers or victims responded before the instigator had a chance an average of 13.5 percent of the time for the peer group and free-play settings. Thus, adults, observers, and victims responded before the instigator could react 20 percent of the time in peer group and 50 percent in free-play conflicts.

One of the most interesting findings pertained to the way children resolved conflicts in each setting. Children generated more resolutions to conflicts in the peer group session (36 percent) than in the free-play setting (19 percent). However, more conflicts were left unresolved in the peer group sessions (60 percent) than during free play (23 percent). The low number of unresolved conflicts during free play was due to the high number of conflicts resolved by adults. Teachers, who were not present during the peer group sessions, intervened in 58 percent of the conflicts in free play. Thus, while more child-generated resolutions occurred during the peer group sessions than in free play, more conflicts were also left unresolved in this setting. In the free-play sessions, adults intervened in conflicts over physical harm and social order most often and in psychological harm least often.

Free-play Comparisons.

Table 6.2 shows that there were differences among the three free-play settings with respect to types of conflicts, but not to the percentage of child-generated resolutions or outcomes. One hundred and ninety-three conflicts (61, 63, and 69 at Preschool A, B, and C, respectively) were recorded for children during free-play sessions. Table 6.2 shows that, at Preschools A and C, conflicts over school rules were much lower (18 percent and 12 percent, respectively) than at Preschool B (where they constituted 54 percent of the conflicts). Preschools A and C also had higher percentages of conflicts that were instigated by acts of physical or psychological harm (42 percent and 46 percent, respectively) than Preschool B (11 percent). The results for the types of outcomes to conflicts in the three free-play settings show that instigators responded to protests from victims by chang-

Table 6.2.   Percent of Sources of Conflicts, Outcomes, and Resolutions for Children at Three Preschools

	Free-Play Settings		
	Preschool A[a]	Preschool B[b]	Preschool C[c]
Sources of Conflicts*			
Physical harm	29	6	19
Psychological harm	13	5	27
Distribution of toys	33	27	19
Rights	7	8	23
Social Order	18	54	12
Outcomes**			
Instigator responds	37	58	25
Instigator ignores	13	25	32
Adult intervenes	38	9	35
Vic/Obs responds	12	7	8
Resolutions***			
None	23	34	35
Child-generated	19	10	18
Adult-generated	58	55	47

[a]$N = 18$
[b]$N = 34$
[c]$N = 17$
*$X^2 = 56$, df $= 8$, p $< .0011$
**$X^2 = 27$, df $= 6$, p $< .0011$
***$X^2 = 4.3$, df $= 4$, n.s.

ing their behavior to accommodate to the victim's complaint in 37 percent, 58 percent, and 25 percent of the conflicts for Preschools A, B, and C, respectively.

The pattern for types of resolutions was strikingly similar, however, at all three schools: adult-generated resolutions occurred more often than child-generated ones. During free play, an average of 53 percent of the resolutions were adult-generated, while 16 percent were child-generated (with no significant difference between schools). Less than half—27 percent of the conflicts at each school—were left unresolved. Adult-generated resolutions occurred for conflicts over rules about social order and acts of physical harm most often (66 percent and 60 percent, respectively), followed by rights, distribution of toys, and psychological harm, (48 percent, 48 percent, and 27 percent, respectively).

Group Processes.

In addition to analyzing how children resolve conflicts, aspects of the social structure of the peer group context were analyzed at Preschool A (videotape recordings were not made of peer groups at Preschool B and C in Study I). In particular, how children entered and exited their peer groups were examined. These "entrance and exit rituals" are part of the social structure that the children create themselves. Two types of entrance rituals were observed: (a) methods of distribution of the toys, and (b) seating patterns at the table. For the majority of the groups, the method of distribution was a grab-and-huddle procedure. Each child would run to the table, grab a bunch of the objects, and put their arms and head over them until everyone had claimed their share. Exchange of toys and objects began after this initial ritual. When a child took a toy from another during the "huddle" period there was much protest; there was less protest once the play was underway. After the initial entrance, there was a lot of exchanging and trading of the toys. Thus, as children formed a group, they used conventional procedures for distributing the toys—a procedure that was generally recognized and carried out by each member of a group. Whether these procedures were established during these sessions or were introduced during preschool play is an open question and will be addressed in comparisons of peer group and free-play interaction (not yet analyzed).

The second entrance ritual observed pertained to the seating pattern. In the majority of cases, children sat in the same chairs during each session. When one child sat in another child's place there was verbal reference to it but little protest (in some groups, the exchange of seating places became a game). This observation is not remarkable on its own but is interesting in comparison to the way children responded to violations of the methods of distribution. Children were much more vocal about changes in the method of distribution of toys than in seating positions. Few exit rituals were observed during the peer group sessions. Observations of four- and five-year-olds show that exit rituals are more common with peer groups composed of children older than three years of age.

Reflective Judgments.

So far, children's explanations for their actions have been analyzed qualitatively. Following are two excerpts, one from the free-play setting and the other from the peer group context:

Free-Play Setting. Carol, Laura, and Elice have been sitting at a table playing with Playdo for about one minute. A teacher is close by but isn't paying particular attention to the children, who each have equal-sized lumps of clay.

Action:

C: Let's make animals.

L: No, let's make hotdogs.

C: Not hot dogs. Let's make french fries, right?

E: Yeah, We're making french fries. We're making french fries.

L: Yeah.

(They all giggle. They are busy silently making things for about 10 seconds).

E: (To C) Here's some french fries. Would you like some french fries? (She holds them out to C, proudly).

C: (Pushes E's Playdo away and looks upset). No! I want my own.

E: (Offering her Playdo to C again). No. You can take these and then you have more.

C: (Rejecting E's Playdo again) NO!

(E takes her playdo back and looks down at it. C and L both look down at theirs. Rachel and Ian walk up to the table. R sits at the spare seat, which has its own lump of Playdo which C, L, and E have not touched. I takes half of the lump for himself and leaves half for R, who picks it up. I stands next to R and molds his Playdo.)

I: I want some more Playdo.

C: You can't have mine.

(Cloe has walked up and stands between C and E).

CL: I need some.

R: We all need to have more Playdo.

L: Yeah, we all need to have more Playdo.

E: Well, all of us don't and I don't have, that's not fair to me. We all want more Playdo.

CL: Yeah.

(The teacher standing a few yards away overhears this and walks over to the table.)

Teacher: Well, it looks as though I've got to make more Playdo. (She smiles and goes to the cupboard. All the children get very excited and they jump up and down, shouting, ''Yeah'' repeatedly. They calm down when the teacher quickly returns).

Teacher: There's no more Playdo, you guys, so it looks as though you're going to have to share what's on the table.

CL: I need more Playdo.

E: I need more Playdo.

R: I need more Playdo.

C: I need more Playdo.

Teacher: (To CL) You take this over here. (She gives CL some of Carol's Playdo). You've got too much, Carol. Let's give some to Cloe. (She takes some more away from Carol and gives it to Cloe. No one reacts or responds at all. They Play).

Duration: Four minutes.

In this four-minute free-play sequence, a conflict arises about sharing Playdo and the teacher intervenes to resolve it. The following sequence occurs during the peer group session:

Peer-Group Setting. Laura is the first to enter the room. She runs in giggling. She immediately goes to her usual seat but then stops and moves directly opposite it. Upon sitting down, she begins to take some of the cars from the pile of toys, one at a time. Carol enters next. She runs in and sits down. Rachel enters as well. Carol begins to indiscriminately shovel as many toys as she can into her area, using both arms. When Laura sees this, she also begins to sweep the toys into her area. Rachel takes the remaining toys.

L:	Could you give me some of your people? (To C, referring to Fisher-Price people)
C:	No.
L:	I need one.
C:	No.
R:	Me too.
C:	I can't . . .
R:	I'll give you . . .
C:	But I have the daddy.
L:	But, but . . . you don't have to give the daddy to us.
C:	Yeah, because there's only one daddy, I only . . .
L	No, you *don't* have to give me the daddy.
C:	Here, OK?! (shrieks and holds up two toys).
L:	Could you give me one?
C:	No, well, I'll give you . . . two of this one. One (gives a doll to L) and this one (gives a doll to R).

(All three appear content and play with their toys.)

Duration: Two minutes.

In this two-minute exchange, the three-year-olds work out a satisfactory swap for the toys and resolve their conflict. Their explanations are not solely based on selfish desires. Carol responds to what she perceives to be a request for a "daddy" doll by telling the others that there is "only one daddy"; in other words, there is a limited number of the desirable toy. She then complies with Laura's request by giving a doll to each group member and the three play contently. These excerpts provide evidence for children's ability to reason about sharing in ways that are not strictly selfish or hedonistic. Yet, children's moral orientation is typically characterized as selfish or pragmatic, particularly in regard to sharing and working out conflicts. Part of this characterization may stem from the typical setting used to assess such abilities, one in which adults intervene before children have a chance to work out problems on their own. The results of this first study indicate that the social structure has an influence on the types of conflicts that arise and the ways in which they are or are not resolved.

Preliminary Results for Study II

The aim of Study II was to examine how the structure of social exchanges bears on children's methods of conflict resolutions. Analyses were conducted to determine the social interactional antecedents of conflicts, the relation of friendship alliances to conflict resolutions, and children's preferences for resolvers of conflicts (as articulated in follow-up interviews). In order to analyze social interactional states, the videotapes of the peer group triads were coded for one of four mutually exclusive states: solitary, dyadic, triadic, or conflictful. Using a lag sequential analysis (Bakeman & Gottman, 1986), transitional probabilities were calculated to assess systematic patterns in behavioral states for 38 peer groups. Results showed that solitary and dyadic states occurred more often than triadic and conflictful, and that dyadic and triadic states significantly predicted conflictful states more often than solitary ones, as measured by transitional probabilities. The vast majority of conflicts preceded by dyadic states involved the excluded member of the triad. Thus, these data support the theory that dyadic states reflect uncoordinated exchanges. Triadic states were shown to precede conflicts less often than expected by chance, supporting the proposition that these states reflect coordinated exchanges.

The results for friendship alliances showed that active resolutions occurred more often among friends than nonfriends. When interviewed, children judged moral conflicts among both friends and nonfriends as wrong; however, conflicts with nonfriends were considered more wrong than ones with friends. Overall, children preferred teachers, rather than peers, as resolvers of conflicts. Peers, more often than teachers, however, were preferred as resolvers of conflicts with friends than those with nonfriends.

The results for the social interactional analyses extend the findings of McLoyd et al. (1984) discussed earlier in which it was shown that 3-year-olds have more difficulty maintaining triadic states than 5-year-olds. Here it was shown that there is a systematic relation between social coordination and the occurrence of conflicts in the flow of interaction. This has an important bearing on the hypothesis that young children's conflict behavior may reflect a lack of coordination rather than selfish behavior.

The findings for the relation between friendship alliances and conflict behavior relates to the theory that the history of interaction bears on how children resolve conflicts and develop social and moral categories. Current analyses pertain to other aspects of children's conceptualization of conflicts such as their preferences for types of resolutions.

Rituals

Preliminary results with the four- and five-year-old groups suggest that there are subtle and important ways in which their rituals differ from those of three-year-olds. Four- and five-year-olds use more explicit and direct ways of distributing the toys at the beginning of the sessions than three-year-olds. In addition, there is a greater establishment of entrance and exit rituals in the older groups than in the younger groups. There is also an increase in the variety of strategies developed for resolving conflicts by older, rather than younger, peer groups.

In sum, the preliminary results from these two studies indicate that aspects of the context, such as the presence or absence of adults and the types of activities engaged in by the children, are influential in the way children resolve conflicts and structure their interactions. While adults intervened in the majority of conflicts in the free-play setting, they did not intervene for all types of problems. Adults intervened in object disputes less often than physical harm and social order problems. These disputes provided the major source of conflicts in the peer groups sessions and engendered the highest number of child-generated resolutions. One of the explanations for a low number of child-generated resolutions in the free-play setting may be that there is a high rate of transition from activity to activity. Other contexts during free play, such as juice time and story time, may reveal more child-generated resolutions and remains to be examined.

CONCLUSIONS

The research described in this chapter indicate that it is important to identify the context within which one is studying social exchanges and how specific aspects of the context bear on social reciprocity. The notion that the context influences the behavioral outcomes in development is not new. What is being proposed that is new is the way in which the context is investigated and how these influences are related to social cognitive outcomes of early experiences, that is, to the development of social and moral knowledge.

Analyses of social behavior need to consider features of the context with greater systematicity than has previously been the case. In the past, context was usually defined fairly globally, either as the general learning environment or as the cultural milieu. In the work described in this chapter, context was defined in terms of the social structure of specific settings and the history of interactions. The social structure included the activities (e.g., singularly-focused tasks or school-time free play), the participants (e.g., adults, peers), and the locale (e.g., home, school). The history of interaction referred to the familiarity and level of acquaintance among the participants. In this way, context is not defined broadly but includes a complex array of different variables that impinge on social outcomes of behavioral exchanges.

That context bears on the types of judgments children develop does not imply that a particular set of experiences produce a set of judgments. Rather such experience is one of many sources that influences how children develop a range of judgments. For example, that children generate resolutions to conflicts in adult-absent settings does not mean that peer exchanges produce moral outcomes but that the presence of adults is influential in how children resolve conflicts. In addition, conducting analyses of the context does not imply that the judgments themselves are contextual. Judgments are contextual or universalistic depending on the type of issue at stake. Figuring out what issues are central to a particular problem involves detailed analyses of the context. Once that assessment has been made, universalistic and relativistic judgments are formed depending on the interpretation of various components in a given problem.

Research which has analyzed contextual features of behavioral exchanges or cognitive problems provides information that is essential for constructing characterizations about the nature of early social and moral development. Children who appear to be premoral or asocial in one setting demonstrate other abilities in other contexts. How children coordinate their behavior in order to establish equality in peer groups is most likely related to their ability to conceptually weigh different situational factors in moral conflicts. Investigating this issue will address some of the important developmental questions about relations between social interaction and the development of social knowledge.

REFERENCES

Arsenio, W.F., & Ford, M.E. (1985). The role of affective information in social-cognitive development: Children's differentiation of moral and conventional events. *Merrill-Palmer Quarterly, 31,* 1–17.

Bakeman, R., & Brownlee, J.R. (1982). Social rules governing object conflicts in toddlers and preschoolers. In K.H. Rubin & H.S. Ross (Eds.), *Peer relationships and social skills in children* (pp. 99–111). New York: Springer-Verlag.

Bakeman, R., & Gottman, J.M. (1986). *Observing social interaction: An introduction to sequential analyses.* New York: Cambridge University Press.

Bar-Tal, D., Raviv, A., & Goldberg, M. (1982). Helping behavior among preschool children: An observational study. *Child Development, 53,* 396–402.

Barton, E.J., & Ascione, F.R. (1979). Sharing in preschool children: Facilitation, stimulus generalization, response generalization, and maintenance. *Journal of Applied Behavior Analysis, 12,* 417–430.

Baskett, L.M., & Johnson, S.M. (1982). The young child's interactions with parents versus siblings: A behavioral analysis. *Child Development, 53,* 643–650.

Bearison, D.J., Magzamen, S., & Filardo, E.K. (1986). Sociocognitive conflict and cognitive growth in young children. *Merrill-Palmer Quarterly, 32,* 51–72.

Becker, J.M.T. (1977). A learning analysis of the development of peer-oriented behavior in nine-month old infants. *Developmental Psychology, 13*, 481–491.

Berkowitz, M.W. (1985). The role of discussion in moral education. In M.W. Berkowitz & F. Oser (Eds.), *Moral education: Theory and application* (pp. 197–218). Hillsdale, NJ: Lawrence Erlbaum.

Blatt, M., & Kohlberg, L. (1975). The effects of classroom moral discussion upon children's level of moral judgment. *Journal of Moral Education, 4*, 129–161.

Brenner, J., & Mueller, E. (1982). Shared meaning in boy toddlers' peer relations. *Child Development, 53*, 380–391.

Bronson, W.C. (1981). *Toddler's behaviors with agemates: Issues of interaction, cognition and affect.* Norwood, NJ: Ablex.

Broughton, J.M. (1978). Development of concepts of self, mind, reality and knowledge. In W. Damon (Ed.), *New directions for child development. Vol. 1: Social cognition* (pp. 75–100). San Francisco: Jossey-Bass.

Brownell, C.A. (1986). Convergent developments: Cognitive-development correlates of growth in infant/toddler peer skills. *Child Development, 57*, 275–286.

Brownell, C.A. (1987, April). *Social context and the construction of social knowledge.* Paper presented at symposium entitled, "Contextual constraints on social interaction and cognition," M. Killen (Chair) at the Biennial Meetings of the Society for Research in Child Development, Baltimore, MD.

Camras, L.A. (1984). Children's verbal and nonverbal communication in a conflict situation. *Ethology and Sociobiology, 5*, 257–268.

Colby, A., & Kohlberg, L. (1987). *The measurement of moral judgment.* New York: Cambridge University Press.

Corsaro, W.A. (1979). "We're friends, right?": Children's use of access rituals in a nursery school. *Language in Society, 8*, 315–336.

Corsaro, W.A. (1985). *Friendship and peer culture in the early years.* Norwood, NJ: Ablex.

Damon, W. (1977). *The social world of the child.* San Francisco: Jossey-Bass.

Damon, W. (1983). The nature of social-cognitive change in the developing child. In W. Overton (Ed.), *The relationship between social and cognitive development* (pp. 103–141). Hillsdale, NJ: Lawrence Erlbaum.

Damon, W., & Killen, M. (1982). Peer interaction and the process of change in children's moral reasoning. *Merrill-Palmer Quarterly, 28*, 347–367.

Davidson, P., Turiel, E., & Black, A. (1983). The effect of stimulus familiarity on the use of criteria and justifications in children's social reasoning. *British Journal of Developmental Psychology, 1*, 46–65.

Doyle, A.B., Connolly, J., & Rivest, L.P. (1980). The effect of playmate familiarity in the social interactions of young children. *Child Development, 51*, 217–223.

Eisenberg, N., & Hand, M. (1979). The relationship of preschooler's reasoning about prosocial moral conflicts to prosocial behavior. *Child Development, 50*, 356–363.

Eisenberg-Berg, N., Haake, R.J., & Bartlett, K. (1981). The effects of possession and ownership on the sharing and proprietary behaviors of preschool children. *Merrill-Palmer Quarterly, 27*, 61–68.

Furth, H. (1978). Children's societal understanding and the process of equilibration. In W. Damon (Ed.), *New directions for child development. Vol. 1: Social cognition* (pp. 101–122). San Francisco: Jossey-Bass.

Gewirth, A. (1978). *Reason and morality*. Chicago: University of Chicago Press.

Hartup, W.W. (1983). Peer relations. In E.M. Hetherington (Ed.), P.H. Mussen (Series Ed.), *Handbook of child psychology: Vol. 4. Socialization, personality, and social development, 4th ed* (pp. 103–196). New York: Wiley.

Hartup, W.W., & Laursen, B. (1987, April). *Friendship and conflict: Synergies in child development*. Paper presented at the Biennial Meetings of the Society for Research in Child Development, Baltimore, MD.

Hay, D.F. (1984). Social conflict in early childhood. In G. Whitehurst (Ed.), *Annals of child development. Vol. 1* (pp. 1–44). Greenwich, CT: JAI.

Helwig, C. (1985). Psychological conceptions of harm. Unpublished Master's Thesis, University of California, Berkeley.

Hinde, R.A., Easton, D.F., Meller, R.E., & Tamplin, A. (1983). Nature and determinants of preschoolers' differential behavior to adults and peers. *British Journal of Developmental Psychology, 1*, 3–19.

Jeffers, V.W., & Lore, R.K. (1979). Let's play at my house: Effects of the home environment on the social behavior of children. *Child Development, 50*, 837–841.

Keil, F. (1985). On the structure dependent nature of stages of cognitive development. In I. Levin (Ed.), *Stage and structure: Reopening the debate* (pp. 144–163). Norwood, NJ: Ablex.

Killen, M. (1985). *Children's coordination of moral, social and personal concepts*. Unpublished doctoral dissertation, University of California, Berkeley.

Killen, M. (1986, May 29). *The construction of social categories in young children's social interaction patterns*. Paper presented at the 16th Annual Symposium of the Jean Piaget Society, Philadelphia, PA.

Killen, M., Rende, R. & Slomkowski, C. (in preparation). Social conflicts in early development.

Killen, M., & Turiel, E. (1985, June 6). *Conflict resolutions in preschoolers' social interactions*. Paper presented at the 15th Annual Meeting of the Jean Piaget Society, Philadelphia, PA.

Killen, M. (1987, April 25). *Children's evaluations of exceptions to moral rules*. Paper presented at the Biennial Meetings of the Society for Research in Child Development, Baltimore, MD.

Krantz, M. (1982). Sociometric awareness, social participation, and perceived popularity in preschool children. *Child Development, 53*, 376–379.

La Freniere, P., & Charlesworth, W. (1983). Dominance, attention and affiliation in a preschool group: A nine-month longitudinal study. *Ethology and Sociobiology, 4*, 55–67.

Laupa, M., & Turiel, E. (1986). Children's conceptions of adult and peer authority. *Child Development, 57*, 405–412.

Masters, J.C., & Furman, W. (1981). Popularity, individual friendship selections, and specific peer interaction among children. *Developmental Psychology, 17*, 344–350.

McLoyd, V.C., Thomas, E.A.C., & Warren, D. (1984). The short-term dynamics of social organization in preschool triads. *Child Development, 55*, 1051–1070.

Moshman, D. (Ed.). (1986). *New directions for child development. Vol. 33: Children's intellectual rights*. San Francisco: Jossey-Bass.

Nagel, T. (1982). The unreasonable demands of morality. Unpublished manuscript, New York University, New York.

Nucci, L. (1981). The development of personal concepts: A domain distinct from moral or societal concepts. *Child Development, 52*, 114–121.

Nucci, L.P. (1984). Children's conceptions of morality, social conventions, and religious prescription. In C. Harding (Ed.), *Moral dilemmas: Philosophical and psychological reconsiderations of the development of moral reasoning* (pp. 138–174). Chicago: Precedent Press.

Nucci, L.P., & Turiel, E. (1978). Social interactions and the development of social concepts in preschool children. *Child Development, 49*, 400–407.

Piaget, J. (1932). *The moral judgment of a child.* London: Routledge & Kegan Paul.

Putallaz, M., & Gottman, J. (1981). An interactional model of children's entry into peer groups. *Child Development, 52*, 986–994.

Rawls, J. (1971). *A theory of justice.* Cambridge, MA: Harvard University Press.

Renninger, K.A. (1987, April). *Child-environment interaction: Play interests and sociability.* Paper presented at the symposium "Social constraints on the development of children's understanding", F.F. Strayer (Chair) at the Biennial Meetings of the Society for Research in Child Development, Baltimore, MD.

Renshaw, P., & Asher, S. (1983). Children's goals and strategies for social interaction. *Merrill-Palmer Quarterly, 29*, 353–374.

Rheingold, H.L., Hay, D.F., & West, M.J. (1976). Sharing in the second year of life. *Child Development, 47*, 1148–1158.

Rogoff, B., & Lave. J. (Eds.). (1985). *Everyday cognition: Its development in social context.* Cambridge, MA: Harvard University Press.

Rubenstein, J., & Howes, C. (1979). The effects of peers on toddler interaction with mothers and toys. *Child Development, 47*, 597–605.

Sackin, S., & Thelen, E. (1984). An ethological study of peaceful associative outcomes to conflict in preschool children. *Child Development, 55*, 1098–1102.

Searle, J.R. (1969). *Speech acts.* London: Cambridge University Press.

Selman, R. (1980). *The growth of interpersonal understanding: Development and clinical analyses.* New York: Academic Press.

Shantz, C.U. (1987). Conflict between children. *Child Development, 58*, 283–305.

Shantz, C.U., & Shantz, D.W. (1985). Conflict between children: Social-cognitive and sociometric correlates. In M.W. Berkowitz (Ed.), *Peer conflict and psychological growth: New directions for child development* (pp. 3–21). San Francisco: Jossey-Bass.

Smetana, J.G. (1981). Preschool children's conceptions of moral and social rules. *Child Development, 52*, 1333–1336.

Smetana, J.G. (in press). Toddlers' moral and conventional interactions with mothers and peers. *Development Psychology.*

Smetana, J.G. (1988). Concepts of self and social convention: Adolescent's and parent's reasoning about hypothetical and actual family conflict. In M.R. Gunnar & W.A. Collins (Eds.), *Minnesota Symposium on Child Psychology, Volume 21* (pp. 79–122). Hillsdale, NJ: Lawrence Erlbaum..

Smetana, J.G. & Braeges, J.L. (1987, April). *The development of toddlers' moral and conventional judgments.* Paper presented at the Biennial Meetings of the Society for Research in Child Development, Baltimore, MD.

Smetana, J.G., Killen, M., & Turiel, E. (1987, August). *Interpersonal and moral conflicts: Children reasoning about social situations.* Paper presented at the Annual Meeting of the American Psychological Association, New York City.

Smith, P.K., & Connolly, K.J. (1977). Social and aggressive behaviour in preschool children as a function of crowding. *Social Science Information, 16*, 601–620.

Strayer, F.F., & Strayer, J. (1976). An ethological analysis of social agonism and dominance relations among preschool children. *Child Development, 17*, 980–989.

Strayer, F.F. (1980). Social ecology of the preschool peer group. In W.A. Collins (Ed.), *Development of Cognition, Affect, and Social Relations, Minnesota Symposia on Child Psychology* (pp. 165–196). Hillsdale, NJ: Lawrence Erlbaum.

Tisak, M. (1986). Children's conceptions of parental authority. *Child Development, 57*, 166–176.

Tisak, M., & Turiel, E. (1984). Children's conception of moral and prudential rules. *Child Development, 55*, 1030-1039.

Turiel, E. (1966). An experimental test of the sequentiality of developmental stages in the child's moral judgment. *Journal of Personality and Social Psychology, 3*, 611–618.

Turiel, E. (1983). *The development of social knowledge: Morality and convention.* New York: Cambridge University Press.

Turiel, E. (in preparation). Judgments and action in practical social situations.

Turiel, E., & Hildebrandt, C. (in preparation). Judgments about controversial social issues. University of California, Berkeley.

Turiel, E., & Smetana, J. (1984). Social knowledge and action: The coordination of domains. In W.M. Kurtines & J.L. Gewirtz (Eds.), *Morality, moral behavior and moral development: Basic issues in theory and research.* (pp. 261–282). New York: Wiley.

Vandell, D.L., & Mueller, E.C. (1980). Peer play and friendships during the first two years. In H.C. Foot, A.J. Capman, & J.R. Smith (Eds.), *Friendship and social relations in children.* New York: Wiley.

Winegar, L.T. (1986, May). *Role of adults in children's understanding of social events.* Paper presented at the 16th Annual Meeting of the Jean Piaget Society, Philadelphia, PA.

Youniss, J. (1980). *Parents and peers in social development.* Chicago: University of Chicago Press.

CHAPTER 7

Individual Patterns in Children's Play Interests*

K. Ann Renninger

Research on individual patterns in children's play interests suggests that children distinguish between both play objects[1] and others in their play even as early as three-years-of age. Findings from these studies suggest that the process by which children come to particular actions rather than other actions during free play at nursery school is a function of what they perceive as the possibilities for action[2] with both objects and others. Thus, what a child sees in choosing to engage with a train, what the train as a physical object offers as possibility for action, what the child sees in engaging with another around a train, beating out another to get the train for play, or choosing to fashion a train out of Legos, and what the child sees in playing with another child who plays trains or in allowing another child to

* Portions of this chapter have been presented as parts of papers at the meetings of the Conference on Human Development (1986), the Jean Piaget Society (1985, 1986), and the Society for Research in Child Development (1987). This chapter was written while the author was supported by a Eugene M. Lang Faculty Grant. The research reported in this chapter has been supported through grants from the National Academy of Education Spencer Fellowship Program, Educational Testing Service Postdoctoral Fellowship Program, and the Swarthmore College Faculty Research Fund. I would like to thank Ann S. Morgan who was a co-investigator on the second study discussed; Hubert Chang, Wendy Davidson, Herbert Kerns, Barbara L. Klock, Christina B. Maybee, Anastasia Norpel, Sherry Hartenstine Levy, and Kenneth Pitts who were research assistants on the studies presented; and Lucien T. Winegar for his insightful comments on an earlier draft of this manuscript. Correspondance should be addressed to K. Ann Renninger, Program in Education, Swarthmore College, Swarthmore, PA 19081.

[1] Play object, or simply object, will be used throughout this chapter to refer to the class of objects or events with which children might engage in a nursery school class. Thus, object could refer to trains, playdough, a doll, or dramatic play among other play "objects."

[2] Action refers to discrete behaviors which can be reliably coded. Thus, the child putting blocks in the cargo car of a train is one action, taking the blocks out of the car is another action. Activity, on the other hand, is used to refer to sequences of actions with an object.

share in the train play is a function of the interest of that child, the play object, and the other(s) in interaction.

In this chapter, children's play interests will be used to discuss the interdependence of both the individual and the other in the development of children's understanding. First, a theoretical description of interest is presented which details the importance of the individual child's understanding of possibilities for action as an influence on how the child engages with the objects available to him or to her in nursery school. The stored knowledge and value, or interest, which the child brings to action is described as having an individual definition, even though it is developed in coordination with others. Following this, two studies which address some of the ways that individual interests are influenced by others and, in turn, some of the ways that individual interests influence interactions with others, are presented. Finally, implications of the interest/object/other relation are discussed.

WHAT IS INTEREST?

Interest is here conceptualized in the tradition of both Piaget (1968) and Vygotsky (1967) as including both the stored knowledge and value which influences the activity of individuals. What the child brings to action/interaction with an identified interest such as, say, the play object train, is a combination of both that child's previous experience with trains and that child's feelings about the experience. This combination of stored knowledge of and value for trains leads to increasing differentiation and reintegration (Werner, 1978) of understanding about trains in relation to what the child already knows and values about trains, as well as the other objects in his or her environment. At first, this developing understanding is associated with the class of objects called train. Later, the activity characteristic of these engagements with trains influences subsequent actions (question asking, challenge setting, and activity) with other classes of objects (events or ideas). Thus, the way in which the child plays with the train and the kinds of challenges he or she sets for him- or herself, influences the kinds of things he or she does with other play objects even when no train is present.

From this perspective, interest is conceptualized as a psychological state which influences the way in which the child represents possibilities for action to him- or herself. As such, interest influences the way in which the child engages in activity. However, it is not the identified object of interest, for example, train, which is "interest," rather train is the content of the activity, the object with which interest is identified. Interest is the individual's cognitive and affective engagement with the identified object of interest, perception of possibilities for action, representation of these possibilities to the self, making of choices about activity, and finally the setting, resolving, and resetting of challenges.

The knowledge and value components of interest derive from what the individual brings to present action from past engagements with both objects and others. Thus, the knowledge and value components of interest can be described as individual in the sense that it is the individual who constructs and reconstructs the possibilities for his or her activity. The knowledge and value components of interest also can be described as social in the sense that what comes to be represented as possible action is influenced by others.

Stored Knowledge

The stored knowledge component of interest refers to the way in which children have represented their previous actions to themselves. This involves the way in which they perceive possibilities for action with the play object, in particular, the possibilities for action which they understand that object to include. It also involves the child's sense of what it is that others do with this object, as well as the importance of the specific kinds of challenges which potential actions hold for that child.

There are at least three ways in which children can represent the features, or functional properties[3], of a play object to themselves (Renninger, 1984). These include whether the play object leads to reengagement in investigative play (Renninger & Sigel, 1986), whether it leads to social exchange, and whether it leads to transformational play. Briefly, *leading to reengagement in investigative play* refers to the probability that some of the play actions of a child with a given play object will involve investigative or manipulative play behaviors as well as more sophisticated play behaviors even when the child has had quite a lot of experience with that object. Examples of some objects which often do lead to reengagement in investigative play include: dramatic play, painting, pasting, playdough, and water play. Examples of some objects which often do not lead to reengagement in investigative play include: blocks, books, cars, dishes, dolls, fire trucks, puzzles, and trains.[4]

Thus the child playing with playdough (an object which leads to reengagement in investigative play) is just as likely to use playdough to build something as he or she is to be squeezing it, poking it, or rolling it around. In contrast, once the child begins using a train as a train (an object which is not as likely to lead to reengagement in investigative play) the child no longer plays by spinning the

---

[3] Rather than using Gibson's (1979) term *affordances* which suggests that the play object itself projects possibilities for action, the term *functional properties* is used to refer to the features of the play object which the child represents to him- or herself. It is thought that the functional properties of play objects are a kind of shared knowledge about the affordances of these play objects and will vary by cultural context. However, as Hartup (1983) points out, few universal assertions can be made about the constraints on peer relations in the development of the child at this time.

[4] Identification of the functional properties of objects is based on a previous sample of three-year-old children's actions with objects in the classroom under study. It is assumed that the particular organization of the classroom influences whether objects are observed as leading to social exchange.

wheels or flicking the coupler. Once the child has explored trains in investigative play, trains are rarely again explored in investigative play. Instead, trains are usually used to carry things, for loading or unloading, or trips.

Leading to social exchange refers to the probability that some of the play actions of a child in a given play area will be combined with chatting behaviors and/or sharing of actions. Examples of some objects which often do lead to social exchange include: blocks, dishes, dramatic play, playdough, and water play. Examples of some objects which often do not lead to social exchange include: books, cars, dolls, firetrucks, painting, puzzles, and trains.

Thus, social exchange is more likely with playdough than it is with trains at least partially because playdough, as children engage it in the nursery school under study, is an object with which it is possible to observe and try out what others are doing (e.g., rhythmic pounding, making pancakes, or rolling snakes). There are seats for children around the playdough table and children come and go at will. Quite often they chat about birthdays and friendships as they play with the playdough. Their proximity to one another at the table also facilitates the sharing/copying of actions with playdough.

The actions of children in train play, on the other hand, suggest that there is not as much likelihood that trains will be perceived as affording social exchange as there is that playdough will. There are at least two reasons for this. First, trains are usually used as trains so shared actions are not so apparent. And, second, there are only two trains available in the nursery school which places a limit on the number of children playing with trains at any one time. (Of course, there is a sense in which the presence of only two trains could suggest the need to share, but for three-year-old children behaviors which might suggest such a representation are not commonly observed.)

Leading to transformational play refers to the probability that some of the play actions of a child with a given object will involve "play" with that object, although the objects represented in play are not present. Thus, for example, the child might play with blocks, using them to represent a truck. While the child is playing "truck", his or her play activity is considered transformational because he or she is transforming the apparent object of play such that it becomes some other object (Renninger & Klock, 1986). The functional properties of the play area are described as leading to transformational play if there is a likelihood that children's play with that object will actually represent play if there is a likelihood that children's play with that object will actually represent play with another (nonpresent) object. Examples of some objects which often lead to transformational play include blocks, dramatic play, playdough, and water play. Examples of some objects which often do not lead to transformational play include books, cars, dishes, dolls, firetrucks, puzzles, painting, pasting, and trains.

Thus, playdough is considered to lead to transformational play, since playdough is often used to represent other objects (e.g., the child can make a truck out of playdough). (However, playdough is not as likely to be used in transformational play because other play objects are not likely to be used to represent playdough in transformational play.) Alternatively, trains are rarely used as something other than trains. Therefore, trains are not considered to lead to transformational play. (Instead, trains are often played with in transformational play [e.g. a boat might become a train, chairs might be lined up to form a train, or Legos might be used to make a train].)

It is not immediately apparent what a child is extracting from the functional properties of an object in choosing (whether this is a reflective choice or not) to play with one object or another. What is more clear is that an object could afford a somewhat different set of potential actions to each child. Given that what the child represents to him- or herself as potential actions with each play object appears to be related to what the object is, previous activity with that object (and with other objects identified as having similar functional properties), and by the kind of parental, teacher, and/or peer input to which that child is subject, it is more clear that an object could afford a somewhat different set of potential actions to each child.

The range of possible actions with a play object and the way in which the child represents these potential actions to him- or herself and is then able to act on them influences the child's representation of that object. It is assumed that there is not necessarily a one-to-one correspondence between what the child intends in activity and how the activity is executed. Instead, as the child experiments with duplicating his or her own actions of those of others, and either runs into difficulty or discovers an alternate set of potential actions, the child's activity begins to include actions which can be distinguished from the next child's actions. This contributes to the individual quality of children's representations, as do the differences between children in the individual range of their experiences and the way in which their representations are continually being revised as a function of experience (Karmiloff-Smith, 1979).

The specific nature of each child's revision is tied to previous representations, and these in turn school what for that child is discrepant or novel, complex, conflicting, surprising, and uncertain (Berlyne, 1960) with respect to that object. In other words, the kinds of actions/potentials the child comes to take/ask for are an outgrowth of how that child has come to represent potential actions with that object and his or her activity with that object. This also begins to explain why two children identified as having the same play interests will not necessarily have the same pattern of action with the same object. The variation in their actions can be attributed to each child's particular understanding of that object.

In engaging with an object, the child differentiates between and integrates possibilities for action around what is perceived as possible action. From the perspective of the observer, it appears that some play areas such as playdough offer the potential of more varied actions than do others such as trains. However, the activity of children in play suggests that some children are more likely to explore the full range of these possibilities than are others. It is very common to see a child sit and squeeze playdough for long stretches of time, while another child in the same time period might have squeezed the playdough, built a highway through the desert, fashioned a car, and carried on an extensive narrative to describe his or her activity. It may be, of course, that each child perceives a similar number of possible actions with each object, but that what these actions are vary between children as a function of prior activity and the kinds of actions with which they engage other play objects.

What the child understands as possibility for action is informed by the functional properties of the play object, as well as the culturally prescribed use of the play object and the others in the environment. Even though the process by which the child comes to represent information to him- or herself is individual, the content of these representations is a product of his or her social milieu. The train, for example, is fashioned in the image of real trains. Once the child investigates and identifies an object as a train, trains are generally played with as they are used in the culture—as trains. The range of possible actions available to the child with trains appears to have been previously determined by others. Unlike the social exchange characteristic of playdough play, where sharing/copying others is appropriate, driving a train by the caboose would almost never be copied. More likely, the inappropriateness of this action (for an increasingly rule-conscious age group) would be loudly pointed out. It is the culturally prescribed properties of trains to which the child attends and with which the child engages.

In contrast, there is no cultural prescription for play with an object such as playdough. While squeezing, flattening, and molding are typical of playdough play, there are no specific actions which characterize use of playdough by adults. Similarly, there is no specific set of actions which characterize use of playdough by children. What a child does with playdough appears to develop out of the possibilities for manipulating playdough and what others are doing with playdough in that classroom. If playdough is being patted on the face as makeup by one child, there is a high probability that others at the table will also incorporate this action into their play with playdough. In playdough play, the child shares/copies ideas for actions with other children as a matter of course. Therefore, playdough is described as being more facilitative of social exchange than an object such as a train.

In both playdough play and train play, there are constraints on the actions that a child comes to identify with each object. These constraints come primarily from the functional properties of the objects, although they are imposed by others as well. In the nursery school under study, for example, the teacher clearly determined that each of the play objects should stay in its own prescribed area. Thus, playdough is usually kept at the playdough table and is not carried to the radiator, or stuffed into a pair of shoes. A constraint of this type serves to limit the range of possible actions available to the child, and as such the functional properties of playdough (or trains, etc.) which can be perceived by the child (or us, as observers, for that matter).

Teachers, or others who may buy the child presents, also make decisions about which and how often play objects are available to the child. The child who only has available play objects which afford the possibility of reengagement in investigative play (e.g., paste, playdough, water, etc.) may, in fact, be constrained when engaging in tasks which do not provide the opportunity for alternating between manipulative play behaviors and other types of play. The assumption here is that given the existence of functional properties peculiar to play objects, there are particular kinds of actions available to the child with one play object which are not available to the same child with the next play object. By limiting the types of objects available, a constraint is placed on the kinds of challenges the child may end up setting for him- or herself and a source for alternate representations of possible actions.

In summary, the child's stored knowledge can be described as an evolving base in which possibilities for action are generated and tested in relation to the representations of others. The others in the class who are also moving between and engaging in different play areas with their respective responses to the possibilities for action with available play objects influence the content of the child's representations and subsequent actions. In addition, what the play object as a product of the culture represents to the child and how the teacher/other organizes the child's play environment also influences that which the child comes to represent to him- or herself.

Stored Value

The value component of interest refers to the feelings abut the potential for action which the child perceives, as well as the activity in which he or she engages with the play object. Specifically, the feelings are linked to the feelings of competence (White, 1959) the child has in setting and meeting particular challenges for him- or herself, the child's sense of self (Mead, 1934), and the child's representations of others' goals for him- or herself.

Having a lot of knowledge about something does not necessarily mean having interest in it. Rather, the child who is identified as having an interest in an object has high levels of both knowledge and value for the identified object of interest. A child is identified as having a noninterest in an object if he or she has knowledge but low value for that object.[5] As such, both knowledge and value are important and interdependent components of interest. Just as the child stores knowledge of potential actions in train play, so the child simultaneously stores

---

[5] In other research currently being conducted, knowledge, value, and action components for individually identified interests were determined. Findings indicate that having knowledge for something does not predict to value for that same object, but conversely, having value for an object heightens the probability that the individual will have knowledge of it. For the purposes of the present research, high levels of both knowledge and value are necessary for an object to be identified as an object of interest.

knowledge about his or her value for that action and/or about train play more generally.

Others have discussed the importance of interestingness of the object as an affect inherent in stimuli. (For a comprehensive review, see Hidi & Baird, 1986). What the present discussion stresses is the individual perception of particular possibilities for action with play objects, in particular, the impact of interest on possibilities for action. As such, knowing a lot about trains and feeling positive about train play is thought to influence and be influenced by the way in which the child subsequently engages with trains.

Presumably, it is the complexity of the particular challenges that the child can set for him- or herself with particular play objects which leads the child to be interested in them. It appears that the level of competence attained with what are eventually identified as objects of interest actually propels a drive for mastery of increasingly complex challenges with these play objects. The facility of setting and resolving challenges with identified objects of interest increases the value of engagement in play with those objects relative to other available objects.

Similarly, practice in challenge setting means that challenges that the children set for themselves with their identified objects of interest are optimally discrepant (Hunt, 1961). They are challenging, but not overwhelming. Of course, repeated engagement with an identified object of interest means that the child has a larger reserve of possible actions on which to draw in trying to resolve these challenges than would be available with objects identified as noninterests. But there is also a sense in which engagement in this kind of problem resolution takes on a value larger than a simple reserve of possible tacts for problem solving. This reserve means that the child can identify a goal/problem and work to attain it/solve it through a variety of ways. It also means that any difficulty encountered in immediately reaching a goal/finding a solution to a problem becomes part of the challenge of engaging with that identified object of interest. In fact, unexpected twists in problem solution actually serve to peak and further support the child's interest (Claparede, 1951).

As Schank (1979) suggests, people come to recognize that certain things have been interesting in the past and mark these. Yet, while these preexisting values inform engagement, interest is further stimulated in response to novelty and unexpectedness of information (the result of action) while a presumed item of interest is being engaged. Knowledge and value for something leads to a well-honed set of expectations for possible actions. When these expectations are violated this presents an extraordinary challenge, a challenge which leads to reengagement in search of resolution, and which both contributes to and extends the knowledge base of the child with respect to that play object. Given the child's stored knowledge of potential actions and value for an object, the kinds of challenges which he or she sets for him- or herself take on a novel or unexpected quality for that child—a quality which the same set of observable circumstances might not represent to another child. Thus, each child can be described as developing individual patterns of action with respect to particular objects and these characterize that child's engagement with those objects.

It appears that the child, at least with respect to his or her identified object of interest, develops an increased facility for challenge setting in play with his or her identified object of interest and is able to pose problems that both are engaging and which push him or her to take on even more difficult tasks much in the way that another such as a teacher or parent might either distance information (Sigel, 1982), adjust instruction (Rogoff & Gardner, 1984), or mediate learning (Feurstein, 1980). In fact, the kinds of challenges that the child can set for him- or herself may be more valued by the child than are those set by others. The challenges which the child sets for him- or herself are more are attuned to his or her own representations than are those of others as they strive to engage the child in particular activity. However, this is not to suggest that another might not open up possibilities for subsequent action that the child's particular challenge setting/ questioning had yet to suggest. Rather, it appears that there is an important interdependence between the development of understanding about an object through resolving challenges, the fact that challenges are set by the child him- or herself, and the value which the child has for these challenges/actions with these objects. In fact, the value the child has for objects identified as interests appears to hold over time, influencing the actions with which they reengage new objects.

Krapp and Fink (1986) report that the structure of interests, or "accustomed and highly preferred person-object-relationships," remain largely unaffected as a child moves from the family into kindergarten. Although there is an initial period of exploring the novelty represented by the new setting, only subtle changes in interests are detected after a period of months. It seems that the patterns of the child's actions with an identified object of interest actually are "re-played" in the patterns of their subsequent actions, regardless of whether this involves another object, or involvement with another person. Which actions will be observed across time is not predictable (at least at this time), but there is a high probability of determining reliable post hoc connections between present and past patterns of actions on a case by case basis. Krapp and Fink found that the new setting did not alter the impact of the particular person-object-relationship, or interest, on the child's pattern of actions, although it did foster the incorporation of new elements into existing person-object-relationships and within and among different person-object-relationships.

These data suggest that the child's process of knowledge acquisition is both cummulative and individual. The child's present interests can be thought of as developing out of his or her prior interests, rather than simply being replaced by them. In other words, the developing child incorporates his or her experience with particular actions, especially those with objects of interest, into subsequent actions. However, as Schiefle (1986) observes, it is not possible for the child to be interested in everything; the child "stresses certain aspects and defines his[her] own limits" in developing understanding. The child differentiates the object environment according to its meaning and this impacts on his or her activity.

The way in which the child engages an identified object of interest at three-years-of age probably influences how and what may then come to be identified as objects of interest later in life. However, it probably is not the case, for example, that a child identified as having an interest in trains is going to be an engineer. More likely, the way in which the child acts/poses challenges contributes to and becomes part of the way in which that child subsequently engages with other objects and/or tasks posed by others. From this perspective, more developed patterns of interest may be most accurately identified with particular kinds of actions, rather than in terms of train actions generally. Thus, with respect to an identified interest in trains, a pattern of action might include repeatedly loading the train, driving it around, and unloading it in the same spot with only minor variations in the loading/unloading process until the addition of a new component such as driving the train to a place across the room under a table. At this point, the child might begin unloading and reloading only a portion of the load, paying attention to an aspect of symmetry of the load, the possibilities presented for building in the new area with what was unloaded, and so on. This repetition of actions is not simply any train-related action. There is careful attention to the structure of the load in the process of loading and unloading.

Among three-year-old children, interests can almost always be identified with particular play areas. However, it is not just the content of the play area identified as the object of interest, but the child's co-constructions within these play areas which is important for a description of the child's developing understanding. The choices reflected in the individual patterns of children's play with objects suggest a kind of self-monitoring which is informed by culturally accepted actions with that play object, what others may choose as actions with those play objects, and experimentation in the process of problem solving—conversing with the self about the options for resolving the problem at hand, running into dead ends, trying out things that work in other situations.

The child's choices about action are informed by others. These others can be thought of as helping the child to place his or her own actions in perspective relative to those in the rest of the nursery school class, his or her family, and/or other significant persons. By helping to define who the child is, the "generalized other," to borrow Mead's (1934) terminology, leads the child to take on a sense of appropriate action for him- or herself and to distinguish these actions from what is appropriate for others. An example of this occurred when one child saw another heading to play with the trains and exclaimed, "those are Ivan's." (As noted earlier, this nursery school class has two train sets, neither of which belonged to Ivan.) At least from the perspective of this child, Ivan had come to be identified with trains and in some sense they had become his. Interestingly enough, trains were an identified interest object for Ivan. He generally started his day playing with trains and returned to them at some point during the morning.

The unanswerable question, of course, is whether he was in fact choosing trains as his actions here or whether they were in fact chosen for him in some far more subtle set of interactions around who he was and what his patterns of actions (and sense of self) were within the group. The probable answer is that his play with trains was co-determined.

This is not to say that Ivan's actions are self-conscious. The child in free play is in the process of exploring and developing an understanding of possible action. At such, the child has knowledge about the immediate pursuit, but whether he or she is aware of a set of actions as specific responses to another is not clear. From study of children's patterns of actions, it seems that what the child comes to value in action is entwined with feelings of efficacy and, as a result, with a particular set of actions. Thus, a child for whom blocks were an identified interest stays with a goal of balancing a block on an angle (defying gravity) for as long as 35 minutes. (Two-and-a-half minutes is a long time for a three-year-old child to play with one play object continuously.) A friend, who, "was supposed to be helping to make a building," might walk away. Presumably, "building" did not involve challenge(s) with which the friend felt either competent or connected.

It seems that the individual child influences the extent to which another can have an impact on what actions the child will take. For the three-year-old child identified as having an interest in block play, it seems that his friend's boredom does not influence what he does. Although, across the videotaped play sessions this same child would frequently ask his friend to "come play." This request appears to have been interpreted by the friend to mean "come chat while I build" and on occasion he would join the child at block play. However, despite his attraction for his friend, the child for whom blocks were an identified interest did not shift his actions. Instead, he presumed that the other child would/should do so and he often did. It seems that for the three-year-old child the value of the self-directed challenge characteristic of interest is a primary determinant of action.

In a related situation, a mother who decided her daughter spent too much time in playdough play asked the teacher to encourage her daughter to do something else. The teacher gave the child some time in playdough play and then asked her what she would like to do next. The child chose pasting and block play—both of which have functional properties in common with playdough. (They both lead to social exchange and do not lead to transformational play, although, playdough and pasting are more likely to lead to reengagement in investigative play than are blocks.) Both pasting and blocks enabled the child to employ a similar pattern of actions to those on which she had focused in her playdough play. What the mother and teacher accomplished was a shift in the object of the child's play. It is not clear at all that there was any substantial shift in the child's actions.

Both of these instances suggest that the value a child has for particular actions while developed within a social milieu are not simply the result of interactions with others. Rather, it appears that as the child comes to value a pattern of actions and has increased practice with these, it is increasingly difficult for another to reorganize the child's actions. The knowledge/value system which evolves in conjunction with the kinds of actions in which the child engages might be said to be formed and tested in relation to others and to take on meaning in relation to others but, at least with respect to activity with identified objects of interest, it is not directed by others. Rather, the value of the identified object of interest to the child appears to influence the way in which the child as individual engages in activity whether this be with objects or others.

INDIVIDUAL INTEREST OBJECTS AND OTHERS

In order to further examine the role of value in the actions of the child, findings from a study of the structure of children's play actions are discussed (Renninger, 1987). This study involved two parts. First, children's play actions were studied as either identified objects of interest or noninterest for a child regardless of what the content of the identified object of interest or noninterest was. Thus, the first part of the study was an evaluation of play actions by differences in value. Following this, to evaluate the influence of others on the action patterns of children, the particular actions of the children within each of the samples under study were evaluated for differences between the types of actions employed with each of the play objects. Thus, the second part of the study was an evaluation of play actions by sample.

This study was designed to evaluate the kinds of actions in which children are engaged in play, the extent to which their actions with objects vary within and between objects, and the role of others in the classroom in determining what are potential actions with play objects both within and between classrooms. All of the play actions of each child were first studied so that it was possible to compare how each child played (in each identified type of play) with each of the available objects.[6] Then, by comparing the types of action patterns which characterized children drawn from one classroom with children drawn from the next, it was possible to evaluate the extent to which specific actions were peculiar to the classroom of these children and their particular patterns of play with that play object, rather than play with that play object given its functional properties. In other words, this study provided an opportunity to evaluate to what extent the tendency to, say, squeeze playdough between fingers is more common to play with playdough generally or to a particular group of children who play together each day more specifically.

Briefly, the sample for this study consisted of a total of 44 children (22M,

---

[6] There are 16 discrete play objects available in the classroom. These objects were "equally" available to all of the children throughout all of their free play periods.

22F) drawn from three groups of children. Sample 1 consisted of 16 children (8M, 8F). Sample 2 consisted of 12 children (6M, 6F). Sample 3 consisted of 16 children (8M, 8F). The children studied ranged in age between 2.9-and-4.2 years. Their mean age was 3.5 years.

The data for all groups of children were collected during free play in the same classroom with the same play objects during the second half of the children's school year under teachers sharing the same "whole-child" approach to education. Each child was individually videotaped for six 40-minute (Samples 1 & 2) or twelve 20 minute (Sample 3) sessions of naturally-occurring free play in the nursery school class. Backup observer notes were also collected by an observer stationed across the room from the camera.

In order to evaluate the role of objects and others in children's actions, two independent codings of the same videotapes of children in free play were employed. The first coding involved identification of children's objects of interest and noninterest because this distinction permitted evaluation of individual differences in value for particular play objects. The second coding involved study of the structure and variation of children's play actions within and between objects identified as interests and noninterests of the children. Evaluation of between group differences in children's actions with play objects permitted evaluation of the influence of others on play actions with particular play objects.

Identification of Children's Interests

Two interest objects and two noninterest objects were identified for each child. Operationally, children were identified as having an interest in a particular class of play objects if over the videotaped play sessions (a) they played with an object more frequently than they did with other objects, (b) they returned to play with that object over several observations, (c) they demonstrated an ability to play with the object using something besides manipulative play, *and* (d) they could play with the object by themselves. Children were identified as having a noninterest in a particular class of play objects if over the videotaped play sessions (a) they did spend time in these play areas, (b) they could use something other than manipulative play with the noninterest object, *and* (c) the children did not spend as much time as they did in the areas in which they were identified as having an interest, and/or (d) they did not play with the objects in solitary play.

Structure of Children's Play Actions

To study the influence of individual patterns of children's interest on their play actions with objects, a taxonomy of play actions was developed which made possible comparison of each child's play with their individually identified objects of interest and noninterest. Five types of play were first identified for each of the play objects available to the children. Then, for each of the videotaped sessions of each child's play, type of play and the specific actions within each type of play were continuously coded. All coding was conducted by a single rater who reviewed all of the data available on a given child before coding the structure and variation of that child's actions.

The five types of play selected for study include investigative, functional, operational, transformational, and facilitative play (Renninger, 1984). In investigative play, children's actions reflect exploration of the physical attributes of an object. Thus, in investigative train play a child might drop the train, push it sideways, or play with the coupler. In functional play, children continue to explore the properties of a class of objects, but the exploration reflects conventional use. In functional train play, a child might hook cars together, push the train (engine first), or load and unload the train. With functional play children demonstrate a culturally-consistent understanding of what is and is not a train.

In operational play, children's actions on objects are sometimes ones of exploration, but this exploration reflects preoccupation with relations such as counting, dividing, ordering, and so on. Superficially, children's play may appear to be either investigative or functional; however, continuous monitoring of the play often reveals repetition of sequencing, counting, dividing, adding, subtracting, balancing, or attention to regularities of motion. For example, in operational train play the child might connect and disconnect cars repeatedly, get down to eye level with the train, and pull it forward and backward while focusing on the wheels, or order the cars by size, color, and so on.

In transformational play, children's actions reflect the use of one object to represent another object. In transformational train play a child might make tickets out of paper, use a line of chairs to denote a train, or step out of a large rocking boat and announce, "We're at the train station, Bill." Train is the object of play even though there are no trains or model trains being used.

Finally, in facilitative play, the object supports children's actions in other play areas. In facilitative train play, the train might be carried to the easels and placed on a nearby window ledge. A child might paint and, when finished, pick up the train and move with it to another play area.

Particular actions within each type of play refer to what the child was doing. Thus one child's investigative play with trains might involve holding the engine upside down and spinning one wheel and then another wheel, whereas another child's investigative play with trains might include pushing a train with one car sideways, stopping the pushing motion, pushing again, and then reorganizing the way the train was connected so that the wheels would allow the train to be pushed more smoothly. All shifts in action were also coded so that it was possible to evaluate the sequence of the child's actions both between and within play objects. Thus, for example, "pushing the train" and "stopping the pushing motion" would count as two actions. An action sequence might include "pushing the train," "stopping the train," "pushing the train," "reorganizing the connections" and would be considered a repeated action sequence if it were employed by the child more than once.

For the evaluation of structure in children's play, all of the children's play types and actions were coded regardless of how long or short the duration of play with that object. This coding contrasts with that for identification of interests and noninterests in which the only play evaluated was that with objects which lasted 2.5 or more minutes. It further contrasts with the identification of objects of interest and noninterest in that it focuses on the process of children's engagement with each play object such that it is possible to compare the individual child's investigative (functional, etc.) play with one object with his/her investigative (functional, etc.) play with another object.

By comparing each child's types of play (and actions within types of play) with both his and her identified objects of interest and noninterest, it is possible to evaluate the influence of individual patterns of interest and noninterest, or value, on the structure of the children's play actions. Because interest previously had been found to influence the way in which the children process information (Renninger & Wozniak, 1985), it was expected that children might be able to represent more possibilities for action to themselves with their identified object of interest than with their identified object of noninterest.

Study of differences in the structure of each child's types of play (and actions within type of play) as a function of value—interest or noninterest[7]—reveal that (a) Children have a wider range of types of play available to them when playing with their identified objects of interests than when playing with objects identified as noninterests; (b) Children are more likely to play longer amounts of time repeating particular sequences of action with their identified object of interest than when they play with objects identified as noninterests; (c) Children's actions within play types are more likely to include more variations of action with their identified object of interest than with their identified objects of noninterest; (d) Children who shared the same identified object of interest did not necessarily share the same action sequences in play with identified object of interest; (e) Children in play with objects identified as noninterests are more likely to either repeat no prior action within play types, or only repeat prior actions with no incorporation of changes in action sequences. (See also, Renninger, in press.)

Findings from this study indicate that children may see more possibilities for action when playing with an identified object of interest. This explanation serves, in turn, to explain the increased variation in the types of play and repetition of particular action sequences in the children's play with identified objects of interest. These findings indicate that particular play objects appear to represent

---

[7] Although it might be argued on the basis of the method used to identify interests and noninterests that children should be employing more types of action with their identified objects of interest than with their identified objects of noninterest, coding of interest only specifies that the child's play must involve some other type of play beside manipulative play (investigative play). Clearly it would be inappropriate to compare length of time of play or frequency of occurence of play with play objects identified as interests and noninterests; however, it is possible to evaluate mean proportion of time played with identified objects of interests and noninterest by type of play and change in actions of play.

possibilities for action to children which are not found in the other play objects with which they engage. That the children continue to re-engage their identified objects of interest, to repeat particular patterns of action which incorporate systematic variations in these actions, and that these actions vary even when children share the same identified object of interest further suggests that children are responding not only to the challenges which the play object affords, but that they are setting challenges for themselves with these play objects which build on their prior actions.

The finding that children who shared the same identified object of interest did not necessarily share the same patterns of action within play types supports the contention that representations for actions are individual, the fact that there is overlap in what actions children employ also suggests that what the child represents to him- or herself is probably related to both the functional properties of the object and what others do with that play object. Repetition of particular patterns of action in play with identified objects of interest suggests that children are able to coordinate types of play in pursuit of a goal and even when a particular goal is "unrealistic" (e.g., defying gravity in the effort to balance a block on an angle) to stay on task and reorganize their goals as alternative possibilities for action are explored. That play lasts longer when the object is an identified object of interest suggests further that the child is more engaged in play, needs time to explore and employ actions, and may even be less distractable when playing with an identified object of interest than when playing with an identified object of noninterest.

Finally, the finding that children either do not repeat actions or only repeat the same actions with their identified objects of noninterest suggests that they are not representing as many possibilities for action to themselves with these objects and that they are not invested in the exploration which representation of more possibilities for action would entail.

Differences in individual patterns of action with play objects indicates that the value of the play object to the child influences what that child does with the play object. To further evaluate the influence of others on the action patterns of the children, differences between the samples employed in the study were evaluated. Findings from this component of the study reveal interesting differences in the specific content of actions characteristic of play with each object area between the samples studied.

For each of the play types coded in each of the play object areas in the nursery school class, there were actions characteristic of that play area generally, and there were also actions characteristic of that sample of children which did not appear in the play of the other samples of children. For example, in playdough play across the samples, it was common to find children flattening playdough with their stomachs and squeezing playdough between their fingers, but playdough was used as makeup in only one sample and was an identified action of several children in that sample. Similarly, house play in one sample involved family roles—mother, father, and children, and dress-ups in the "house corner;" in another sample it involved family roles, stuffed animals, no dress-ups, and the sand or art tables.

The design of the present study permitted evaluation of the child-object-other children relations both within and between the samples by controlling differences between the objects, the physical space, and teacher organization of the classroom in which the children were engaged. The findings suggest that while there is a set of actions afforded by play objects as a function of their specific functional properties, there is also a class of actions with these objects which appears to be associated with particular children in the class, with particular objects. In addition, the findings suggest that the child probably is not only in the position of setting challenges for him- or herself in play, but also is being challenged by others in the class to the extent that he or she is responsive to these challenges.

These data suggest that shared experience effects the repertoire of actions the child brings to subsequent activity. In particular, the specific others in the classroom in which a child develops his or her facility with play objects will influence and be influenced by that child. It seems plausible that who—and with what representations—is in the given play area as the child is engaging in setting and resolving challenges may make a substantial difference in whether the child assimilates a given action.

What contributes to reorganization of the child's action patterns with a play object appears to be something which is picked up by at least some group members and shared such that it becomes characteristic of the group. As such, classroom grouping becomes an important component of what is understood as possibility (and perhaps even a priority) for activity. Membership in a class appears to influence both the emergence of what potential actions are perceived and what may become understood as possibilities for action even when the object for which these new possibilities is an identified object of interest for the child. Given this kind of finding, it is probable that were a class of children to take on a particular action, this would act to facilitate reorganization of action patterns in a way that neither another child, nor the teacher could. In a similar vein, it seems reasonable to suggest that the content of new interests as well as the kind of challenge setting in which children engage are also influenced both by the functional properties of the objects available to the child and the identified interest object as well as the action patterns of the others in the class.

INDIVIDUAL INTEREST OBJECTS AND INTERACTION

In order to evaluate the role of objects and others in interaction more specifically, a study of child-child-object interaction was undertaken (Renninger & Morgan, 1986). This study was designed to evaluate the interaction of naturally occurring dyads of nursery school children around play objects as a joint function of both the children and their shared activity. After identifying all reciprocal dyadic exchanges around play objects, the presence of interest in the object of play and the level of affiliation of each member of the dyad for the other member of the dyad was determined.

For the purposes of this study, interaction was defined as involving at least three relational exchanges (verbal and/or nonverbal) between two children around a class of objects or events. In contrast to the rather fleeting give and take which often characterizes the play of three-year-old children, the present study focused on more sustained interactions among these children.

Take, for example, two children named Billy and David who have been in the same nursery school class for six months. They are familiar both with each other and with the play objects available in the nursery school. During free play,

> Billy is playing with one horse figure; another stands to the side of where he sits. David walks across the room to where Billy is playing. Billy says to David, ''Let's play with two little horses.'' David sits down and touches one. Billy says, ''No, I'm using that one,'' but he lets David take it. Billy begins to gallop his horse around a small area and David follows with his horse. David turns around and says something to Billy. Billy goes back and gets other horses. He returns and repeats, ''Put your horsie there. Put your horsie there. Put your horsie there.'' David keeps moving across the floor. Billy clenches his fists and jumps up and down. He wants the horse ''back here.'' (Billy M. III, Tape 6)

In this example, Billy and David are playing with the horses. This excerpt is a portion of an even longer interaction between Billy and David around the horses. Their play is considered an interaction because it involves *at least* 3 relational exchanges (the action shifts from one child to the next and is used to structure subsequent action). In this example, the first three relational exchanges include shifting of action from David approaching Billy, to Billy suggesting that he and David play horsie, and back to David reaching over and touching one of the horses. However, it is not clear (a) whether Billy and David usually play together or whether this was an isolated instance of play, (b) whether either Billy or David, or both Billy and David are interested in horses—in other words, do they return to play with horses frequently? Do they play more competently with horses than with other play objects? Will they play with horses by themselves? And, (c) what the specific verbal and nonverbal actions which take place in this interaction are and how Billy in particular gets away with some of them—is Billy directing the action? If so, how is he able to do this?

This study was designed to address the interrelation of these questions—questions which address the role of the other, the object, and specific behaviors in interaction among three-year-old children. The sample for this study consisted of 16 children (8M-4 older, 4 younger, 8F-4 older, 4 younger) in the same nursery school class.[8] Each child was individually videotaped during six 40-minute sessions of naturally occurring free play, during the second term of the school year. Thus all children were familiar with both the other children in the class and with the play objects available to them.

Evaluation of the effect of both interest and affiliation on interactions among children required three independent codings of the same set of videotapes of children in free play. The first type of coding identified all instances of relational exchanges between dyads and assessment of these interactions as synchronous or asynchronous. The second type of coding identified the individual interests of children. The third type of coding evaluated the relative frequency of affiliative behaviors among children.

Identification of Interactions and Rating of Synchrony/Asynchrony

All dyadic exchanges between the focal child and other children around an object on each of the videotapes of the children in free play were first identified. Interactions were identified as those exchanges which had a minimum of three relational exchanges.

Following this, rating of synchrony or asynchrony of the identified interaction was determined using categories of behavior which were empirically derived from pilot data through both observation and available literature (e.g. Wertsch, McNamee, McLane, & Budwig, 1980). These categories are presented as independently identifiable categories which, in combination, are employed to identify the interaction of dyads as synchronous or asynchronous. Categories of behaviors include directing, following, and rejecting. Briefly, *directing behaviors* include those behaviors in which one child verbally or nonverbally gives instruction to the other child (e.g., Billy initiated galloping the horse); *following behaviors* include those behaviors in which one child verbally or nonverbally supports the emerging organization of the play (e.g., David then galloped his horse); and *rejecting behaviors* include those behaviors in which one child verbally or nonverbally alters the prior organization of the play (e.g., David kept moving his horse across the floor even though Billy had told him to "put it there").

The interaction of a dyad was rated synchronous if neither child had significantly more directing, following, or rejecting behaviors than the other. The interaction of a dyad was rated asynchronous if one child had significantly more directing *and* rejecting behaviors than the other, or if one child had significantly more directing behaviors than the other and there were no rejecting behaviors by the other child.

Thus, Billy and David's interaction was identified as asynchronous because

---

[8] The sample studied in this research was the same as Sample 1 from the previously reported study. All raters for each study were unaware of either the coding employed or the findings of the other study.

Billy had significantly more directing and rejecting behaviors than did David—Billy told David not to play with one horse and let him play with the other; Billy repeatedly demanded that David not put his horsie in one place; and later in the interaction (not transcribed here), the teacher intervened because Billy scooped up all of the horses and refused to let David play with any of them.

Identification of Interests

The play objects of interest to each child were identified based upon that child's play behaviors across the six video tapes for which that child was the focal child. As in the previously described research, objects were identified as interests of a child if (a) the child returns to that object repeatedly, (b) the child spends more time playing with that object than with other play objects, (c) the child at times plays with that object in solitary play, *and* (d) the child at times plays in other than manipulative play with that object. In this study, the identified object of interest for one child acted as a control for the identified object of interest of the next child. In this way it was possible to compare children's interactions around objects identified as being of interest for one or both of the children with interactions around objects which were not identified as being of interest to either of the children.

Horses were an identified interest for Billy—Billy returned to play with horses more frequently than he played with other available play objects; he spent more time playing with horses than he did with other play objects; he would play with horses by himself; and in his play, horses were galloped, grazed, and needed to travel in horse trailers. In the example of Billy and David, the object—the horse(s)—was an identified interest for Billy, but it was not an identified interest for David. Therefore, their interaction was classified as an interaction around an identified interest for only one child.

Identification of Affiliative Behaviors

The children's ongoing patterns of affiliation were determined by coding the signal behaviors of one child to another child across all of the videotapes of the children in free play. Signal behaviors include each child's (a) approach to another child, (b) nonverbal gestures to another child (pointing, waving, smiling, etc.), (c) physical contact with another child, and (d) talking to another child (Blicharski & Strayer, 1985). Then, frequencies of signal behaviors for each child with every other child across all of the videotapes was determined. Finally, interactions identified as being reciprocal were rated as high, low, or unidirectional in amount of affiliation on the basis of both the proportion of each child's signal behaviors toward every other child in the class *and* the proportion of their signal behaviors to the other member of the dyad in relation to the proportion of that child's signal behaviors to him or her.

Thus, interactions rated as high in affiliation involved children who were matched in the relatively high number of signals to each other compared to signals for every other child in the class when signal behaviors were identified using the videotapes in which they were the focal child. Similarly, interactions rated low in affiliation were those in which the children were matched in the relatively low number of signals they had for each other across the videotapes, and interactions rated unidirectional in affiliation were those in which one child had more signals for the other child relative to the number of their signal behaviors for every other child in the class. On the basis of each child's number of signal behaviors relative to the other child in a given dyad; each dyad then was classified as being either high, low, or unidirectional in affiliation.

Billy and David's interaction, for example, was rated as unidirectional in level of affiliation because Billy had higher levels of signal behaviors with other children relative to those with David, but David had high levels of signal behaviors with Billy relative to his signal behaviors with other children in the nursery school class.

It should be stressed that coding of affiliation was carried out across all of the videotapes (almost all of the free play during the entire second term of the second year) and was assessed relative to ongoing classroom behaviors. Thus, although Billy in the portion of the interaction transcribed, and as initiator and director of the interaction may seem to have more signals to David than David does to him, this finding is not based on all of the available data on Billy and David in free play. It should also be noted that since coding for affiliation was conducted using a combined scan and sequence sampling procedure, the coding scheme for assessing levels of affiliation among dyad members was not the same as that for coding back-to-back shifts of relational exchanges identified as interactions.

Across 72 hours of videotaped free play, a total of 53 sustained interactions were identified, involving 26 dyads of children. (All children in the study participated in at least one dyad pair. Only six dyad pairs had more than one interaction. One dyad pair had 11 interactions.) Findings reveal that (a) older children are more likely to engage in sustained interactions and to have more than one sustained interaction in the same dyad pair than are younger children; (b) children are more likely to engage one another in sustained interaction if they have high affiliation for each other; (c) children are more likely to engage in asynchronous than synchronous sustained interactions; (d) synchronous sustained interactions tend to last longer than asynchronous sustained interactions; (e) asynchronous sustained interactions occur most frequently around a play object identified as an interest of one child, but not the other child; (f) in asynchronous sustained interactions, children for whom the play object is an interest are more likely to initially direct action, direct actions throughout the interaction, and use nonverbal rather than verbal directives; (g) the sustained interactions of dyad pairs which had more than one sustained interaction with each other were equally likely to be identified as being synchronous as asynchronous.

These findings suggest that sustained interactions of the type studied in this research are not common among children at three-years-of age, at least in the nursery school under study. In fact, the findings indicate that when these children have interactions they usually do so with different children. While it could be argued that the inconsistent pairing of dyads indicates an inability to discriminate between peers and proof of random behavior in sustained interaction, better support exists for a thesis that both the other and the play object are important to the development of children's understanding of interactions. Furthermore, once children have participated in an interaction, they have their value for the behaviors in that interaction, in addition to their value for both the other and the play object as a basis upon which to engage in another interaction. Thus movement from a sustained interaction in one dyad to sustained interaction in another dyad may actually provide the basis of very systematic engagement in future sustained interactions and an emerging understanding of social process.

In this study, dyads of children rated as high in affiliation were more likely to engage in interaction than were dyads rated as either low or unidirectional in affiliation. This indicates that these children have some prior knowledge (even if this is not a reflective knowledge) of who the other is in their interactions and what their own affiliative patterns with others have been. That most dyads did not engage in more than one interaction suggests that the children may well be exploring the process of sustained interaction, much as they explore play objects. In fact, the finding that older dyad pairs had more sustained interactions and engaged in more than one sustained interaction further supports this interpretation. That these sustained interactions were as likely to be synchronous as asynchronous further suggests that factors beside mere practice with interacting influence the distribution of directing, following, and rejecting behaviors within a sustained interaction.

The specific relation between the other, the play object, and behaviors in interaction is not clear and probably varies from dyad to dyad as a function of individual differences in value for the other and the object. It may be that children's sustained interactions are at least to some extent products of attractions to objects of interest of other children and that this attraction guided them toward interactions around particular objects. By definition, children do spend more time playing with their interest objects than with other available play objects. Given that these children also have a greater repetoire of actions available to them in play with their interest objects, they presumably care more about how to play with them than do children for whom the object(s) is not of interest.

There is a clear influence of interest on behaviors in sustained interaction. In particular, in asynchronous sustained interactions, children for whom the object is an interest both initiate the action and use more directing behaviors than other children. Billy, for example, wanted to decide where the horses were going to gallop. His repeated directive, clenched fists, and jumping up and down indicated that he really wanted his plan to be followed. Whether he could have articulated it or not, David's willingness to allow Billy to direct the actions suggests both that he knew that Billy had an interest in horses and that Billy would have specific ideas about how horse play should "go."

As a complement to David's understanding about Billy's feelings for horses, Billy acknowledged David's walking across the room towards him by inviting David to play. He probably knew that he played with horses more than David did and that David preferred boats. But there was something about sharing play with the horses that was more attractive to him than continuing to play by himself. It is not simply the object of interest which is being valued here. It appears to be an interest in the other, perhaps in relation to an attraction to horses, which is important to the organization of the children's interactions.

The horse was Billy's turf. Billy and David together negotiated an interaction which was informed by this fact. Billy's overt dismay at David's inattention to his wishes had to challenge both David and Billy's understanding of what they each could do. Presumably Billy thought that play with David and the horses meant doing things his way. David, on the other hand, appears to have assumed that there was a license to expand on Billy's directions. This impass stopped the interaction later on when Billy scooped up all of the horses.

It is not surprising that asynchronous sustained interactions such as Billy and David's are shorter than synchronous sustained interactions. If a child joined another child because of the opportunity to play with a play object and/or the opportunity to play with the other child *and* this child monopolized what went on in the interaction, then the original goal in joining that child was not met. However, it is interesting that the child for whom the object is not an identified interest stays with the exchange long enough for it to be identified as an interaction. The object must have some value to the child. In addition, the object-other relationship may be important as well.

When children perceive that their play is not what they had hoped it would be, their understanding of sustained interaction is challenged. They then must make a choice based on their value for the object and the other about whether to continue the exchange. Since dyads which had more than one interaction revealed similar amounts of synchronous and asynchronous interactions, and prior knowledge of other, object, and sustained interaction are known to the child, then asynchronous sustained interactions must be either comfortable for or at least expected by these children. Thus, others, objects, as well as behaviors in prior interactions appear to inform children's movement from interaction in one dyad to repeated interaction in that dyad. They also may inform children's movement from an interaction in one dyad to interaction in another dyad.

CONCLUSIONS

The preceeding discussion of children's play actions suggests that the content of individual representations of objects varies. In particular, what children represent to themselves as possibilities for action with objects and/or others appears to vary between children as a function of individual differences in their interests, or their stored knowledge and value.

It might be expected that children with the same identified object of interest would be employing similar actions and involved in the same kinds of challenge-setting in their actions, since the functional properties of each object more commonly leads to some, rather than other actions. This expectation is accurate. There is a consistency to the kinds of actions one sees when children are playing with each play object. However, in addition to those actions which are common to play with an object, children also incorporate actions into their play with objects which vary from that which might be considered typical.

The actions a child undertakes in play are presumed to be based upon what the child has previously explored and what the child understands to be possibilities for action with that object. The sequence or pattern in which children employ actions is thought to be influenced by prior interest, the functional properties of the object, and the others with whom the child is involved. In short, the child has a lot of available information about possibilities for action. However, differences in how children engage play objects suggests that they are more focused on some of these possibilities than they are on others.

Findings from the studies reported here indicate that a substantial amount of variance is introduced into the actions and the interactions of children by individual differences in their identified object(s) of interest. Specifically, interest influences the way in which children of approximately the same age and same amount of familiarity engage with play objects, as well as their actions in sustained interactions around play objects.

Such findings suggest that the child's value for an object influences what he or she understands to be possible with that play object since it influences to what the child attends and how he or she represents the play object's possibilities to him- or herself. Presumably, the value that such understanding holds for the child is linked to prior engagements with that object and leads to repetition and elaboration of these experiences in subsequent activity. This value also serves to both focus and limit the child's actions since the child in selecting one set of actions, or attending to one kind of challenge, is by definition eliminating several others.

The fact that children's play appears to be more fully developed with respect to identified objects of interest than with identified objects of noninterest attests to the impact of both stored knowledge and value on patterns of action. In particular, children seem to be selecting with what object and with which others they will play based on individual interests. They are also engaging with both objects and others differently as a function of individual interests.

Consider again the examples of the children patting playdough on their faces as makeup and the child driving the train, caboose first. Not all of the children in the sample used playdough as makeup. The influence of others on the particular content of action suggests that social exchange (whether this is an actual discussion or whether the child copies the behaviors of another child at the playdough table) can, but does not necessarily, lead to particular action patterns with a play object. One might ask what would have happened if another child had been first to employ this action. Similarly, what would have happened if another child had driven the train by its caboose? This action could have been understood as a great joke.

It appears that who does what (and probably when) forms the basis of children's emerging understanding. Controlling for differences between children in the content of their representations appears to be a useful first step for detailing the process of children's understanding generally and the implications of individual patterns in children's play interests more specifically. Clearly, longitudinal study of interests and friendship is needed to determine what individual profiles of understanding include, how individual understanding varies from that of the group as a whole, and how understanding of possibilities with both interest objects (and interesting others) and noninterest objects (noninteresting others) develops.

REFERENCES

Berlyne, D.E. (1960). *Conflict, arousal, and curiosity*. New York: McGraw-Hill.

Blicharski, T., & Strayer, F.F. (1985). Procedures and taxonomy for observation of preschool social ecology. Unpublished coding manual.

Claparede, E. (1951). *Le developpement mental*. Neuchatel: Delachaux et Niestle.

Feurstein, R. (1980). *Instrumental enrichment: An intervention program for cognitive modifiability*. Baltimore, MD: University Park Press.

Gibson, J.J. (1979). *The ecological approach to visual perception*. Boston: Houghton Mifflin.

Hartup, W.W. (1983). Peer relations. In E. Mavis Hetherington (Volume Ed.), *Socialization, personality, and social development*. In Paul H. Mussen (Ed.), *Handbook of child psychology*, Vol. 4, New York: John Wiley & Sons.

Hidi, S., & Baird, W. (1986). Interestingness—A neglected variable in discourse processing. *Cognitive Science, 10*, 179–194.

Hunt, J.M. (1961). *Intelligence and experience*. New York: Ronald Press.

Karmiloff-Smith, A. (1979). Problem-solving procedures in children's construction and representations of closed railway circuits. *Archives de Psychologie, XLVII*, 180, 37–61.

Krapp, A., & Fink, B. (1986, October). *The transition from family to kindergarten and its impact on person-object-relationships*. Paper presented at the meeting of the International Association for the Study of People and their Physical Surroundings, Haifa, Israel.

Mead, G.H. (1934). *Mind, self, and society from the standpoint of a social behaviorist*. Chicago: University Press.

Piaget, J. (1968). *Six psychological studies*. New York: Vintage Books.

Renninger, K.A. (1984). Object-child relations: Implications for both learning and teaching. *Children's Environments Quarterly, I*(2), 3–6.

Renninger, K.A. (1987, April). *Child-environment interaction: Play interests and sociability*. Paper presented at the meeting of the Society for Research in Child Development, Baltimore, MD.

Renninger, K.A. (in press). Children's play interests, representation, and activity. In R. Fivush & J. Hudson (Eds.) *What young children remember and why. Emory Cognition Series, Vol. III.* New York, NY: Cambridge University Press.

Renninger, K.A., & Klock, B.L. (1986, April). *Effect of individual patterns of interest on transformational play of young children*. Paper presented at the International Conference on Infancy Studies, Beverly Hills, CA.

Renninger, K.A., & Morgan, A.S. (1986, May). *Other and play object as value in social understanding*. Paper presented to the Jean Piaget Society, Philadelphia, PA.

Renninger, K.A., & Sigel, I.E. (1986, April). *Effect of functional properties of play interests on the cognitive organization of young children*. Paper presented to the Conference on Human Development, Nashville, TN.

Renninger, K.A., & Wozniak, R.H. (1985). Effect of interests on attentional shift, recognition, and recall in young children. *Developmental Psychology, 21*, 624–632.

Rogoff, B., & Gardner, W.P. (1984). Adult guidance of cognitive development. In B. Rogoff & J. Lave (Eds.), *Everyday cognition: Its development in social context* (pp. 95–116). Cambridge, MA: Harvard University Press.

Schank, R.C. (1979). Interestingness: Controlling inferences. *Artificial Intelligence, 12*, 273–297.

Schiefele, H. (1986). Interest: New answers to an old problem. *Zeitschrift fur Padagogik, 32* (2), 153–162.

Sigel, I.E. (1982). The relationship between parents' distancing strategies and the child's cognitive behavior. In L.M. Laosa & I.E. Sigel (Eds.), *Families as learning environments for children* (pp. 47–86). New York: Plenum.

Vygotsky, L. (1967). Play and its role in the mental development of the child. *Soviet Psychology, 3*(2), 62–76.

Werner, H. (1978). Process and achievement: A basic problem of education and developmental psychology. In S.S. Barten & M.B. Franklin (Eds.), *Developmental processes: Heinz Werner's selected writings, Vol. I: General theory and perceptual experience* (pp. 23–40). New York: International Universities Press, Inc. (Originally published in 1937)

Wertsch, J.V., McNamee, G.D., McLane, J.B., & Budwig, N. (1980). The adult-child dyad as a problem-solving system. *Child Development, 51*, 1215–1221.

White, R. (1959). Motivation reconsidered: The concept of competence. *Psychological Review, 66*, 297–333.

CHAPTER 8

Socially-Shared Cognition: The Role of Social Context in the Construction of Knowledge*

Celia A. Brownell

As the preceding chapters have made clear, in recent years a new emphasis in developmental psychology has emerged. This view regards it as necessary to consider the role of the child's social context in describing and explaining her development, including her cognitive development. One of the strongest forms of the argument seems to go something like this: Cognition never occurs in a social vacuum. It always takes place in some social/affective context. Although the learner, problem solver, thinker may at any given moment be solitarily involved with the nonsocial world, what she brings to bear on her interactions with the world at that moment is directly affected by the knowledge, biases, affect, problem-solving style, and so forth that she has acquired during socially supported activity. Knowledge is culturally constructed and constrained. Complementarily, one can argue that when two or more knowledge systems interact, they are certain to alter one another's knowledge. Hence, in any social interaction knowledge is acquired, whether it is knowledge about self, about other, about the physical world, about nonpresent events, or about knowledge itself. And that knowledge is inevitably and continuously co-constructed, just because it is knowledge simultaneously agreed upon by interacting individuals. Further, for individual cognitive systems to interact with one another in the first place requires at least some initial component of shared, socially-founded knowledge. This implies that cognition itself is fundamentally social; that knowledge—of all

---

* The term "socially shared cognition" was borrowed from a faculty/student seminar by the same name, organized by Lauren Resnick and John Levine at the University of Pittsburgh in 1987–1988. This group explored multiple literatures concerning reciprocal relations between cognition and social interaction, and many of the citations in the present chapter are a product of that productive and stimulating discourse.

kinds, social as well as nonsocial—is "co-constructed," is socially shared, is a form of social agreement. One possible broader implication is that knowledge cannot be considered general over individuals or over contexts. Rather, knowledge and its acquisition and use are intimately tied up with quite specific contexts—those social situations, interactions, and individuals that have given rise to and support the knowledge.

The chapters in this volume have taken up different positions on this general argument and have raised different issues regarding the fundamental role of the child's social context in understanding development. Questions addressed both implicitly and explicitly by these writers include those about the universality of cognitive processing and mechanisms of acquisition, and the independence of cognition from the individual's interpersonal, socioemotional context. How much of what is learned during childhood, and how much of the knowledge acquisition process itself is a function of the learner's social context? Do the relations between knowledge acquisition and context change with age, becoming more, or less, interdependent? What are the implications of such questions for the actual study of the child's construction of his world?

In addition to motivating the chapters in this volume, these sorts of questions have also motivated a fair amount of scholarly activity in a variety of otherwise somewhat independent domains of thinking, including anthropology, sociology, education, and social psychology, as well as cognitive and developmental psychology. Further, although variations on these questions are especially timely right now, they have been asked quite cogently in one form or another by psychologists throughout the century. One purpose of this concluding chapter is to provide some perspective for thinking about the preceding chapters, in a broad and somewhat cursory review of related scholarly activity. A second aim is to identify the strands of agreement among the quite different arguments, methodologies, and empirical reports represented in this volume. In so doing, points of disagreement will also emerge, as will a set of issues yet to be resolved. The discussion will not dwell on criticism, though questions deserving further inquiry will be noted. Nor will shortcomings in methodology or design be emphasized. Rather the focus will be to identify and discuss the higher order themes that emerge from the chapters taken both individually and as a whole. The initial part of the discussion will provide some larger perspective, setting the stage for the second part which will focus on the individual chapters.

SETTING THE STAGE

The common thread running through the various chapters in this volume has been that different social contexts provide different inputs to the child's construction of social knowledge. On the face of it, that perspective appears straightforward, perhaps even so obvious as to be trivial. But with only a few exceptions this theme has not been directly recognized in most research on the development of understanding. Research in conceptual development has instead typically focused on the description and explanation of age-related universals in acquisition, universals across contexts, independent of context. Few have considered potential context-specific contributions to the child's construction of knowledge. In a related vein, whereas most researchers in cognitive development assume that the child actively constructs knowledge, and they look for age differences in children's ability to use varying cues or sources of information in building knowledge, making inferences or solving problems, only a handful of investigators has considered how a child's perception or interpretation of different social contexts might contribute to the construction of knowledge. The present chapters have brought together investigators whose research and thinking has placed in the foreground the roles that context might play in the child's conceptual development.

Impetus for the study of context in development has come from diverse sources, a few of which will be briefly noted. Perhaps one of the most far-reaching changes in experimental child psychology over the last decade or so has been the move out of the laboratory. This shift has not been unique to developmental psychology; both social psychology and cognitive psychology also have strong and productive lines of research conducted in the everyday environment. There have been multiple reasons for this shift. Some have come from the recognition, empirically, that we obtain an underestimate or a misestimate of basic competencies in the laboratory. For example, researchers in infant development have been struck many times over by the finding that laboratory-based data often do not completely mirror the infant's everyday functioning. This has included developments in memory (Ashmead & Perlmutter, 1980), object search (DeLoache, 1984), motor skills, (Lockman, 1988), social interaction (Kaye, 1982), event knowledge (Nelson, 1981), and so forth. Rogoff, et al. (1984) have effectively argued, in fact, that the laboratory is itself a context affecting our observations of development, rather than being context-free as it traditionally has been viewed. Other influences on the shift to naturalistic research have been more theoretically grounded. For example, ethologists have contended that the detection of both proximal and distal causal mechanisms must begin first in the animal's natural environment (Hinde, 1974; Tinbergen, 1963).

Regardless of the source of influence, however, it has now become quite clear that the laboratory is but one context in which to observe behavior and development (Rogoff et al., 1984). And it can be argued that it is due in part to our relocation of a portion of our research efforts into the real world that we have come to see that our explanations must consider context. The natural environment is not a simple, single, unitary context. It is constituted of multiple, interdependent contexts, any of which can have important, systematic influences on multiple aspects of development.

That point has probably been made most clearly by Bronfenbrenner and

Crouter (1983) and Sameroff (1983) in their complex models of the environment as it exists on several intertwined and interdependent levels. The child's development is conceived of as embedded in a variety of mutually interacting social systems. Social interactions function within families; families constitute multiple, different contexts for development; these, in turn, are embedded within multiple varieties of social institutions; these are themselves embedded in still higher order contexts such as culture. And each of these separate but interdigitated systems is involved in multiple feedback networks with each of the others.

Of course, major social systems are not the only dimensions along which one can categorize contextual influences in development. Existing research has shown that various aspects of the situation affect children's performance and, by implication, their development. Perhaps most convincingly in cognitive development we've been shown by many investigators now that task-specific demands can alter our views of the child's apparent competence. These include memory demands, attention demands, knowledge-base demands, verbal facility demands, demands made by the unfamiliarity of the materials or the setting, and so on (e.g., Gelman & Baillargeon, 1983).

We also know that various aspects of the immediate social context contribute to performance and development. Vygotsky's theory, and research inspired by it, has shown that much of the child's activity in the world is embedded in a variety of social interactional contexts (Wertsch, 1985). Social partners variously "scaffold" the child's acquisition of knowledge in the "zone of proximal development." And this scaffolding often contributes differentially to the child's mastery. Other Soviet psychologists have held similar positions—that the meaningfulness to the child of the task context is an essential contributor to much of cognitive performance, and that cognitive development occurs in contexts that are meaningful to the child (cf., Brown, 1975).

It has become evident within social development that the relationships that are often studied as outcomes (friendships, peer groups, parent-child relationships) are themselves contexts for development (Hinde, Perret-Clermont, & Stevenson-Hinde, 1985). Piaget proposed a central role for peer relationships in certain aspects of cognitive development (cf., Musatti, 1986). Damon (1981, 1987) has gone further to show that different types of peer relations contribute differently to different aspects of social–cognitive understanding. A few years ago, Hartup (1980) described the different roles played by peers and parents in the development of various aspects of social competence. More recently, he has proposed that close, socially and emotionally important relationships serve as contexts for the development of cognitive regulatory functions such as planning, task involvement, and monitoring (Hartup, 1985). These relationships are marked by more effective, finely tuned dialogues supportive of cognitive development than are other kinds of interactions. Hence, different types of relationships as well as different qualities of relationships may differentially influence the development of a variety of conceptual competencies. Of course, the dynamics of these relationships themselves vary over contexts, whether the context is as general as the culture (Whiting, 1986), or as specific as situations which promote self-interest vs. equality among friends (Berndt, 1986). Hence, the complexity of the problem of defining context begins to become evident. Contexts exist at multiple levels simultaneously.

The focus heretofore has been on fairly recent conceptualizations of context in development, but it must be acknowledged that this interest has its genesis in earlier eras. Thinkers including Mead, Piaget, and Vygotsky began publishing their proposals for the interdependence of cognition and social settings in the early part of the century. And over three decades ago researchers such as Lewin (1954), Barker & Wright (1955), and Sears (1951), called for a consideration of social context in theories of development, and in fact began to incorporate such considerations into their empirical research as well as in their explanatory systems.

Although this discussion, and the chapters in this volume, emphasize developmental psychology, recognition of the importance of context in the construction of knowledge is not unique to developmental psychology. Both social psychologists and cultural anthropologists have begun in recent years to study the social distribution or sharing of knowledge in groups and cultures, as well as the functions of such shared knowledge and the mechanisms of its distribution. Culture is described as a growing pool of socially learned information, supplemented and transmitted from generation to generation. This information includes fundamental concepts about the world and its organization, down to what objects are and how they are to be interpreted (D'Andrade, 1981). Further, this "culturally constituted reality" also includes "behavioral environments," which we, as psychologists, typically study as the contexts of development (Whiting, 1986, makes a similar distinction). What is especially interesting about this perspective is the proposal that an immense pool of information is shared among members of human society, and must be actively managed by its members. "There is a major division of labor in who knows what, (which) entails remarkable engineering problems. How can things be arranged so that all this information gets learned again and again without serious loss or distortion? How could one know if the information were lost? How can procedures be established so that the person who has the appropriate information is there when needed? (D'Andrade, 1981). These questions are nearly identical to those raised by Minsky (1986) in his recent speculations about "the society of mind." That is, the same engineering problems of information distribution, access, and transfer are characteristic of the individual mind. Thus, culture, or human society more broadly, may be the ideal metaphor for the individual mind.

In responding to the engineering problems he raised, D'Andrade notes that cultural knowledge is transmitted by a process of "guided discovery" and that people appear to be much better at learning through this process than on their own. "This curious combination of self-initiated yet other-dependent learning

. . . appears to yield properties of both flexibility and sharedness.'' So new knowledge can be selectively added to the cultural pool, but knowledge remains shared insofar as people need others for learning through guided discovery. Hence, D'Andrade makes an insightful and provocative case for cognition being fundamentally socially shared, and necessarily (from the learner's perspective) socially acquired. Other anthropologists have begun to explore empirically the nature of collective knowledge and how it is acquired and used by individuals to govern everyday behavior (Boster, 1986, 1987; Hutchins, cited in Resnick, 1987; Mathews, 1987).

An independent literature in social psychology makes points remarkably similar to those of the cultural anthropologists. This literature is derived from traditional research in group processes, but has broken the boundaries of tradition to resurrect the notion of a "group mind." Here the goal is to be able to predict both individual and group behavior from knowing how groups organize and process information. The catchy neologism coined for the mechanism by which individuals in groups share information is "transactive memory" (Wegner, Guiliano, & Hertel, 1987; Wegner, 1987). Transactive memory is based on communication among individual memories, where "other people can be locations of external storage for the individual . . . This allows people to depend on each other for the enhancement of their personal memory stores. At the same time, however, this interdependence produces a knowledge-holding system that is larger and more complex than either of the individuals' own memory systems.'' Wegner argues further that transactive memory cannot belong to an individual, rather it is a property of the group. It therefore influences not only what the group as a whole can remember, but also what individuals can remember as participants in the group. Thus transactive memory is constructed within groups by individuals in concert, and as a group process it also affects the knowledge of individual group members. For example, within couples each member typically takes responsibility for different aspects or kinds of information. In a memory task, couple members who believed their partner was not expert on a topic took greater responsibility for remembering information about that topic. The individual's memory was transactively constrained by knowledge about the social partner's memory ability. Although this new trend in social psychology is not as conceptually detailed or as empirically advanced as the corresponding perspective in anthropology, the parallels are clear. In both instances it makes a great deal of sense to consider cognition as fundamentally socially shared.

If knowledge is socially shared, one question is just how general it is beyond the immediate social context. Some anthropologists, sociologists, and others have gone quite far to contend that knowledge is, in fact, uniquely situated within specific, quite constrained social groups (e.g., Gergen, 1986; Lave, in preparation). The argument is that mental activity is a function of situation-specific supports and demands, and cannot be described in terms of context-free strategies, algorithms, or knowledge. And these situations are socially embedded, socially defined, socially valued. Others have made similar arguments— "that human problem solving procedures are highly local and content specific, rather than global and formal" (D'Andrade, 1981); "that cognitive development is characterized by the mastery of context-specific knowledge about the world" (Laboratory of Comparative Human Cognition [LCHC], 1983). There are any number of empirical demonstrations of the lack of transfer of strategies and other general principles of knowing or problem solving across even quite similar contexts (see LCHC, 1983; Resnick, 1987, for reviews). There are also several convincing empirical reports of detailed and expert use of complex problem-solving strategies in specific, socially and culturally defined contexts. Scribner's (1984) analyses of the situation specificity of complex problem-solving algorithms used in blue-collar jobs such as loading and inventory-taking in a dairy are exemplary. We are unavoidably directed by these kinds of data to consider in much greater detail the nature and organization of the social and practical settings which structure cognitive change.

Finally, educators, instructional psychologists, and cognitive psychologists as well as developmental psychologists have begun to capitalize on notions inspired by Vygotsky such as the zone of proximal development and scaffolding. A number of researchers have shown clear effects of group problem solving with either peer or adult-child interactions, and have begun to detail some of the processes entailed (Azmitia & Perlmutter, 1987; Doise & Mugny, 1979; Perret-Clermont, A., 1980; Resnick, 1987; Saxe, Guberman, Gearhart, 1987; Wertsch, McNamee, McLane, Budwig, 1980). These researchers typically contrast the traditional view of the child as a self-directed learner with a perspective that emphasizes the social origins of cognitive change. They posit social processes such as internalization as the mechanism of change. This work has begun to make some real progress in identifying the range of processes that mediate the effectiveness of group learning over solitary learning. Among peers these include the sharing of expertise, externalization of basic epistemic activities, sharing of responsibility for thinking, distribution of the cognitive load among several individuals, airing alternative points of view or alternative solution strategies (and other forms of conflict that can lead to cognitive restructuring), and co-construction of new solutions which take into account differences as well as similarities among the participants (Brown & Palincsar, in press).

THE INDIVIDUAL CHAPTERS

What should be evident at this point is that there is widespread scholarly interest in the relations between cognition and the social setting. Many scientists from a variety of disciplines have become increasingly convinced that the study and explanation of cognition requires explicit consideration of the social context in which knowledge is acquired and used. Correspondingly, there are probably equally as many, and widely diverse, conceptualizations regarding the nature of the relations between cognition and social context. Finally, the empirical work that has generated this perspective, or that has derived from it, is still in its early stages. Hence it is largely illustrative in nature. That is, we know little about the processes governing socially embedded cognition simply because most scientists are still at the stage of demonstrating its existence or relevance.

In this context, then, let's turn to consider what the chapters in the present volume bring, individually and collectively, to this emerging perspective. The discussion of the individual chapters is organized thematically, rather than according to their order of appearance in the volume. Several possible organizations suggest themselves. One is to compare the group of chapters that consider parent-child or adult-child relations as contexts for development (Valsiner (Chapter 1); Strayer, Moss & Blicharski (Chapter 2); Winegar (Chapter 3); Packer & Mergendoller (Chapter 4)) with those that focus on the contributions of peer interactions to conceptual development (Killen (Chapter 6); Renninger (Chapter 7); Gauvain (Chapter 5)). However, there exists a still higher order theme that both integrates and distinguishes the chapters. That theme is the relation between the individual child and the social context. This theme gets played out in definitions of context as well as in the hypothesized roles of context in development. Ultimately it comes down to just what is meant by socially shared cognition, what the functions of the social surround are for conceptual development, and how to study the processes and the outcomes of social influences on cognition.

Strayer, Moss, and Blicharski

Like all the authors, Strayer, Moss, and Blicharski argue that variations in social contexts produce variations in the development of the individual child's understanding. However, they uniquely derive this position from a powerful evolutionary argument. In so doing they provide a convincing theoretical rationale for the centrality of social settings to the growth of understanding. These authors' position is that "social adaptation is the prime mover of cognitive development," at both the phylogenetic and the ontogenetic levels. Phylogenetically, the argument goes, ancestors of humans were subject to ecological pressures not only from the physical ecology but also from the social ecology entailed in group living. That is, the physical ecology presumably made it advantageous for evolutionarily early forms of our ancestors to live in groups. Group living, then, placed particular kinds of adaptational pressures on individuals, including pressures for cognitive adaptations to permit the representation of relationships and group processes. Over evolutionary time, those individuals who possessed the cognitive abilities that permitted the maintenance of complex social relationships, including reciprocity, cooperation, social regulation of conflict, and so forth were more likely to survive and reproduce in an ecology where group living was necessary. As group living became more complex, it placed additional evolutionary pressures on human cognitive and representational abilities. Thus, we have evolved as a social species, that is to depend on and contribute to the social group for our own individual reproductive success. That evolution has resulted in our ability to share and coordinate representations or knowledge. Those individuals who failed to participate in such sharing, first as learners and then as teachers, would have been less successful at producing offspring, while those whose representational abilities permitted better, or more efficient, coordination of knowledge would have come to dominate the gene pool.

While it does not necessarily follow that knowledge acquisition must be a social process ontogenetically (we could individually construct our knowledge of the world, and then simply transmit it to one another), it would be a tremendously inefficient system, at both the individual and group level, for knowledge not to be socially acquired given that it must ultimately be socially functional. Thus our evolution has set us up to acquire and to use knowledge in the context of social interactions. The social setting, then, has both motivated cognitive development and structured it in particular ways to optimize adaptation to the social group. The development of understanding, by this argument, is fundamentally, even biologically, social.

Strayer and his colleagues then extend this interesting, and basically convincing argument to draw two important implications: (a) that basic cognitive abilities are first constructed in the social setting and then "progressively extended to the world of objects"; and (b) "that the multiplicity of agents in the infant's social entourage should be as important to early social and cognitive development as the quality of primary nurturing," where the quality of nurturing refers to the parent-infant attachment relationship. From these they derive a set of specific hypotheses regarding the relationships between a child's attachment with the mother (secure vs. insecure) and the child's experience of social demands in different environments (day care vs. home reared), in influencing the child's verbal interactions and problem-solving tactics during semistructured play with the mother. They predict that securely attached two-year-olds in day care should be more skilled at these aspects of problem solving than children raised exclusively at home, because of the social pressures (and presumably the child's successful adaptation to them) experienced in the day-care setting. They also predict certain advantages in problem solving for insecurely attached children who attend day care, specifically, that they should be more advanced in the metacognitive aspects of problem solving such as planning, monitoring, and predicting outcomes.

In contrast to the arguments made for the evolutionary origins of cognition in social activity, these secondary lines of argument lack the force and appeal of the former. In particular, it is not evident how these implications follow directly from an ethological or biosocial theoretical system. There seems to be nothing inherent in the argument that cognition develops in social contexts that dictates that object-related cognition is secondary to understanding of the social world, or

that object representations should follow, developmentally, the acquisition of social representations. Indeed, one might expect understanding of the physical
world to occur in the context of social interactions and simultaneously with similar aspects of social understanding. One might even expect understanding of the
physical world to precede similar understanding of the social world in those instances where physical objects may offer greater predictability and less variability than social objects. Regardless, the point simply is that to accept that cognitive development is driven by social demands is not to exclude the demands
made by the physical world, nor to dictate the developmental sequence of physical world and social understanding. Of course, these objections do not dilute the
prediction of variability in cognitive outcomes from variability in the social settings in which cognitive developments are embedded.

Strayer, Moss and Blicharski indeed present empirical evidence for a link between children's social experience in day-care settings with multiple caregivers,
and certain aspects of their cognitive development as exhibited during social
problem solving with their mothers. Specifically, they show that children with
extended day-care experience are more active in problem solving with their
mothers than are children reared exclusively at home. In particular, children with
supplemental social experiences (i.e., day-care children) tend to be more sophisticated in their use of metacognitive strategies such as predicting consequences,
stating goals, and so on. Further, broader social experiences were shown to compensate for poorly adapted, insecure mother-infant relationships.

To the extent that the social experiences children get in day care either directly
support problem-solving skills, or indirectly contribute to them by the kinds of
adaptations children must make and the social strategies they construct, it makes
some sense to predict carryover into social problem solving with the mother. Following this interesting and timely demonstration of the positive effects of day-
care experience on the young child's cognitive development, Strayer's analysis
would benefit from a fuller perspective on what it is in the day-care social setting
that is presumed to contribute to advancement in problem-solving skills. Is it the
experience in having to coordinate behavior with other children? Is it that day-
care adults are more expert at scaffolding the child's incipient problem-solving
abilities, or perhaps provide more variability in such scaffolding?

It should also be noted that despite the appeal of this particular biological argument, a different and similarly appealing one can be made. Some scholars
(e.g., Flavell, 1985; Scarr-Salapatek, 1976) have proposed that if the child were
forced to depend on the social environment to provide the appropriate challenges, novelty, and structure for learning to occur, many youngsters all over the
world would not acquire basic cognitive skills. The social environment is simply
too variable to guarantee involvement sufficient to promote acquisition of many
skills. Instead, these authors contend, the child must come into the world ready
to engage it, motivated to set her own challenges, and to meet them. Hence, the

efficient and well-adapted biological organism comes prepared to engage and to structure the world.

Of course, a moment's reflection leads to the recognition that these two posi-·tions are not mutually exclusive, rather they are complementary. Flavell's proposal provides a much more active child than does Strayer's, while Strayer's child can benefit (or suffer) from variations in social settings. Indeed, the child of Strayer, Moss and Blicharski has built-in propensities to take advantage of whatever the social world offers. But the contrast does raise additional questions for the analysis of Strayer and his colleagues. For example, are all children assumed to adapt similarly to day care or other varieties of nonparental social experiences? Presumably not. What explains variation in adaptation, and to what does such variation predict?

Regardless of the force or lack of it for the biosocial basis of their predictions, the research by Strayer and his colleagues is unique and fresh for two reasons. First, few researchers have explicitly considered the possibility that extraparental social adaptations may induce the construction by very young children of more sophisticated behavior with the parent. It is more typical to consider the parent-child social system the primary one at this age and to ignore or downplay social experience in other social systems, or to treat the adaptations the child makes in the parent-infant system as independent of those made in other social systems (e.g., peer interaction, or day care). Second, in line with the other authors in this volume, these authors' explicit consideration of the role of the social context in cognitive development has enriched both their conceptual and their empirical approach. For example, while a few authors have begun to study parental scaffolding of infant games (Bruner, 1977; Crawley, Rogers, Friedman, Iacobbo, Criticos, Richardson & Thompson, 1978; Gustafson, Green & West, 1979; Hodap, Goldfield, Boyatzis, 1984), Strayer, Moss and Blicharski uniquely conceptualize the mother as a coparticipant in the young child's construction of problem-solving strategies (see also Rogoff, in press, a, b). The dominant view of the correspondence between the mother-infant relationship and the child's acquisition of problem-solving competence has conceived of the infant's attachment to the mother as the primary determinant, facilitating effective engagement with the world. A reasonable corpus of research has supported this conception and Strayer's arguments are not in disagreement with this approach. But the conceptualization by Strayer and colleagues of cognitive development as motivated by social experience, and of the mother and child as co-constructing understanding, demands much closer scrutiny of the mother-child interaction. This has led Strayer, Moss, and Blucharski to enormous richness and originality in their operationalization of social problem solving within this age group. Further, their analyses of maternal responses to the child's problem-solving communications provide a much fuller picture of the interactional system itself, as well as a better view of the particular kinds of interactions that mediate the effects found by traditional attachment researchers. There are few other observational systems that so flexibly capture the dynamic correspondence between social and cognitive activity in very young children.

Killen

Perhaps the most straightforward and uncontroversial presentation of social settings as contexts for the development of understanding is Killen's. Killen defines context in terms of the social and physical setting in which children's interactions are embedded. In a broad-ranging review, she reminds us of the various ways that such contexts for interaction have been conceived. The social characteristics of interactional settings that she herself concentrates on are the identity of the interactants, especially peers vs. adults, and the familiarity of the interactants with one another. She shows throughout that these kinds of variations in social settings can produce quite interesting differences in children's social interactions. For example, young children appear more socially competent with adult or older peer partners—especially if the partner is familiar—than they do with same age or unfamiliar partners. In this view, the role of social context in development is to affect the performance of skills possessed by the child. Killen limits her discussion to social and social-cognitive skills, but the argument can easily be extended to traditional cognitive or problem-solving performance. In Killen's view, then, social contexts function as windows onto the range of competencies possessed by children. By implication, without an adequate sampling of the range of contexts in which children's interactions occur, scientists will have an incomplete and inaccurate picture of the development of social understanding and social skill.

Although she does not explicitly discuss it, Killen's review implies a second important role for social context in the development of understanding. Specifically, different kinds of interactions may serve as different inputs to the construction of social knowledge. For example, in her review of Turiel's recent work, she shows that the physical setting affects the kind of interactions that children witness or become engaged in. These different kinds of interactions, in turn, contribute to the construction of different kinds of social knowledge. Participation in some kinds of interactions leads to reasoning about implicit moral norms, while participation in others leads to reasoning about social conventions and rules. Hence, the types of interactions in which children become engaged can be considered a contextual variable with farreaching developmental implications (see also Chandler, 1980; Higgins & Parsons, 1983).

Killen illustrates both of these principles with observations of children's conflicts and conflict resolutions in different contexts. In one case she defined the social context by whether adults were present or absent during the children's play. In the second, the context was defined by the particular preschool attended by the children, with three different sites observed. Over preschool sites there were both similarities and differences in social behavior. Whereas site affected the type of conflict observed, the proportion of resolutions generated by the children themselves remained constant over preschools. In contrast, children's self-generated resolutions to conflict differed quite markedly between adult-structured and child-structured play, as did the particular types of conflict observed.

These findings confirm those of prior investigators of early peer interaction— that children interacting with peers do indeed structure their social behavior, without benefit of adult input. Moreover, the finding that children's interactions with one another are quite different across social settings implies that it is the children themselves who structure their interactions differently as a function of the context. This interpretation is buttressed by Killen's analysis of entrance and exit rituals. These analyses suggest that children actually invent or construct their own social structure, and regulate their behavior accordingly.

The important implication from these findings is that children themselves contribute to the social contexts in which they find themselves. This, in turn, adds enormous complexity to one's conceptualization of social context. Context now must be defined in terms of a dynamic interaction between the child's own efforts to structure her social world, and the actual social and physical characteristics of any given setting. In other words, influences of setting or context on the development of social understanding are not independent of characteristics of the individual child, including his developmental level. Returning to Killen's initial review, for example, the finding that different partners elicit different levels of social skill in children can be only partly explained in terms of the partner's characteristics. One must also consider the focal child's abilities and interests, including his cognitive developmental status, his motivation to become engaged, and so forth. Additionally, one must consider the symmetry or asymmetry between the child's competencies and those of her partner.

Much of the research on mixed-age interaction is based on these premises. For example, even very young children, 18 and 24 month olds, interact quite differently in same vs. mixed-age peer dyads (Brownell, 1982). This is plainly a social context effect of the sort Killen discussed in her review and illustrated in her data. But it also appears that young children's cognitive development both constrains how sophisticated the younger, 18-month-old partner can become with an older, 24-month partner, and that it facilitates the kinds of accommodations the 24-month-old is capable of making to a younger peer. Hence social contexts do not produce unilateral effects on the child's development; the child herself affects the action of the social setting. The relationship between the child and the contexts of development must be conceived of as a dynamic, mutually constraining one, with the child structuring the context as much as the context structuring the child. This, indeed, is the position taken in several of the chapters, and one to which we will return.

What is unique about Killen's presentation is more implicit than explicit in it. But it is addressed by no other of the papers, and, indeed by few scholars of this perspective (see Clark & Wilkes-Gibbs, 1986). Specifically, her emphasis on conflict and its resolution among jointly engaged peers brings to our attention that in attempts to negotiate, to share, to distribute, or to transmit knowledge there may be failures, miscommunications, misapprehensions. In contrast, most other writers view social exchange as essentially coordinated knowledge-sharing, occurring without effort by the interactants. One is forced to ask upon reading Killen what the outcomes are of the breakdowns she documents, and, further, what positive function such breakdowns might play in the social and cognitive systems that are served by social interaction. This issue is similar to the question of the role of conflict in cognitive change raised by Piaget (1954; 1962) many years ago, and since studied intensively and productively by the Genevans (e.g., Doise & Mugny, 1979). But it is not the same issue, precisely. For the Genevans, conflict, especially among peers, can induce cognitive change. The question raised here is meant to focus on the co-construction of knowledge rather than on the induction of change. The distinction may be subtle, but it is reflected in questions of the following sort. What knowledge is being co-constructed in the face of conflict? That is, what does each child learn from the other during the initiation and resolution of a conflict episode? How does conflict serve to define the boundaries of solutions or strategies for solving interpersonal or physical world problems? How do different levels of participation in conflict affect what is learned by the participants? When conflicts remain unresolved, as a surprising number do according to Killen, what has been co-constructed? Among other things, these questions raise the possibility that not all social interaction may be constructive for knowledge acquisition. On the other hand, one could argue that, if nothing else, conflict permits learning about conflict, and ultimately, perhaps, also something about negotiation, compromise, and the flexibility of group decisions (e.g., Piaget, 1962).

Gauvain; Renninger

Although the chapters by Strayer, Moss, and Blicharski—as well as by Killen—consider the effects of context on the development of understanding in the individual child, neither chapter directly examines the role of the child in shaping or influencing the social context in which he's embedded, that is, the reciprocal relation between the child and the social setting. The two authors who do most directly evaluate what the child brings to the social setting, and how the child's own understanding, interest, or cognitive activity may structure the social setting are Gauvain and Renninger.

Without mentioning Strayer's evolutionary argument Gauvain takes a position similar to his—that individuals' understanding must be coordinated with others in social groups, and that social contexts offer particular opportunities for cognitive growth through children's coordination of their "individual cognitive activities with the behavior of others in everyday situations." Social contexts, then, are motivators of cognitive change for Gauvain as well as for Strayer and his colleagues. Gauvain provides a nice illustration of the interplay between developmental universals or competencies, such as memory, that develop more-or-less across contexts and within individuals (although partly as a function of social input), and the role of particular contexts in supporting, or altering, or perhaps even hindering both the expression of the competence as well as its further development.

The study presented is an observation of individual activity choice and planning in a social context, and contains elements of (a) individual cognitive developmental universals, (b) specific demands, constraints, or facilitation offered by certain characteristics of the context in which the child operates, (c) illustration of how children themselves interpret and renegotiate features of the context, altering its structure from that intended by adults or experimenters, and using it for their own developmental and interpersonal ends, (d) a contrast between individual and socially embedded activity, suggesting that in some instances socially embedded activity is not always easier or more ''natural,'' and that children may have to learn to negotiate the social environment in addition to learning individual cognitive skills (as opposed to learning individual cognitive skills in the supportive, but essentially invisible [to the child] social context). Hence Gauvain retains the duality between cognitive and social activity, between the individual child and the social context. This contrasts with Winegar, Valsiner, and Packer and Mergendoller, whose conceptualizations intentionally blur these distinctions, a perspective to be discussed later.

Gauvain's research provides additional conceptual substance for the arguments made by Strayer. Specifically, she lays out particular kinds of cognitive demands made by social coordination in group activity. She makes it clear, especially, that metacognitive skills such as planning and monitoring activity are crucial to effective social coordination. Conversely, stable differences in children's ability to coordinate their social behavior with others (as indexed by their popularity) affect the nature of the children's activity planning and the correspondence between their plans and their actions. Although not discussed by Gauvain, this illustrates the mutual, reciprocal regulation of cognition and social interaction: children's history of social coordination affects their cognitive activity and, presumably, their development of additional cognitive competencies. Such cognitive or metacognitive skills, in turn, may influence their future social coordinations.

The demands on children's planning made by the immediate social situation—that is ''fitting the action being planned with the context in which the action will occur,''—are ones with which children this young have particular difficulty. Hence, as Gauvain notes, planning in social situations may not only distribute some of the cognitive load, it may also force the child to become more sensitive to the very qualities of social settings that impact on action, including others' plans and actions in relation to ones' own, the social structure of the group, and so on. At the same time, existing characteristics of the social situation affect how the child will make and execute plans, thereby also affecting what she learns about planning itself. The child comes to be able to "coordinate individual and social concerns" through activity in the social setting at the same time as the social setting provides unique opportunities and makes unique demands for developing certain kinds of cognitive understanding. Again, the reciprocity between cognitive activity and the social context becomes evident.

This reciprocity is also evident in Renninger's chapter. In addition, Renninger goes still further than Gauvain in placing the individual thinking and acting child central to the effects of the social context. The child is the director of her own development, actively determining the nature and extent of the influence of social others on her development. In Renninger's scheme the child's knowledge is developed in coordination with and is directly influenced by social others, but is nonetheless individually defined because it is the individual who does the constructing. Further, the child sets his own challenges to his understanding, which then drive further knowledge acquisition. Moreover, his own challenges may be more cognitively motivating than the challenges set by others. Finally, the individual child influences what and how much effect the other will have on him. Some aspects of the child's knowledge are more dependent than other aspects on constraints imposed by the social environment, and as the child's knowledge becomes more practiced it becomes harder for a social other to reorganize that understanding.

To illustrate these arguments Renninger shows how a child's play interests are individually defined by the child, despite having developed partly out of social activity. She also presents data showing not only how others influence the child's play interests, but how the individual child's interests influence social activity with others. Children's activity interests with various playthings such as trains, playdough, or dolls are held to be a joint product of the functional properties of the objects themselves, the child's past and current experiences with the objects, and the past and current social settings in which the child plays with the objects or witnesses others playing with them. Objects differ not only in their functional properties, but also in the degree to which activity with them is culturally prescribed and the degree to which they can support social interaction. Trains, for example, are played with as they are understood in the culture, whereas there is no particular cultural definition of play with playdough. On the other hand, trains often do not support social play, whereas playdough often does. Hence a child's play interests are influenced by multiple aspects of the social system, and different interests may be differently influenced.

The child's own experiences with objects also influence her activity interests. In particular, Renninger introduces the notion of self-set challenges as an important force in determining activity interests. Out of mastery motivation, the child sets challenges for himself around actions with objects (challenge is never more explicitly defined). These, in turn, affect the interestingness of the object. The important point here for Renninger is that these challenges are set by the child himself. Further, they may be even more influential than those set by others because self-set challenges are more likely to be optimally discrepant from the child's existing knowledge and interests. Hence, the individual child not only structures his own activity with objects according to his own interests, but his interests and activity, at the same time, constrain the effects that others can have on his behavior and on his further interests or knowledge. In other words, the child is himself constructing his own ''contexts'' for development, and the impetus to do so comes from the child as well as from motivating qualities of the social surround. Thus, play interests are both individually and socially determined, in a complex interweaving of mutual, but independent influences from within the child and from without.

The strength of the chapters by Renninger and Gauvain is their concentration on the individual's contribution to the social context at the same time as they also recognize the role that social context plays in affecting the development of understanding. The weaknesses of both chapters are also similar. Neither author helps much to clarify the reciprocal interaction between children's understanding and the social settings in which it develops. That is, both authors demonstrate the interdependence of child and context, but they provide few insights into the interpersonal processes that contribute to that interdependence.

Winegar; Valsiner; Packer & Mergendoller

The three chapters by Winegar, Valsiner, and Packer and Mergendoller are addressed more directly to the reciprocal, dialectical relations between the child's activity or understanding and the social environment. In these discussions, the individual child is not central, rather the relation with the social context is central. The social settings in which the child develops are unique and everchanging, in flux moment by moment. The social context provides not only the experience the child must assimilate and make sense of, it also becomes an active, dynamic, and integral source of developmental change, independent of the child yet also constructed by her. Social contexts are both the product of development and the impetus and guide for development. Understanding is conceived of as a joint construction by the child and the social others who participate with the child in activity. Understanding here is genuinely socially shared, and, in fact, cannot be adequately located in the mind of the individual child. Rather, understanding is an active, continuous, and changing negotiation between the child and the social environment. There is, then, no generalized, abstract, decontextualized knowledge. All understanding is context-bound, in both acquisition and use.

As a corollary, the process of development itself is also most explicitly addressed by these chapters. In common, they conceive of development not as powered by forces lying within the child, as for example Piaget or other more traditional cognitive developmentalists would have it. Nor is development conceived of as a product simply of the social transmission of cultural practices, through progressive scaffolding of the child into ever more expert, adult-like performances. Rather, development is conceived of as evolving out of a series of constraints imposed by the social environment, but imposed upon a child who partly determines the nature, the degree, and the direction of those constraints. That is, the environment is not simply responsive to a changing child; the child actively constructs, challenges, and changes the environment at the same time as the environment limits the child's activity in it. Hence the child together with others *co*constructs her own development. The role of the individual child in these three chapters, then, is equal with the role of the social setting in the development of understanding. Both are active. Both are constructive. Both change. They mutually constrain and influence one another. And development is a continuous, dynamic negotiation between the child and the social environment. The boundaries between the individual knower and the social setting in which knowledge is acquired have thereby become blurred. The social context, then, is tied not only to the content of the child's understanding, but to the process of understanding as well. Understanding becomes an inherently social process, rather than an individual process supported by social settings.

Of these three chapters, it is perhaps Winegar's where the roles of the individual and the social setting are most precisely demarcated, and their relationship most plainly explicated. Winegar illustrates the general principles noted above with observations of children's progressive understanding of conventional social sequences (e.g., preschool snack; grocery shopping) as they are embedded in social interaction. In particular, he is interested in elucidating the contributions of social others to the acquisition of this sort of complex, rule-bound understanding. He argues that such contributions must be critical given how complex the rules and conventions to be acquired are, and how quickly and effortlessly even inexperienced three-year-olds acquire them. This could only happen if the information available to the child for inducing the rules has been structured to fit the child's understanding and cognitive abilities. His data point to clear social constraining by adults of the knowledge to be acquired by the child. He also illustrates children's dependence on such adult-imposed constraints. Indeed, children solicit input and feedback from the adult in a situation (the store) where they are aware of their lack of understanding. By experimentally manipulating the amount of adult structuring of the information available to the child, Winegar is able to show as well that at the same time as children rely on adult support for knowledge acquisition, they also take responsibility themselves for using or structuring that support as necessary. Finally, he shows that the nature of the constraints changes as children gain understanding, and the specific actions of child and adult are progressively coordinated to the same ends.

This relates to an important point made early in the chapter by Winegar. To explain children's acquisition of social understanding, one must posit constraints in the child as well as in the social environment. That is, the child must bring some sort of preference for or sensitivity to particular aspects of the social situation, an aptitude for learning from just the sort of constraining or instructing or scaffolding that adults and other social partners provide. Similar to the way that children are assumed to have a biologically-based readiness to learn a complex linguistic system from organized input, so also might we assume that the child brings a biologically-based predisposition to become a socially adapted individual, and a corresponding readiness to be socialized, to build up certain kinds of social understanding in interaction with certain kinds of adult activity, points similar to Strayer's.

Central to Winegar's discussion is the insight that scripts, or any systematic cognitive constructions, are not acquired independent of the social context. More than being context-sensitive, children's scripts are also representations of unique social meaning. D'Andrade (1981) has similarly pointed out that the construction of scripts is a process of guided discovery of knowledge. As does Winegar, D'Andrade further argues that the knowledge embodied in scripts is more than simply shared—it is part of the institutionalized knowledge of the culture, and members of the culture are expected to acquire it. The children in Winegar's sample do not have the option of not learning the snacktime routines if they are to be socially and culturally successful and well-adapted.

As a consequence the child's social systems are themselves adapted to the child as a learner/discoverer through such processes as "differential constraining/progressive empowerment." These supports for acquisition of sociocultural scripts influence the likelihood that children will learn and remember culturally important events, but that is not all, Winegar argues. Because the events that children come to represent and remember are uniquely socially embedded, additional meaning is given them by the social context. Further, such meaning is not passively absorbed by the child, and is not just socially transmitted by the adults or experts. Rather the social and cultural meaning of events is negotiated or co-constructed by the child during the social interactions in which events are embedded.

In exploring this guided discovery of conventional procedures, Winegar provides several insights about what adults actually do in their role as guides. For example, the teacher sets very general goals while the children negotiate (both "intraindividually" and "interindividually") exactly how to fill the more specific slots. Teachers' methods include externalizing their own competence by modeling, providing verbal and nonverbal feedback, offering options for action, direct tuition, and so forth. Interestingly, many of these very same principles have begun to be incorporated into alternative forms of teaching traditional academic subjects in instructional settings (see Brown & Palincsar, in press, for an example). Their success in elementary school classrooms speaks to the generality and power of Winegar's observations in the much less formal, but perhaps more representative social setting of preschool snacktime.

Although here and elsewhere Winegar has empirically illustrated the principles he discusses, the actual processes of acquisition in the child remain elusive. How does acquisition differ by age, by differentially socially constrained settings, by the child's investment in the social situation? What is general over settings? Over children? Are there differences among adults, settings, or children that produce important differences in what's learned or how it's acquired? For example, Ross (1988) reported data recently which suggests that mothers may in some contexts "misguide" development. That is, the child must overcome (or at least ignore) the mother's explicit and systematic "teaching." The context in which this occurs is toddler-object conflicts. Mothers' goals are to teach rules about possession, cooperation, and justice, but they also apparently wish to "keep the peace." In their mediation of object-conflict mothers almost always side with the other child, even if their own child has a principled "right" to the object according to the mother's justifications! Several things are happening here—mother has several goals, mother and child do not at this moment share goals, mother does not accept the child's goals. The point is that adult guidance is not always the finely tuned, child-sensitive, complementary and supportive system it is assumed to be. What is the child learning in these situations, and how? These are concerns for which it is too soon to expect answers. But they should perhaps be more directly recognized and discussed.

Valsiner's and Winegar's arguments are quite similar in many ways. Valsiner is less explicit about what the child brings to the task of constructing social understanding, but he does make it evident just how complex a task it is. The information confronting the child, in even so circumscribed a space as a set of caregiver rules about child conduct, becomes immense as soon as one recognizes the multiplicity of socialization agents in the young child's experience. Add to that the fact that caregivers share only a part, not a constant part, of their caregiving style and activity, and the enormity of the problem to be solved by the child is quickly evident.

Thus, Valsiner argues on the one hand that constraints in the child's social environment "limit the possible course of development" and "eliminate excess uncertainty at every moment." But at the same time he goes to great lengths to demonstrate, using a straightforward hypothetical example, just how numerous, complex, heterogenous, and uncoordinated the constraints provided by the child's social environment actually are. Clearly this is not a simple problem for the child—nor for the scientist trying to understand how the child understands, or how all children come to similar understandings, how developmental uniformity emerges from such heterogeneity. As argued in Winegar's paper, one must posit some constraints and/or predispositions in the child as she actively participates in and learns from these complex social environments. Valsiner proposes two complementary means by which structure or homogeneity might emerge from inconsistencies in social constraints. First, caregivers may attempt planfully to coordinate their behavior, imposing consistency between themselves as well as over time and situations. But even among individuals whose goals at some level are similar, such purposeful coordination results in only limited homogeneity. The second source of regularity, then, could come from the child himself. Valsiner suggests several possible general strategies the child might bring to socialization that would impose structure on inconsistent input. The child could respond differentially to whatever aspect of the social context is currently most salient, most adaptive, most powerful, and so on. ("Maximal Contextual Exploitation"). Or the child could be governed by or conform to the most common element(s) in the social context ("Undifferentiated Majority Rule"). Or the child might try to negotiate changes in the social context by setting one part off against another ("Weak Link Rule"). While these strategies are probably all characteristic of children's responses to social constraints at one time or another, they don't entirely capture the dynamic co-construction of context to which Valsiner seems committed. These are response strategies more than they are constructions. They also don't speak to the central problem Valsiner is attempting to resolve—how is homogeneity in outcome derived from heterogeneity of input? Does homogeneity emerge because the child is consistent in strategy choice over different adults, or over situations or time? Where do these homogeneous, consistent response strategies come from, and what are the decision processes in applying them to a given situation? Is it not unavoidable to propose some more general, pan-species, information-processing constraints within the individual child?

Another central issue for Valsiner is how to operationalize "bounded indeterminacy," how to conceptualize it closely enough to study it directly and to document the processes and their effects during development. This notion seems to hinge on a different scientific model of the relation between "input" and "output," respectively environment, and knowledge or behavior. The traditional model is that input determines output through the operation of some specifiable set of rule-bound mediating processes. Insofar as one is able to discover and specify those mediating processes and their principles of operation, an explanation is possible and reasonable predictions about input/output relations can be made. One alternative is that outcomes may be dependent on input, but not directly predicted by any particular pattern of input. This is because the mediating processes change dynamically in local response to one another, in some sense independent of the initial input. Input functions to engage or "start up" the system, but the ensuing processes are not a directly predictable product of the particular pattern of input, hence "indeterminacy." But the system also does not operate chaotically, because there are constraints or "boundaries" on the kinds of responses different parts of the system can make. Each part of the system itself is constrained, and imposes constraints on other parts of the system. Hence, "bounded" indeterminacy.

This description of a knowledge system is not inherently limited to a socially embedded one. It could equally well describe the mind of the individual learner, and the internal, dynamic cognitive processes that constitute thinking and learning (see, for example, McClelland, Rumelhart & Hinton, 1986). Such parallels across systems lend Valsiner's arguments greater strength, cogency, and credibility. However, comparisons with well-developed models of cognitive processing that embody some of the same general principles as Valsiner's system also point up how inadequately specified such a system is when applied to socially influenced knowledge change. It is one thing to posit the existence of social constraints on the development of understanding, but quite another to operationalize them precisely, to explain their origins, and to model how they operate dynamically to produce knowledge. How, exactly, does regularity or predictability in development emerge from "bounded indeterminacy"?

Valsiner's presentation has begun to address these kinds of challenging issues by starting to map out the complex terrain which must be covered. The questions raised by Valsiner's discussion are provocative and fundamental to a contextualist perspective. More so than most of the other chapters, they point to the *process* of social influence. Certainly we cannot hope to explain the role of social context in development without an adequate model of the processes of influence. The next steps are clear, and are sure to provide powerful new models of development. Empirical research must begin to identify concretely the constraints in both the child and in the social structure, how those constraints mutually affect one another over time, and how they together determine outcome.

Both Winegar and Valsiner present socialization as a complex problem for the child to solve, in the sense of having to organize and represent only partially overlapping, incomplete, and often contradictory information. They further argue that socialization is ultimately a joint effort, a socially negotiated and shared understanding between the child and the socialization agents. This perspective stands in sharp contrast to the traditional socialization literature in which child rearing is usually described in terms of a limited set of universal parenting styles and global individual differences within them. It also goes beyond recent permutations of the traditional position, in which the child is recognized as influential in the parents' child rearing style but where the mechanism is ultimately the same—internalization. In these chapters, internalization of parental norms is considered only part of the socialization process. Socialization can also be conceived of as a set of cognitive and social-cognitive achievements by the child, a complex problem of coordinating and organizing information, and negotiating understandings with multiple, often independent socialization agents. The child's efforts to solve this problem, to induce parental norms for conduct, are always joint co-constructions with a social environment whose constraints limit and channel the possible solutions for the child. Hence, these two chapters raise questions critically important to this perspective: How is the social context organized and represented by the child, how does that correspond to the actual organization of the context, and how does the child's representation of the social context impact on socialization?

We come, finally, to the chapter by Packer and Mergendoller. While in the same spirit as the other chapters, it also goes beyond them in conceptually criti-

cal ways. Both Winegar and Valsiner meld together the construction of knowledge by the individual child and the social context in which understanding is constructed. They do so insofar as they hold understanding to be co-constructed, a
set of meanings with social others and therefore not standing alone in a single
child's head, rather held socially, shared. They also, however, reject a situation-
ist perspective in which all knowledge is completely unique to a given situation
and given participants. All the authors assume some amount of generality across
children and across social settings.

Packer and Mergendoller, however, come closest to rejecting generality in
favor of situationism. Their exposition of the child/social context relationship is
probably the most complete of any of the chapters, as is the mapping of their
conceptual system onto an appropriate methodology. In many instances, their
reasoning fills in the gaps left by the authors of the other chapters: what is meant
by action or activity; the social environment as mediating meaning rather than
materially causing change (the latter would require the social environment to be
materially separate from meaning, a position these authors reject); the equiva-
lence of social interchange and everyday ways of acting in the world; the organization of social activity as semantic and polysemous, and also intrinsically temporal; the implicit, holistic knowledge that constitutes and derives from everyday
activity.

The immediate methodological implications as well as the larger scientific implications of this position are deep. The argument is that it makes little sense to
explain behavior except with respect to its local activity setting, and with respect
to the social interactions in which everyday activity is embedded. The meaning
of the activity to the participants *is* the explanation. Hence, one's methodology is
to describe the situation-bound activity of the participants, and to inquire of them
as carefully as possible about the meanings or goals of their activity. Obviously,
there are limits on the ages and kinds of activities that will yield to this methodology. There also may be a paradox of sorts here. The observer/scientist must be
part of the meaning of the situation, insofar as his presence is defined within and
changes the situation. He must, then, include the scientific enterprise itself in his
explanation of the situation, and he must include himself as well. Indeed, in this
view, science as practical activity should have particular, situated meanings itself, and should not be acontextual. Yet, the perspective adopted by these writers
is an objective one, characterizing children generally, by extrapolating from their
behavior over situations within the classroom. They also characterize science
and explanation generally, extrapolating across objects of explanation ("situations") to argue for a particular, appropriate scientific approach. But is it possible to have a generalized science, or a science of generalities, if knowledge is
completely situated? Is not the value of one scientific approach as meaningful to
its participants as another approach is to its practitioners?

Perhaps this is stretching the implications of these authors' arguments beyond
the ones intended. But either one argues for general scientific principles that

serve to organize and explain the specifics in objectively observed data, or one must be willing to give up the privileged status of scientist/objective investigator. In the latter case, the "scientific" construction of meaning is no different from any other construction of meaning, and is context- and person-bound. That is, of course, a radically different view of both knowledge and science, in essence a rejection of an objective science as it has been construed over hundreds of years. But perhaps these authors mean more simply to inspire science to be more self-reflective, to encourage scientists to model explicitly the role of the investigator in constructing presumably objective "truths." In either case, the position taken by Packer and Mergendoller is a bold one, and certain to provoke considered evaluation of a science of context.

One of the strengths of this approach is its focus on how children's engagement in practical, everyday action structures or gives meaning to children's thought. It is by becoming engaged in particular activities that children acquire and change their goals, and their understanding of behavior and action. These activities, in turn, are embedded in a social network. With Lave and others, Packer and Mergendoller argue that the study of general cognitive skills, removed from their embeddedness in routine and everyday behavior, is pointless. Indeed, the argument is that there exist no such general, decontextualized, disembedded cognitive skills, and, further, that such general purpose, "widely transportable" skills cannot be successfully taught. Instead, cognition and learning are more profitably construed as "practices," activities inherently a part of routine, everyday experience. If cognition is part of everyday practices, it must be studied in terms of the activities and social contexts of which it is a part. Hence the classroom that Packer and Mergendoller study is a context for everyday activity, rather than a strictly pedagogical setting. Children structure and are structured by their routine activity in this setting. This view obviously calls for careful analysis of the organization of the context, including the children's contributions, and how that organization constrains activity, hence cognition. As Scribner (1984) recommends, "if cognitive skills are closely tied to the intellectual requirements of the practices in which they are embedded, one way to determine their characteristics is to study them as they function in these practices, [i.e.], the practices themselves need to become objects of analysis." That is exactly what Packer and Mergendoller set out to do. Their observations were largely conversations with children in a classroom whose environment was meant to induce changes in understanding indirectly, through particular kinds of social engagement, rather than didactically as in traditional classrooms. The conversations of the investigators with the children made it evident that children seldom were aware of their own understanding, yet most of them had constructed that understanding through guided social activity with which they had become voluntarily engaged.

A second insight offered by these data is that the child's interpretation of the social context often fails to correspond to the adult's. The child constructs her own meaning of the situations. Even in situations explicitly planned by adults for particular ends, children take from them what they wish, interpreting them in unique and individual ways. As expected, then, the child's understanding is not general across settings or held in common with other children in the setting. Thus it is the child's own construction of meaning, as much as the scientist's, that is central to our research interests. And any child's understanding, by the arguments in this chapter, is meaningful only in its immediate social context.

SUMMARY AND CONCLUSIONS

In pulling these quite diverse chapters together, finally, what are the common themes and issues that emerge? Each has gone far beyond the simpler position of just a few years ago, that the proper place for a developmental science is in the contexts of development and not in the laboratory (except as it also constitutes a context for development). Instead, each chapter has defined carefully and explicitly which particular aspects of the social context are under scrutiny, and why these specific delineations of context are central to the study of development. Further, each has grappled in one way or another with the most difficult issue of determining relations between the individual child and the larger social environment in the construction of understanding. The fundamental agreement is that cognition and understanding emerge out of social interaction.

The social context has been defined in these chapters as variously as culture (Renninger), the particular preschool classroom (Killen), social roles of the participants (Killen, Winegar, Valsiner), number of social partners or demands (Strayer), past interactive and play history (Renninger), and the social structure and practical activity within the classroom (Packer).

Similarly, the hypothesized functions of the social context in the development of understanding have included (a) variation in context serves to reveal variations in children's understanding (Killen); (b) variations in social context contribute to variations in children's understanding (all authors); (c) the social context motivates, facilitates, and structures children's understanding (all authors); (d) the social context *is* children's understanding (Packer & Mergendoller). Complementarily, the presumed role of the individual child in relation to the social context has ranged from (a) the child as active in constructing knowledge, but essentially irrelevant to the definition of social context which can be defined independent of the child, to (b) the child's understanding is both affected by and affects the social context, to (c) the child and social others are coparticipants in the construction of knowledge, and no knowledge lies solely within the individual child, rather all knowledge and understanding is socially shared.

From this diversity of perspectives, however, emerges a set of larger issues held in common. With the recognition that development, including conceptual development, is not independent of the individual's social, emotional, and cultural contexts, the difficult problem becomes to specify (a) how context is to be defined; (b) which aspects of context play what roles in development, and which aspects of the social context are most important for which aspects of development; (c) what is the role of the individual child, her cognition, affect, and behavior in constraining or facilitating the action of the social context; (d) what are the mechanisms or processes of influence in the interaction between the child and the social setting.

It is no small matter to provide a definition of context, and, as has been evident in these chapters, contexts may be defined in multiple, quite different ways. Contexts are not uniform. They run the gamut from specific task demands or other situation-specific demands, constraints, or supports, to social and cultural institutions that are nearly universal. Even within a given social context—for example, the mother-child system, constraints and supports vary over time and situation (e.g., Saxe, Guberman, & Gearhart, 1987). What aspects of context, which particular settings, are the important ones to study? And how is context to be conceptualized more broadly? On the one hand, context has been conceived of as a main effect, as a determinant of behavior and development, along with other, age-related variables. In this view context is often imposed from without. The child finds herself in a given context and must adapt to it cognitively, socially, emotionally. These adaptations, in turn, result in the child's construction of particular aspects of knowledge. Contexts affect conceptual development directly by providing different kinds of information, experience, support to the developing system. A second view is that context itself forms an integral part of the child's understanding, in the sense that the context is part of what the child knows. Children construct their own contexts. They do so by choosing settings and partners that provide them with different demands and supports. They also do so by virtue of their perception, representation, and understanding of different aspects of multiple contexts. Children build up context-specific knowledge during the social negotiations or coconstructions of meaning with others. Hence, the child dynamically contributes to and structures his own experiences at the same time as he is affected by them. Contexts are within the child as well as outside of him. Clearly there is no single, most appropriate level or dimension along which to define context. The definition will follow from the purpose of any particular scientific enterprise. Nevertheless, an explicit theory of context would go far in bringing coherence to this emerging perspective.

Perhaps a more compelling reason to begin to construct a theory of context is because without such a theory, we run the risk of trivializing the study of context by "discovering" that development depends on everything. Although in some sense it does, the traditional model of science is one in which higher-order principles permit us to discern (and explain) regularity and systematicity in the workings of the world. When explanations begin unparsimoniously to approach the complexity of the data for which they try to account, scientists become uncomfortable. Of course, this goal of science is also a basic operating principle of the human mind. In labeling both Pekingese and Great Danes as dogs, we gloss over or discount a multitude of dissimilarities. So too, in science. Explanations must always gloss over some amount of diversity. The hard question is just how much it is appropriate or useful to gloss over. For many years in the recent history of the discipline, most of social context has been glossed over, relegated to the error term. Children have been studied as if they uniformly and sensibly responded to uniform and constant "contexts." Powerful, general, within-child structures and processes have been held to account for this sort of acquisition and performance. While these developed in social contexts, they were assumed to be little affected in obvious ways by the contexts in which they developed, as long as the contexts were within the normal range of human environments. Whatever variation in development was produced by variation in context was not scientifically important or interesting. Whatever support or constraint in the social context contributed to the individual's development was secondary to within-child mechanisms. This view, predominant over the last few decades, contrasts markedly with that of the middle decades in psychology's recent history. Those middle years were characterized by the view that variations in the child's environment could account for everything, both regularity and diversity, in the growth of competence. While the chapters in the present volume offer the beginnings of a synthesis of these two perspectives, at the same time they reveal just how difficult an enterprise that will be—just because there is no well-developed conceptual system in which context is an integral determinant of theoretically relevant outcomes.

A second issue, particularly for developmental psychology, is the problem of discerning which aspects of development are most sensitive to which aspects of context. For example, language development at one level is completely determined by the context in which it is acquired—a child learns only and all of the language in the linguistic environment(s) in which he is reared. However, there are also surprising and intriguing similarities in development across quite dissimilar linguistic environments, extending even to the "language" invented by deaf children of hearing parents (Goldin-Meadow, 1984). Hence, some aspects of language development may be more or less sensitive to variations in particular features of the context. It is not unreasonable to suppose that this principle holds across other aspects of development as well.

Complementarily, higher-order developmental changes may themselves constrain the influence of the social context. Peer collaborations, for example, are relatively ineffective in producing changes in problem-solving performance among preschoolers (Azmitia & Perlmutter, 1987). But peer interaction during this period does support the acquisition of a wide variety of interactional competencies, including the cognitive and representational skills entailed in complex social pretense (Bretherton, 1984). Hence, the social context can serve a wide variety of functions for development, from motivating to structuring, but the process of influence must be considered a reciprocal one. Different aspects of development may be differentially responsive to and affected by social constraints, at different points in the developmental process. And at the same time as the social context constrains development, a child's development constrains the influence of social context.

Although age-related developmental questions have not arisen in these chapters, concerns have been raised more generally about the role of the individual child in the action of the social context. Children develop individual cognitive processes, with powerful mechanisms and structures for representing and interpreting the contexts of development. As more and more research empirically testifies, however, the child's social surround contributes to development of the mind. The social system carries some of the cognitive load. Not all of what is commonly presumed to be "in" the child's head is really located there exclusively; some knowledge is socially shared. At some level all knowledge is sociocultural in origin, rather than individually generated, including physical world knowledge. In newly analyzed protocols of everyday life among the !Kung bushmen, Adamson and Bakeman (1988) have shown that the adults in infants' environments provide a cultural interpretation of objects and object play as soon as babies begin to manipulate objects. For the !Kung objects are defined as things for sharing rather than as things for manipulating, in relation to the economic and social reciprocity in the culture. Accordingly, adults provide no support for the development of object manipulation skills. There are no toys for children, and no object manipulation games, even informal ones. However, adults do encourage, model, and reward object sharing with infants long before the infants begin to understand or control sharing or exchange. Hence the world of objects for the !Kung child is a very different one than for the Western child.

Despite the sociocultural origins of knowledge, an important question is how socially shared knowledge is represented by the individual child. Further, how does the child's representation or interpretation of the social context affect the influence of context? Few have examined what the child knows about social contexts, what aspects of contexts are salient and are encoded and interpreted, and how representation of contexts changes with age. Arsenio (1987) has provided an initial analysis of children's sensitivity to, understanding of, and evaluation of different socioaffective contexts. Arsenio found that children possess distinct representations of different social contexts. Further, they evaluate or interpret the particular events that occur in given social contexts, as well as both their own roles and the roles of other participants. Finally, in a true co-construction, both partners bring something to the interactional context, and both partners take something new away. A complementary question, then, is what the adult (or other participants in social settings), as an individual cognitively separate from the child, learns from the child. How does the "expert's" knowledge change as a function of this co-constructive process? At the same time, then, as we recognize and model the social processes that contribute to the construction of socially shared knowledge, it is important to consider both the constraints imposed by the individuals involved in the process and the individuals' own understanding of contexts.

One final issue, and perhaps the most challenging one, is to determine what the processes of action and influence are between the individual and the social environment, and how those processes can be described, modeled, and explained. How is information actually socially transmitted? What affects the transmission/acquisition process itself, as well as the outcome of that process? What are the specific constraints on the process and how do they operate? How is socially distributed knowledge accessed by the individual, or modeled by the scientist? How does it "add up" to the emergent sociocultural, practical knowledge that is studied by scientists? The chapters in this volume all make a first attempt at specifying aspects of this larger process. Other scholars have made similar efforts, as reviewed briefly above. But the mechanisms of socially sharing knowledge remain somewhat elusive.

One highly speculative, but interesting analogy can be generated from a recently proposed model of how the individual mind constructs and represents knowledge. The essence of this model, referred to as "Parallel Distributed Processing" (McClelland, Rumelhart & Hinton, 1986), is that mental representation actually lies in the patterns of "communication" among individual components of knowledge. These individual components of knowledge are not themselves so complex as "concepts," "rules," or semantic networks. But together, interactively, they can specify these more complex aspects of representation. In other words, higher-order knowledge is distributed across a system of smaller units, the nature of whose interactions cause the higher-order knowledge to emerge. These interactions are simple, quantifiable relationships, some stronger, some weaker. Further, the action of one unit of knowledge constrains the actions of other units, dynamically, over time (processing time, or learning time). What is especially intriguing about these PDP systems is that they are not governed by a set of rules or a priori principles, yet they generate behavior or knowledge that appears rule-governed. In other words, the system operates as if it were rule-governed although it is not. Regularity emerges from the dynamic interaction of multiple, mutually influencing, individually specified components of information: "Each aspect of the information in the system can act on other aspects, simultaneously influencing other aspects and being influenced by them . . . [and] . . . each constraint may be imperfectly specified and ambiguous, yet each can play a potentially decisive role in determining the outcome of processing." Systems based on these principles have been able to account for a wide range of apparently rule-governed behavior, including some fairly complex language phenomena such as the acquisition of the past tense in English.

The parallels to interacting social systems that generate regular, predictable outcomes from socially distributed knowledge are fairly obvious. It is not necessary in this sort of model to generate a set of rules or principles that govern the behavior of individuals in some predetermined way to produce regular patterns of outcome. Rather, by knowing something about the patterns of transmission and influence among the individuals in the system, and the constraints that operate between individuals, regularities in outcome can be predicted. Of course, this is only an analogy, and as with any analogy it is not a perfect fit. In particular, such a system cannot capture the full complexity of socially interacting minds, with complex affective and motivational variables factored in. The individual "units" in a social system are themselves complex individuals, whereas in a cognitive system they can be much simpler, such as pieces of concepts or words. Nonetheless, such precisely modeled systems within the cognitive domain might at least offer the beginnings of an operational framework within which to begin to empirically specify some of the constructs proposed in the present volume's chapters.

In the beginning of this discussion it was suggested that the operation of social systems may constitute a good metaphor for the operation of the human mind. Here, it is the complement: current models of the human mind may offer good empirical frameworks for modeling the influence of social interaction on the acquisition and representation of knowledge within social systems. But these two views converge on a still higher order principle: that conceptual systems and social systems do not operate independently of one another. It should come as no surprise, really, that they can serve as metaphors for one another. As Strayer and others have pointed out, cognitive systems and social systems are coadapted. Each has evolved under pressures from the other. They have reciprocally influenced one another over evolutionary time and it is reasonable to suppose that they do so over ontogenetic time as well. The reason it is unique to consider these possibilities, however, is because historically scientists have divorced minds and social systems. Cognitive development and social development have seldom met in our theories of development, and when they have it typically has been to consider how a child brings his self-contained, asocial intellectual processes to bear on the objects and events of the social world. But even so, the two systems, conceptual and social, are not usually presumed to interact with one another, to reciprocally influence the actions, structures, and processes of one another. It has been the goal of this volume to call attention to just this reciprocity of influence, and to begin to reveal empirically—as well as conceptually—the fundamentally social bases of knowledge acquisition, representation, and use.

REFERENCES

Adamson, L., & Bakeman, R. (1988, April). *Guiding infants toward cultural understanding.* Paper presented at International Conference on Infant Studies, Washington, DC.

Arsenio, W. (1987, April). *Context effects on children's judgments of the affective consequences of sociomoral events.* Paper presented at Society for Research in Child Development, Baltimore, MD.

Ashmead, D., & Perlmutter, M. (1980). Infant memory in everyday life. *New Directions in Child Development, 10,* 1–16.

Azmitia, M., & Perlmutter, M. (in press). Social influences on children's cognition: State of the art and future directions. In H. Reese (Ed.), *Advances in child development and behavior*. New York: Academic Press.

Barker, R., & Wright, H. (1955). *Midwest and its children*. New York: Harper & Row.

Berndt, T. (1986). Sharing between friends: Contexts and consequences. In E. Mueller & C. Cooper (Eds.), *Process and outcome in peer relationships* (pp. 105–129). Orlando, FL: Academic Press.

Boster, J. (1986). Exchange of varieties and information between agaruna manioc cultivators. *American Anthropologist, 88*, 428–436.

Boster, J. (1987). Why study variation? *American Behavioral Scientist, 31*, 150–162.

Bretherton, I. (Ed.). (1984). *Symbolic Play*. Orlando, FL: Academic Press.

Bronfenbrenner, U., & Crouter, A. (1983). Evolution of environmental models in developmental research. In P. Mussen (Ed.), *Handbook of Child Psychology* (4th ed., pp. 357–414). New York: Wiley.

Brown, A. (1975). Knowing, knowing about knowing, knowing how to know. In H. Reese, (Eds.), *Advances in child development and behavior*, (vol. 10). New York: Academic Press.

Brown, A., & Palincsar, A. (in press). Guided, cooperative learning and individual knowledge acquisition. In L. Resnick (Ed.), *Knowing and learning: Issues for a cognitive science of instruction*. Hillsdale, NJ: Erlbaum.

Brownell, C. (1982, April). *Effects of age and age mix on toddler peer interaction*. Paper presented at International Conference on Infant Studies, Austin, TX.

Bruner, J. (1977). Early social interaction and language acquisition. In H. Schaffer (Ed.), *Studies in mother-infant interaction*. London: Academic Press.

Chandler, M. (1980). Social knowledge and social structure. *International Journal of Psycholinguistics, 7*, 41–57.

Clark, H., & Wilkes-Gibbs, D. (1986). Referring as a collaborative process. *Cognition, 22*, 1–39.

Crawley, S., Rogers, P., Friedman, S., Iacobbo, M., Criticos, A., Richardson, L., & Thompson, M. (1978). Developmental changes in the structure of mother-infant play. *Developmental psychology, 14*, 30–36.

Damon, W. (1981). Explaining children's social cognition on two fronts. In J. Flavell & L. Ross, *Social-cognitive development*. Cambridge, Mass: Cambridge University Press.

Damon, W. (1987, April). *Peer relations as contexts for psychological growth*. Paper presented at Society for Research in Child Development, Baltimore, MD.

D'Andrade, R. (1981). The cultural part of cognition. *Cognitive Science, 5*, 179–195.

DeLoache, J. (1984). Oh where, oh where: Memory based searching by very young children. In C. Sophian (Ed.), *Origins of cognitive change*. Hillsdale, NJ: Erlbaum.

Doise, W., & Mugny, G. (1979). *The social development of the intellect*. New York: Oxford University Press.

Flavell, J. (1985). *Cognitive development*. Englewood Cliffs, NJ: Prentice Hall.

Gelman, R., & Baillargeon, R., (1983). A review of some Piagetian concepts. In P. Mussen (Ed.), *Handbook of Child Psychology* (pp. 167–230). New York: Wiley.

Gergen, K. (1986). The social constructionist movement in modern psychology. *American Psychologist, 40*, 266–275.

Goldin-Meadow, S. (1984). Gestural communication in deaf children: Effects and non-effects of parental input on early language development. *Monographs of the Society for Research in Child Development*, No. 207. Chicago: University of Chicago Press.

Gustafson, G., Green, G., & West, M. (1979). The infant's changing role in mother-infant games. *Infant behavior & development, 2*, 301–308.

Hartup, W. (1980). Two social worlds: Family relations and peer relations. In M. Rutter (Ed.), *Scientific foundations of developmental psychiatry*. London: Heinemann.

Hartup, W. (1985). Relationships and their significance in cognitive development. In Hinde, R., Perret-Clermont, A., & Stevenson-Hinde, J. (Eds.), *Social relationships and cognitive development*. Oxford: Clarendon.

Higgins, E., & Parsons, J. (1983). Stages as subcultures: Social-cognitive development and the social life of the child. In E. Higgins, W. Hartup, & D. Ruble (Eds.), *Social cognition and social development: A sociocultural perspective*. New York: Cambridge University Press.

Hinde, R. (1974). *Biological bases of human social behavior*. New York: McGraw-Hill.

Hinde, R., Perret-Clermont, A., & Stevenson-Hinde, J. (Eds.). (1985) *Social relationships and cognitive development*. Oxford, England: Clarendon.

Hodapp, R., Goldfield, E., & Boyatzis, C. (1984). The use and effectiveness of maternal scaffolding in mother-infant games. *Child development, 55*, 772–781.

Kaye, K. (1982). *The mental and social life of babies: How parents create persons*. Chicago: University of Chicago Press.

Laboratory of Comparative Human Cognition. (1983). Culture and cognitive development. In P. Mussen (Ed.), *Handbook of Child Psychology*, 4th ed. New York: Wiley.

Lave, J. (in preparation). *Cognition in Practice*.

Lewin, K. (1954). Behavior and development as a function of the total situation. In. L. Carmichael (Ed.), *Manual of Child Psychology*, (2d ed.). New York: Wiley.

Lockman, J. (1988, April). *Object manipulation and social context*. Paper presented at the International Conference on Infant Studies, Washington, DC.

Mathews, H. (1987). Intracultural variation in beliefs about gender. *American Behavioral Scientist, 31*, 219–233.

McClelland, J., Rumelhart, D., & Hinton, G. (1986). The appeal of parallel distributed processing. In D. Rumelhart, J. McClelland, and PDP Research Group (Eds.), *Parallel distributed processing: Explorations in the microstructure of cognition*. Cambridge, MA: MIT Press.

Mead, G.H. (1934). *Mind, self & society*. Chicago: University of Chicago Press.

Minsky, M. (1987). *The society of mind*. New York: Simon & Schuster.

Musatti, T. (1986). Early peer relations: The perspectives of Piaget and Vygotsky. In E. Mueller & C. Cooper (Eds)., *Process and outcome in peer relationships* (pp. 25–50). Orlando, FL: Academic Press.

Nelson, K. (1981). Social cognition within a script framework. In J. Flavell and L. Ross (Eds.), *Social cognitive development* (pp. 97–118). Cambridge: Cambridge University Press.

Perret-Clermont, A. (1980). *Social interaction and cognitive development in children*. London: Academic Press.

Piaget, J. (1954). *The child's construction of reality*. New York: Basic Books.

Piaget, J. (1962). *The moral judgment of the child*. New York: New Press.

Resnick, L. (1987). Learning in school and out. *Educational Researcher, 16,* 13–20.

Rogoff, B., Gauvain, M., & Ellis, S. (1984). Development viewed in its cultural context. In M. Bornstein & M. Lamb (Eds.), *Developmental psychology: An advanced textbook.* Hillsdale, NJ: Erlbaum.

Rogoff, B. (in press-a). The joint socialization of development by young children and adults. In M. Lewis & S. Feinman (Eds.), *Social influences and behavior.* New York: Plenum.

Rogoff, B. (in press-b). Infants' instrumental social interaction with adults. In S. Feinman (Ed.), *Social referencing and the social construction of reality.* New York: Plenum.

Ross, H. (1988, April). *Mothers as judges, teachers, and keepers of the peace.* Paper presented at International Conference on Infant Studies, Washington, DC.

Sameroff, A. (1983). Developing systems: Contexts and evolution. In P. Mussen (ed.), *Handbook of child psychology* (4th ed.). New York: Wiley.

Saxe, G., Guberman, S., & Gearhart, M. (1987). *Social processes in early number development.* Monographs of the Society for Research in Child Development, 52, (2). Chicago: University of Chicago Press.

Scarr-Salapatek, S. (1976). An evolutionary perspective on infant intelligence. In M. Lewis (Ed.), *Origins of intelligence.* New York: Plenum.

Scribner, S. (1984). Studying working intelligence. In B. Rogoff & J. Lave (Eds.), *Everyday cognition: Its development in social context.* Cambridge: Harvard University Press.

Sears, R. (1951). A theoretical framework for personality and social behavior. *American Psychologist, 6,* 476–483.

Tinbergen, N. (1963). On aims and methods of ethology. *Zeitschrift fur* tierpsychologie, 20, 410–433.

Wegner, D. (1987). Transactive memory: A contemporary analysis of the group mind. In B. Mullen & G. Goethals (Eds.), *Theories of group behavior* (pp. 165–198). New York: Springer-Verlag.

Wegner, D., Guiliano, T., & Hertel, P. (1987). Cognitive interdependence in close relationships. In W. Ickes (Ed.), *Compatible and incompatible relationships.* New York: Springer-Verlag.

Wertsch, J., Ed. (1985). *Culture, communication and cognition: Vygotskian perspectives.* Cambridge, England: Cambridge University Press.

Wertsch, J., McNamee, G., McLane, J., & Budwig, N. (1980). The adult-child dyad as a problem-solving system. *Child Development, 51,* 1215–1221.

Whiting, B. (1986). Effects of experience on peer relations. In E. Mueller & C. Cooper (Eds.), *Process and outcome in peer relationships.* Orlando: Academic Press.

Whiting, B., & Whiting, J. (1975). *Children of six cultures.* Cambridge: Harvard University Press.

Author Index

Subject Index

A

Action
  relationship to cognition, *see* Cognition,
    relationship to action
Attachment, 24–26
  influence on metacognition, 28–29, 31–38,
    38–41, 181–184

B

Bounded indeterminacy, *see also* Dependent
  independence of development, 1, 7,
  193–194

C

Co-construction, 156, 173–174, 189–190
  interindividual, 50, 55, 63, 63–64, 191
  intraindividual, 50, 55, 63, 63–64
Cognition
  bio-social bases of, 21–22, 180–182,
    186–187
  relationship to action, 47, 68–69, 71–72,
    104–107, 129–130
  within care-given environment, 16–17
Conflict
  definition of, 120, 126
  research on, 132–141
  role in development, 126–130, 185–186
Constraints (constraining), 7–8, 22–24, 45–46,
  48, 49, 152–153, 189–191
  partial coordination of, 11–16
Context (contextualism), 119–120, 121–130,
  141–142, 173–180, 184–185, 197–200
  definitions of, 197–198
  history of interactions, as, 124–125
  situationism, compared to, 49, 178–179,
    198–199, 195
  social structure, as, 3, 122–124
Control of action
  internal vs. external, 90–91
  in planning, 96–97
  internalization of, 49, 194

Coordination
  definition of, 130
  of social interaction, 8–11, 120
  role in development, 130–132

D

Daycare, *see* Multiple caregivers
Dependent independence, 49
Differential constraining/progressive
  empowerment, 8, 20, 48–49, 54, 60–61
Distancing, 23–24; *see also* Constraints
Domains of knowledge
  social knowledge 120, 125, 128

E

Empowerment of children, *see* Differential
  constraining/progressive empowerment
Ethology
  cognitive, 21–22, 40–41
  conflict as investigated by, 126–128
  context as defined by, 121
Event knowledge, 46–48

H

Hermeneutics, 2, 68–72, 195–196

I

Intelligence, *see* Cognition
Interest
  affiliation and, 166–169
  challenges and, 154–155, 188–189
  definition of, 148–149
  identification of, 166
  influence on planning, 105–106
  influence on play, 3, 121–122, 147–148,
    161–162, 169–171, 188–189
  influence on social interaction, 161–167
  research on, 158–169
  social influence on, 156–158
  stored knowledge and, 149–153
  stored value and, 153–156